Probabilistic Machine Learning for Finance and Investing

A Primer to Generative AI with Python

Deepak K. Kanungo

Beijing · Boston · Farnham · Sebastopol · Tokyo

Probabilistic Machine Learning for Finance and Investing

by Deepak K. Kanungo

Published by O'Reilly Media, Inc., 1005 Gravenstein Highway North, Sebastopol, CA 95472.

O'Reilly books may be purchased for educational, business, or sales promotional use. Online editions are also available for most titles (*http://oreilly.com*). For more information, contact our corporate/institutional sales department: 800-998-9938 or *corporate@oreilly.com*.

Acquisitions Editor: Michelle Smith
Development Editor: Jeff Bleiel
Production Editor: Aleeya Rahman
Copyeditor: nSight, Inc.
Proofreader: Liz Wheeler

Indexer: Sue Klefstad
Interior Designer: David Futato
Cover Designer: Karen Montgomery
Illustrator: Kate Dullea

August 2023:   First Edition

Revision History for the First Edition
2023-08-14:   First Release

See *http://oreilly.com/catalog/errata.csp?isbn=9781492097679* for release details.

978-1-492-09767-9

[LSI]

To my parents, from whom I learned common sense and what it means to be human.

Table of Contents

Preface... ix

1. The Need for Probabilistic Machine Learning................................. 1
   Finance Is Not Physics   2
   All Financial Models Are Wrong, Most Are Useless   4
   The Trifecta of Modeling Errors   6
      Errors in Model Specification   6
      Errors in Model Parameter Estimates   7
      Errors from the Failure of a Model to Adapt to Structural Changes   10
   Probabilistic Financial Models   10
   Financial AI and ML   12
   Probabilistic ML   16
      Probability Distributions   17
      Knowledge Integration   17
      Parameter Inference   19
      Generative Ensembles   19
      Uncertainty Awareness   20
   Summary   20
   References   21
   Further Reading   22

2. Analyzing and Quantifying Uncertainty...................................... 23
   The Monty Hall Problem   24
   Axioms of Probability   26
   Inverting Probabilities   30

Simulating the Solution   33
Meaning of Probability   35
  Frequentist Probability   36
  Epistemic Probability   37
  Relative Probability   40
Risk Versus Uncertainty: A Useless Distinction   41
The Trinity of Uncertainty   44
  Aleatory Uncertainty   44
  Epistemic Uncertainty   46
  Ontological Uncertainty   49
The No Free Lunch Theorems   51
Investing and the Problem of Induction   54
The Problem of Induction, NFL Theorems, and Probabilistic Machine
  Learning   59
Summary   60
References   61

3. **Quantifying Output Uncertainty with Monte Carlo Simulation**. 63
Monte Carlo Simulation: Proof of Concept   64
Key Statistical Concepts   66
  Mean and Variance   66
  Expected Value: Probability-Weighted Arithmetic Mean   67
  Why Volatility Is a Nonsensical Measure of Risk   68
  Skewness and Kurtosis   69
  The Gaussian or Normal Distribution   70
  Why Volatility Underestimates Financial Risk   71
  The Law of Large Numbers   75
  The Central Limit Theorem   76
Theoretical Underpinnings of MCS   77
Valuing a Software Project   78
Building a Sound MCS   83
Summary   84
References   85

4. **The Dangers of Conventional Statistical Methodologies**. 87
The Inverse Fallacy   88
NHST Is Guilty of the Prosecutor's Fallacy   94
The Confidence Game   98
  Single-Factor Market Model for Equities   100

    Simple Linear Regression with Statsmodels   101
    Confidence Intervals for Alpha and Beta   104
  Unveiling the Confidence Game   105
    Errors in Making Probabilistic Claims About Population Parameters   105
    Errors in Making Probabilistic Claims About a Specific Confidence Interval   106
    Errors in Making Probabilistic Claims About Sampling Distributions   106
  Summary   109
  References   111
  Further Reading   112

5. The Probabilistic Machine Learning Framework. **113**
  Investigating the Inverse Probability Rule   114
  Estimating the Probability of Debt Default   118
  Generating Data with Predictive Probability Distributions   123
  Summary   127
  Further Reading   128

6. The Dangers of Conventional AI Systems. **129**
  AI Systems: A Dangerous Lack of Common Sense   130
  Why MLE Models Fail in Finance   132
    An MLE Model for Earnings Expectations   133
    A Probabilistic Model for Earnings Expectations   136
  Markov Chain Monte Carlo Simulations   142
    Markov Chains   143
    Metropolis Sampling   145
  Summary   149
  References   150

7. Probabilistic Machine Learning with Generative Ensembles. **151**
  MLE Regression Models   153
    Market Model   154
    Model Assumptions   155
    Learning Parameters Using MLE   155
    Quantifying Parameter Uncertainty with Confidence Intervals   156
    Predicting and Simulating Model Outputs   156
  Probabilistic Linear Ensembles   156
    Prior Probability Distributions $P(a, b, e)$ 158
    Likelihood Function $P(Y| a, b, e, X)$ 159
    Marginal Likelihood Function $P(Y|X)$ 159

Posterior Probability Distributions P(a, b, e| X, Y)   160
Assembling PLEs with PyMC and ArviZ   161
   Define Ensemble Performance Metrics   162
   Analyze Data and Engineer Features   164
   Develop and Retrodict Prior Ensemble   168
   Train and Retrodict Posterior Model   176
   Test and Evaluate Ensemble Predictions   185
Summary   188
References   189
Further Reading   189

8. Making Probabilistic Decisions with Generative Ensembles. **191**
Probabilistic Inference and Prediction Framework   193
Probabilistic Decision-Making Framework   195
   Integrating Subjectivity   195
   Estimating Losses   197
   Minimizing Losses   200
Risk Management   201
   Capital Preservation   202
   Ergodicity   202
   Generative Value at Risk   206
   Generative Expected Shortfall   209
   Generative Tail Risk   210
Capital Allocation   211
   Gambler's Ruin   212
   Expected Valuer's Ruin   214
   Modern Portfolio Theory   218
   Markowitz Investor's Ruin   221
   Kelly Criterion   225
   Kelly Investor's Ruin   229
Summary   230
References   231
Further Reading   232

Index. **233**

Preface

Generative AI, and Chat GPT-4 in particular, is all the rage these days. Probabilistic machine learning (ML) is a type of generative AI that is ideally suited for finance and investing. Unlike deep neural networks, on which ChatGPT is based, probabilistic ML models are not black boxes. These models also enable you to infer causes from effects in a fairly transparent manner. This is important in heavily regulated industries, such as finance and healthcare, where you have to explain the basis of your decisions to many stakeholders.

Probabilistic ML also enables you to explicitly and systematically encode personal, empirical, and institutional knowledge into ML models to sustain your organization's competitive advantages. What truly distinguishes probabilistic ML from its conventional counterparts is its capability of seamlessly simulating new data and counterfactual knowledge conditioned on the observed data and model assumptions on which it was trained and tested, regardless of the size of the dataset or the ordering of the data. Probabilistic models are generative models that know their limitations and honestly express their ignorance by widening the ranges of their inferences and predictions. You won't get such quantified doubts from ChatGPT's confident hallucinations, more commonly known as fibs and lies.

All ML models are built on the assumption that patterns discovered in training or in-sample data will persist in testing or out-of-sample data. However, when nonprobabilistic ML models encounter patterns in data that they have never been trained or tested on, they make egregious inferences and predictions because of the inherent foundational flaws of their statistical models. Furthermore, these ML models do it with complete confidence and without warning decision makers of their uncertainties.

The increasing adoption of nonprobabilistic ML models for decision making in finance and investments can lead to catastrophic consequences for individuals and society at large, including bankruptcies and economic recessions. It is imperative that all ML models quantify the uncertainty of their inferences and predictions on unseen data to support sound decision making in a complex world with three-dimensional uncertainties. Leading companies clearly understand the limitations of standard AI technologies and are developing their probabilistic versions to extend their applicability to more complex problems. Google recently introduced TensorFlow Probability to extend its established TensorFlow platform. Similarly, Facebook and Uber have introduced Pyro to extend their PyTorch platforms. Currently, the most popular open source probabilistic ML technologies are PyMC and Stan. PyMC is written in Python, and Stan is written in C++. This book uses the extensive ecosystem of user-friendly Python libraries.

Who Should Read This Book?

The primary audience of this book is the thinking practitioner in the finance and investing discipline. A thinking practitioner is someone who doesn't merely want to follow instructions from a manual or cookbook. They want to understand the underlying concepts for why they must adopt a process, model, or technology. Generally, they are intellectually curious and enjoy learning for its own sake. At the same time, they are not looking for onerous mathematical proofs or tedious academic tomes. I have provided many scholarly references in each chapter for readers who are looking for the mathematical and technical details underlying the concepts and reasoning presented in this book.

A thinking practitioner could be an individual investor, analyst, developer, manager, project manager, data scientist, researcher, portfolio manager, or quantitative trader. These thinking practitioners understand that they need to learn new concepts and technologies continually to advance their careers and businesses. A practical depth of understanding gives them the confidence to apply what they learn to develop creative solutions for their unique challenges. It also gives them a framework to explore and learn related technologies and concepts more easily.

In this book, I am assuming that readers have a basic familiarity with finance, statistics, machine learning, and Python. I am not assuming that they have read any particular book or mastered any particular skill. I am only assuming that they have a willingness to learn, especially when ChatGPT, Bard, and Bing AI can easily explain any code or formula in this book.

Why I Wrote This Book

There is a paucity of general probabilistic ML books, and none that is dedicated entirely to finance and investing problems. Because of the idiosyncratic complexities of these domains, any naive application of ML in general and probabilistic ML in particular is doomed to failure. A depth of understanding of the foundations of these domains is pivotal to having any chance of succeeding. This book is a primer that endeavors to give the thinking practitioner a solid grounding in the foundational concepts of probabilistic ML and how to apply it to finance and investing problems, using simple math and Python code.

There is another reason why I wrote this book. To this day, books are still a medium for serious discourse. I wanted to remind the readers about the continued grave flaws of modern financial theory and conventional statistical inference methodology. It is outrageous that these pseudoscientific methods are still taught in academia and practiced in industry despite their deep flaws and pathetic performance. They continue to waste billions of research dollars producing junk studies, tarnish the reputation of the scientific enterprise, and contribute significantly to economic disasters and human misery.

We are at a crossroads in the evolution of AI technologies, with most experts predicting exponential growth in its use, fundamentally transforming the way we live, work, and interact with one another. The danger that AI systems will take over humanity imminently is silly science fiction, because even the most advanced AI system lacks the common sense of a toddler. The real clear and present danger is that fools might end up developing and managing these powerful savants based on the spurious models of conventional finance and statistics. This will most likely lead to catastrophes faster and bigger than we have ever experienced before.

My criticisms are supported by simple math, common sense, data, and scholarly works that have been published over the past century. Perhaps one added value of this book is in retrieving many of those forgotten academic publications from the dusty archives of history and making readers aware of their insights in plain, unequivocal language using logic, simple math, or code that anyone with a high school degree can understand. Clearly, the conventional mode of expressing these criticisms hasn't worked at all. The stakes for individuals, society, and the scientific enterprise are too high for us to care if plainly spoken mathematical and scientific truths might offend someone or tarnish a reputation built on authoring or supporting bogus theories.

Navigating This Book

The contents of this book may be divided into two logical parts interwoven unevenly throughout each chapter. One part examines the appalling uselessness of the prevailing economics, statistical, and machine learning models for finance and investing domains. The other part examines why probabilistic machine learning is a less wrong, more useful model for these problem domains. The singular focus of this primer is on understanding the foundations of this complex, multidisciplinary field. Only pivotal concepts and applications are covered. Sometimes less is indeed more. The book is organized as follows, with each chapter having at least one of the main concepts in finance and investing applied in a hands-on Python code exercise:

- Chapter 1, "The Need for Probabilistic Machine Learning" examines some of the woeful inadequacies of theoretical finance, how all financial models are afflicted with a trifecta of errors, and why we need a systematic way of quantifying the uncertainty of our inferences and predictions. The chapter explains why probabilistic ML provides a useful framework for finance and investing.

- Chapter 2, "Analyzing and Quantifying Uncertainty" uses the Monty Hall problem to review the basic rules of probability theory, examine the meanings of probability, and explore the trinity of uncertainties that pervade our world. The chapter also explores the problem of induction and its algorithmic restatement, the no free lunch (NFL) theorems, and how they underpin finance, investing, and probabilistic ML.

- Chapter 3, "Quantifying Output Uncertainty with Monte Carlo Simulation" reviews important statistical concepts to explain why Monte Carlo simulation (MCS), one of the most important numerical techniques, works by generating approximate probabilistic solutions to analytically intractable problems.

- Chapter 4, "The Dangers of Conventional Statistical Methodologies" exposes the skullduggery of conventional statistical inference methodologies commonly used in research and industry, and explains why they are the main cause of false research findings that plague the social and economic sciences.

- Chapter 5, "The Probabilistic Machine Learning Framework" explores the probabilistic machine framework and demonstrates how inference from data and simulation of new data are logically and seamlessly integrated in this type of generative model.

- Chapter 6, "The Dangers of Conventional AI Systems" exposes the dangers of conventional AI systems, especially their lack of basic common sense and how they are unaware of their own limitations, which pose massive risks to all their stakeholders and society at large. Markov chain Monte Carlo simulations are introduced as a dependent sampling method for solving complex problems in finance and investing.

- Chapter 7, "Probabilistic Machine Learning with Generative Ensembles" explains how probabilistic machine learning is essentially a form of ensemble machine learning. It shows readers how to develop a prototype of a generative linear ensemble for regression problems in finance and investing using PyMC, Xarray, and ArviZ Python libraries.

- Chapter 8, "Making Probabilistic Decisions with Generative Ensembles" shows how to apply generative ensembles to risk management and capital allocation decisions in finance and investing. The implications of ergodicity and the pitfalls of using ensemble averages for financial decision making are explored. The strengths and weaknesses of capital allocation algorithms, including the Kelly criterion, are examined.

Conventions Used in This Book

The following typographical conventions are used in this book:

Italic
> Indicates new terms, URLs, email addresses, filenames, and file extensions.

`Constant width`
> Used for program listings, as well as within paragraphs to refer to program elements such as variable or function names, databases, data types, environment variables, statements, and keywords.

`Constant width bold`
> Shows commands or other text that should be typed literally by the user.

`Constant width italic`
> Shows text that should be replaced with user-supplied values or by values determined by context.

> This element signifies a tip or suggestion.

> This element signifies a general note.

> This element indicates a warning or caution.

Using Code Examples

Supplemental material (code examples) is available for download at *https://oreil.ly/supp-probabilistic-ML*.

If you have a technical question or a problem using the code examples, please send email to *support@oreilly.com*.

This book is here to help you get your job done. In general, if example code is offered with this book, you may use it in your programs and documentation. You do not need to contact us for permission unless you're reproducing a significant portion of the code. For example, writing a program that uses several chunks of code from this book does not require permission. Selling or distributing examples from O'Reilly books does require permission. Answering a question by citing this book and quoting example code does not require permission. Incorporating a significant amount of example code from this book into your product's documentation does require permission.

We appreciate, but generally do not require, attribution. An attribution usually includes the title, author, publisher, and ISBN. For example: "*Probabilistic Machine Learning for Finance and Investing* by Deepak K. Kanungo (O'Reilly). Copyright 2023 Hedged Capital L.L.C., 978-1-492-09767-9."

If you feel your use of code examples falls outside fair use or the permission given above, feel free to contact us at *permissions@oreilly.com*.

O'Reilly Online Learning

 For more than 40 years, *O'Reilly Media* has provided technology and business training, knowledge, and insight to help companies succeed.

Our unique network of experts and innovators share their knowledge and expertise through books, articles, and our online learning platform. O'Reilly's online learning platform gives you on-demand access to live training courses, in-depth learning paths, interactive coding environments, and a vast collection of text and video from O'Reilly and 200+ other publishers. For more information, visit *https://oreilly.com*.

How to Contact Us

Please address comments and questions concerning this book to the publisher:

O'Reilly Media, Inc.
1005 Gravenstein Highway North
Sebastopol, CA 95472
800-889-8969 (in the United States or Canada)
707-829-7019 (international or local)
707-829-0104 (fax)
support@oreilly.com
https://www.oreilly.com/about/contact.html

We have a web page for this book, where we list errata, examples, and any additional information. You can access this page at *https://oreil.ly/Probabilistic_ML*.

For news and information about our books and courses, visit *https://oreilly.com*.

Find us on LinkedIn: *https://linkedin.com/company/oreilly-media*

Follow us on Twitter: *https://twitter.com/oreillymedia*

Watch us on YouTube: *https://youtube.com/oreillymedia*

Acknowledgments

I would like to thank Michelle Smith, Jeff Bleiel, and the entire O'Reilly Media team for making this book possible. It was a pleasure working with everyone, especially Jeff, whose honest and insightful feedback helped me improve the contents of this book.

I would also like to thank the expert reviewers of my book, Abdullah Karasan, Juan Manuel Contreras, and Isaac Rhea, for their valuable comments.

Furthermore, I would like to thank the following readers of the early releases of the book for their equally valuable feedback: Ian Angell, Bruno Rignel, Jonathan Hugenschmidt, Autumn Peters, and Mike Shwe.

## CHAPTER 1

The Need for Probabilistic Machine Learning

Essentially, all models are wrong, but some are useful. However, the approximate nature of the model must always be borne in mind.

—George Box, eminent statistician

A map will enable you to go from one geographic location to another. It is a very useful mathematical model for navigating the physical world. It becomes even more useful if you automate it into a GPS system using artificial intelligence (AI) technologies. However, neither the mathematical model nor the AI-powered GPS system will ever be able to capture the human experience and richness of the terrain it represents. That's because all models have to simplify the complexities of the real world, thus enabling us to focus on some of the features of a phenomenon that interest us.

George Box, an eminent statistician, famously said, "all models are wrong, but some are useful." This deeply insightful quip is our mantra. We accept that all models are wrong because they are inadequate and incomplete representations of reality. Our goal is to build financial systems based on models and supporting technologies that enable useful inferences and predictions for decision making and risk management in the face of endemic uncertainty, incomplete information, and inexact measurements.

All financial models, whether derived theoretically or discovered empirically by humans and machines, are not only wrong but are also at the mercy of three types of errors. In this chapter, we explain this trifecta of errors with an example from consumer credit and explore it using Python code. This exemplifies our claim that inaccuracies of financial models are features, not bugs. After all, we are dealing with people, not particles or pendulums.

Finance is not an accurate physical science like physics, dealing with precise estimates and predictions, as academia will have us believe. It is an inexact social study grappling with a range of values with varying plausibilities that change continually, often abruptly.

We conclude the chapter by explaining why AI in general and probabilistic machine learning (ML) in particular offers the most useful and promising theoretical framework and technologies for developing the next generation of systems for finance and investing.

What Is a Model?

AI systems are based on models. A model maps functional relationships among its inputs and outputs variables based on assumptions and constraints. In general, input variables are called independent variables and output variables are called dependent variables.

In high school, you learned that the equation of any line in the XY plane can be expressed as $y = mx + b$, where m is the slope and b is the y-intercept of the line. For example, if you assume that consumer spending—the output/dependent variable y— has a linear relationship with personal income—the input/independent variable x— the equation for the line is called a model for consumer spending. Moreover, the slope m and the intercept b are referred to as the model's parameters. They are treated as constants, and their specific values define unique functional relationships or models.

Depending on the type of functional relationships, the parameters, and the nature of inputs and outputs variables, models may be classified as deterministic or probabilistic. In a deterministic model, there are no uncertainties about the type of functional relationships, the parameters, or the inputs or outputs of the model. The exact opposite is true for probabilistic models discussed in this book.

Finance Is Not Physics

Adam Smith, generally recognized as the founder of modern economics, was in awe of Newton's laws of mechanics and gravitation.[1] Since then, economists have endeavored to make their discipline into a mathematical science like physics. They aspire to formulate theories that accurately explain and predict the economic activities of human beings at the micro and macro levels. This desire gathered momentum in the early 20th century with economists like Irving Fisher and culminated in the econophysics movement of the late 20th century.

---

1 David Orrell and Paul Wilmott, "Going Random," in *The Money Formula: Dodgy Finance, Pseudo Science, and How Mathematicians Took Over the Markets* (West Sussex, UK: Wiley, 2017).

Despite all the complicated mathematics of modern finance, its theories are woefully inadequate, almost pitiful, especially when compared to those of physics. For instance, physics can predict the motion of the moon and the electrons in your computer with jaw-dropping precision. These predictions can be calculated by any physicist, at any time, anywhere on the planet. By contrast, market participants—traders, investors, analysts, finance executives—have trouble explaining the causes of daily market movements or predicting the price of an asset at any time, anywhere in the world.

The Political Economics of Misrepresenting a Nobel Prize

In his will, Alfred Nobel did not create a prize in economics or mathematics or any other discipline besides physics, chemistry, medicine, literature, and peace. The Sveriges Riksbank Prize in Economic Sciences in Memory of Alfred Nobel, now commonly and mistakenly referred to as the Nobel Prize in Economics, was created by the Swedish Central Bank in 1968. The central bank funds the award in perpetuity and pays the Nobel Foundation to administer it like it does the Nobel prizes willed by its benefactor.

By elevating the status of economics to that of the natural sciences and by buying the ongoing support of the prestigious Nobel Foundation, the Swedish central bank was able to gain independence in its decision making from the country's politicians to pursue its market-friendly policies. Economic policy decisions were to be left to the economic "scientists," just as health policy decisions were left to medical scientists.[2] However, by doing this, the Foundation disregards the will of Alfred Nobel and misrepresents the fundamental nature of economics as a social science.

In his 1974 acceptance speech, Friedrich Hayek, a pioneer of libertarian economics and advocate for free-market policies, clearly understood how the newly established economics prize could be misused when he said, "The Nobel Prize confers on an individual an authority which in economics no man ought to possess...This does not matter in the natural sciences. Here the influence exercised by an individual is chiefly an influence on his fellow experts; and they will soon cut him down to size if he exceeds his competence. But the influence of the economist that mainly matters is an influence over laymen: politicians, journalists, civil servants and the public generally."[3]

---

2 Avner Offer and G. Söderberg, *The Nobel Factor: The Prize in Economics, Social Democracy, and the Market Turn* (Princeton, NJ: Princeton University Press, 2016).

3 Friedrich von Hayek, "Banquet Speech," Nobel Prize Outreach AB, 2023, *https://www.nobelprize.org/prizes/economic-sciences/1974/hayek/speech*.

Perhaps finance is harder than physics. Unlike particles and pendulums, people are complex, emotional, creative beings with free will and latent cognitive biases. They tend to behave inconsistently and continually react to the actions of others in unpredictable ways. Furthermore, market participants profit by beating or gaming the systems that they operate in.

After losing a fortune on his investment in the South Sea Company, Newton remarked, "I can calculate the movement of the stars, but not the madness of men."[4] Note that Newton was not a novice investor. He served as the warden of the Mint in England for almost 31 years, helping put the British pound on the gold standard, where it would stay for over two centuries.

All Financial Models Are Wrong, Most Are Useless

Some academics have even argued that theoretical financial models are not only wrong but also dangerous. The veneer of a physical science lulls adherents of economic models into a false sense of certainty about the accuracy of their predictive powers.[5] This blind faith has led to many disastrous consequences for their adherents and for society at large.[6] Nothing better exemplifies the dangerous consequences of academic arrogance and blind faith in analytical financial models than the spectacular disaster of LTCM, discussed in the sidebar.

The Disaster of Long-Term Capital Management (LTCM)

LTCM was a hedge fund founded in 1994 by Wall Street veterans and academics Myron Scholes and Robert Merton, inventors of the famous Black-Scholes-Merton option pricing formula. The LTCM team was so confident in its investment models, overseen by two future "Nobel laureates," that it leveraged its portfolios to dangerously high levels. The team intended to magnify the tiny profits that LTCM was making on its various investments. In the first four years, LTCM had very impressive annual returns and had to turn away investor money.

However, the unpredictable complexity of social systems reared its ugly head in 1998, when the Russian government defaulted on its domestic local currency bonds. Such an event was not anticipated by LTCM's models, since a government can always print more money rather than default on its debt. This shocked global markets and led to the rapid collapse of LTCM—and showed that leverage magnifies losses, as it does

---

4 David Orrell and Paul Wilmott, "Early Models," in *The Money Formula: Dodgy Finance, Pseudo Science, and How Mathematicians Took Over the Markets* (West Sussex, UK: Wiley, 2017).

5 J. R. Thompson, L.S. Baggett, W. C. Wojciechowski, and E. E. Williams, "Nobels For Nonsense," *Journal of Post Keynesian Economics* 29, no. 1 (Autumn 2006): 3–18.

6 Orrell and Wilmott, *The Money Formula*.

gains. To prevent the crisis of LTCM from spreading and crashing the global financial markets, the Federal Reserve and a consortium of large banks bailed out LTCM. See Figure 1-1, which compares the value of $1,000 invested separately in LTCM, Dow Jones (DJIA), and US Treasury bonds.

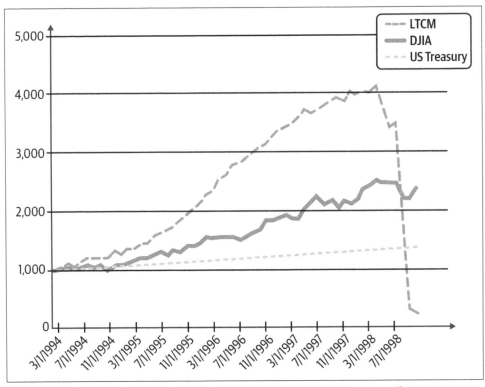

Figure 1-1. The epic disaster of Long Term Capital Management (LTCM)[7]

---

7 Adapted from an image from Wikimedia Commons.

Taking a diametrically different approach from hedge funds like LTCM, Renaissance Technologies, the most successful hedge fund in history, has put its critical views of financial theories into practice. Instead of hiring people with a finance or Wall Street background, the company prefers to hire physicists, mathematicians, statisticians, and computer scientists. It trades the markets using quantitative models based on nonfinancial theories such as information theory, data science, and machine learning.

The Trifecta of Modeling Errors

Whether financial models are based on academic theories or empirical data-mining strategies, they are all subject to the trifecta of modeling errors. Errors in analysis and forecasting may arise from any of the following modeling issues: using an inappropriate functional form, inputting inaccurate parameters, or failing to adapt to structural changes in the market.[8]

Errors in Model Specification

Almost all financial theories use the Gaussian or normal distribution in their models. For instance, the normal distribution is the foundation upon which Markowitz's modern portfolio theory and Black-Scholes-Merton option pricing theory are built.[9] However, it is a well-documented fact in academic research that stocks, bonds, currencies, and commodities have fat-tailed return distributions that are distinctly non-Gaussian.[10] In other words, extreme events occur far more frequently than predicted by the normal distribution. In Chapter 3 and Chapter 4, we will actually do financial data analysis in Python to demonstrate the non-Gaussian structure of equity return distributions.

If asset price returns were normally distributed, none of the following financial disasters would occur within the age of the universe: Black Monday, the Mexican peso crisis, the Asian currency crisis, the bankruptcy of LTCM, or the Flash Crash. "Mini flash crashes" of individual stocks occur with even higher frequency than these macro events.

---

8 Orrell and Wilmott, *The Money Formula*; M. Sekerke, *Bayesian Risk Management* (Hoboken, NJ: Wiley, 2015); J. R. Thompson, L. S. Baggett, W. C. Wojciechowski, and E. E. Williams, "Nobels for Nonsense," *Journal of Post Keynesian Economics* 29, no. 1 (Autumn 2006): 3–18; and Katerina Simons, "Model Error," *New England Economic Review* (November 1997): 17–28.

9 Orrell and Wilmott, *The Money Formula*; Sekerke, *Bayesian Risk Management*; and Thompson, Baggett, Wojciechowski, and Williams, "Nobels for Nonsense."

10 Orrell and Wilmott, *The Money Formula*; Sekerke, *Bayesian Risk Management*; and Thompson, Baggett, Wojciechowski, and Williams, "Nobels for Nonsense."

Yet, finance textbooks, programs, and professionals continue to use the normal distribution in their asset valuation and risk models because of its simplicity and analytical tractability. These reasons are no longer justifiable given today's advanced algorithms and computational resources. This reluctance to abandon the normal distribution is a clear example of "the drunkard's search": a principle derived from a joke about a drunkard who loses his key in the darkness of a park but frantically searches for it under a lamppost because that's where the light is.

Errors in Model Parameter Estimates

Errors of this type may arise because market participants have access to different levels of information with varying speeds of delivery. They also have different levels of sophistication in processing abilities and different cognitive biases. Moreover, these parameters are generally estimated from past data, which may not represent current market conditions accurately. These factors lead to profound epistemic uncertainty about model parameters.

Let's consider a specific example of interest rates. Fundamental to the valuation of any financial asset, interest rates are used to discount uncertain future cash flows of the asset and estimate its value in the present. At the consumer level, for example, credit cards have variable interest rates pegged to a benchmark called the prime rate. This rate generally changes in lockstep with the federal funds rate, an interest rate of seminal importance to the US and world economies.

Let's imagine that you would like to estimate the interest rate on your credit card one year from now. Suppose the current prime rate is 2% and your credit card company charges you 10% plus prime. Given the strength of the current economy, you believe that the Federal Reserve is more likely to raise interest rates than not. Based on our current information, we know that the Fed will meet eight times in the next 12 months and will either raise the federal funds rate by 0.25% or leave it at the previous level.

In the following Python code example, we use the binomial distribution to model your credit card's interest rate at the end of the 12-month period. Specifically, we'll use the following parameters for our range of estimates about the probability of the Fed raising the federal funds rate by 0.25% at each meeting: `fed_meetings` = 8 (number of trials or meetings); `probability_raises` = [0.6, 0.7,0 .8, 0.9]:

```
# Import binomial distribution from sciPy library
from scipy.stats import binom
# Import matplotlib library for drawing graphs
import matplotlib.pyplot as plt

# Total number of meetings of the Federal Open Market Committee (FOMC) in any
# year
fed_meetings = 8
```

```
# Range of total interest rate increases at the end of the year
total_increases = list(range(0, fed_meetings + 1))
# Probability that the FOMC will raise rates at any given meeting
probability_raises = [0.6, 0.7, 0.8, 0.9]

fig, axs = plt.subplots(2, 2, figsize=(10, 8))

for i, ax in enumerate(axs.flatten()):
    # Use the probability mass function to calculate probabilities of total
    # raises in eight meetings
    # Based on FOMC bias for raising rates at each meeting
    prob_dist = binom.pmf(k=total_increases, n=fed_meetings,
    p=probability_raises[i])
    # How each 25 basis point increase in the federal funds rate affects your
    # credit card interest rate
    cc_rate = [j * 0.25 + 12 for j in total_increases]

    # Plot the results for different FOMC probability
    ax.hist(cc_rate, weights=prob_dist, bins=fed_meetings, alpha=0.5,
    label=probability_raises[i])
    ax.legend()
    ax.set_ylabel('Probability of credit card rate')
    ax.set_xlabel('Predicted range of credit card rates after 12 months')
    ax.set_title(f'Probability of raising rates at each meeting:
    {probability_raises[i]}')

# Adjust spacing between subplots
plt.tight_layout()

# Show the plot
plt.show()
```

In Figure 1-2, notice how the probability distribution for your credit card rate in 12 months depends critically on your estimate about the probability of the Fed raising rates at each of the eight meetings. You can see that for every increase of 0.1 in your estimate of the Fed raising rates at each meeting, the expected interest rate for your credit card in 12 months increases by about 0.2%.

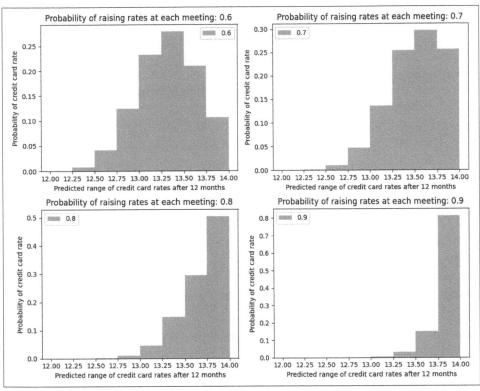

Figure 1-2. Probability distribution of credit card rates depends on your parameter estimates

Even if all market participants used the binomial distribution in their models, it's easy to see how they could disagree about the future prime rate because of the differences in their estimates about the Fed raising rates at each meeting. Indeed, this parameter is hard to estimate. Many institutions have dedicated analysts, including previous employees of the Fed, analyzing the Fed's every document, speech, and event to try to estimate this parameter. This is because the Fed funds rate directly impacts the prices of all financial assets and indirectly impacts the employment and inflation rates in the real economy.

Recall that we assumed that this parameter, `probability_raises`, was constant in our model for each of the next eight Fed meetings. How realistic is that? Members of the Federal Open Market Committee (FOMC), the rate-setting body, are not just a set of biased coins. They can and do change their individual biases based on how the economy changes over time. The assumption that the parameter `probility_raises` will be constant over the next 12 months is not only unrealistic, but also risky.

Errors from the Failure of a Model to Adapt to Structural Changes

The underlying data-generating stochastic process may vary over time—i.e., the process is not stationary ergodic. This implies that statistical moments of the distribution, like mean and variance, computed from sample financial data taken at a specific moment in time or sampled over a sufficiently long time period do not accurately predict the future statistical moments of the underlying distribution. The concepts of stationarity and ergodicity are very important in finance and will be explained in more detail later in the book.

We live in a dynamic capitalist economy characterized by technological innovations and changing monetary and fiscal policies. Time-variant distributions for asset values and risks are the rule, not the exception. For such distributions, parameter values based on historical data are bound to introduce error into forecasts.

In our previous example, if the economy were to show signs of slowing down, the Fed might decide to adopt a more neutral stance in its fourth meeting, making you change your `probability_raises` parameter from 70% to 50% going forward. This change in your parameter will, in turn, change the forecast of your credit card interest rate.

Sometimes the time-variant distributions and their parameters change continuously or abruptly, as in the Mexican peso crisis. For either continuous or abrupt changes, the models used will need to adapt to evolving market conditions. A new functional form with different parameters might be required to explain and predict asset values and risks in the new market regime.

Suppose after the fifth meeting in our example, the US economy is hit by an external shock—say a new populist government in Greece decides to default on its debt obligations. Now the Fed may be more likely to cut interest rates than to raise them. Given this structural change in the Fed's outlook, we will have to change the binomial probability distribution in our model to a trinomial distribution with appropriate parameters.

Probabilistic Financial Models

Inaccuracies of financial models are features, not bugs. It is intellectually dishonest and foolishly risky to represent financial estimates as scientifically precise values. All models should quantify the uncertainty inherent in financial inferences and predictions to be useful for sound decision making and risk management in the business world. Financial data are noisy and have measurement errors. A model's appropriate functional form may be unknown or an approximation. Model parameters and outputs may have a range of values with associated plausibilities. In other words, we need mathematically sound probabilistic models because they accommodate inaccuracies and quantify uncertainties with logical consistency.

There are two ways model uncertainty is currently quantified: forward propagation for output uncertainty, and inverse propagation for input uncertainty. Figure 1-3 shows the common types of probabilistic models used in finance today for quantifying both types of uncertainty.

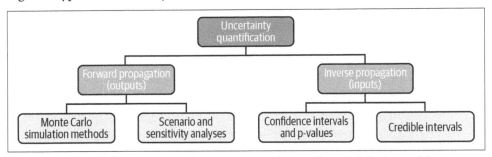

Figure 1-3. Quantifying input and output uncertainty with probabilistic models

In forward uncertainty propagation, uncertainties arising from a model's inexact parameters and inputs are propagated forward throughout the model to generate the uncertainty of the model's outputs. Most financial analysts use scenario and sensitivity analyses to quantify the uncertainty in their models' predictions. However, these are basic tools that only consider a few possibilities.

In scenario analysis, only three cases are built for consideration: best-case, base-case, and worst-case scenarios. Each case has a set value for all the inputs and parameters of a model. Similarly, in sensitivity analysis, only a few inputs or parameters are changed to assess their impact on the model's total output. For instance, a sensitivity analysis might be conducted on how the value of a company changes with interest rates or future earnings. In Chapter 3, we will learn how to perform Monte Carlo simulations (MCS) using Python and apply it to common financial problems. MCS is one of the most powerful probabilistic numerical tools in all the sciences and is used for analyzing both deterministic and probabilistic systems. It is a set of numerical methods that uses independent random samples from specified input parameter distributions to generate new data that we might observe in the future. This enables us to compute the expected uncertainty of a model, especially when its functional relationships are not analytically tractable.

In inverse uncertainty propagation, uncertainty of the model's input parameters is inferred from observed data. This is a harder computational problem than forward propagation because the parameters have to be learned from the data using dependent random sampling. Advanced statistical inference techniques or complex numerical computations are used to calculate confidence intervals or credible intervals of a model's input parameters. In Chapter 4, we explain the deep flaws and limitations of using p-values and confidence intervals, statistical techniques that are commonly used in financial data analysis today. Later in Chapter 6, we explain Markov chain Monte Carlo, an advanced, dependent, random sampling method, which can be used to compute credible intervals to quantify the uncertainty of a model's input parameters.

We require a comprehensive probabilistic framework that combines both forward and inverse uncertainty propagation seamlessly. We don't want the piecemeal approach that is currently in practice today. That is, we want our probabilistic models to quantify the uncertainty in the outputs of time-variant stochastic processes, with their inexact input parameters learned from sample data.

Our probabilistic framework will need to update continually the model outputs or its input parameters—or both—based on materially new datasets. Such models will have to be developed using small datasets, since the underlying environment may have changed too quickly to collect a sizable amount of relevant data. Most importantly, our probabilistic models need to know what they don't know. When extrapolating from datasets they have never encountered before, they need to provide answers with low confidence levels or wider margins of uncertainty.

Financial AI and ML

Probabilistic machine learning (ML) meets all the previously mentioned requirements for building state-of-the-art, next-generation financial systems.[11] But what is probabilistic ML? Before we answer that question, let's first make sure we understand what we mean by ML in particular and AI in general. It is common to see these terms bandied about as synonyms, even though they are not. ML is a subfield of AI. See Figure 1-4.

---

11 Sekerke, *Bayesian Risk Management*.

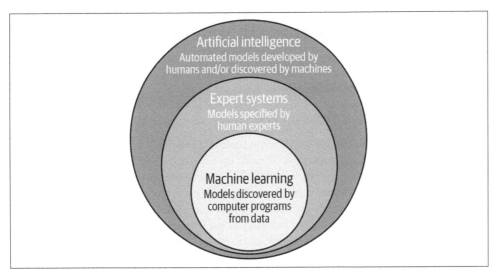

Figure 1-4. ML is a subfield of AI

AI is the general field that tries to automate the cognitive abilities of humans, such as analytical thinking, decision making, and sensory perception. In the 20th century, computer scientists developed a subfield of AI called symbolic AI (SAI), which included methodologies and tools to embed into computer systems, symbolic representations of human knowledge in the form of well-defined rules or algorithms.

SAI systems automate the models specified by domain experts and are aptly called expert systems. For instance, traders, finance executives, and system developers work together to explicitly formulate all the rules and the model's parameters that are to be automated by their financial and investment management systems. I have managed several such projects for marquee financial institutions at one of my previous companies.

However, SAI failed in automating complex tasks like image recognition and natural language processing—technologies used extensively in corporate finance and investing today. The rules for these types of expert systems are too complex and require constant updating for different situations. In the latter part of the 20th century, a new AI subfield of ML emerged from the confluence of improved algorithms, abundant data, and cheap computing resources.

ML turns the SAI paradigm on its head. Instead of experts specifying models to process data, humans with little or no domain expertise provide general-purpose algorithms that learn a model from data samples. More importantly, ML programs continually learn from new datasets and update their models without any human intervention for code maintenance. See the next sidebar for a simple explanation of how parameters are learned from data.

Training a Linear ML System to Learn

Recall the deterministic linear model discussed earlier and expressed by the equation $y = mx + b$. A unique line crosses at least two distinct points in the XY plane. The two points enable us to solve analytically for the exact values of parameters m and b using simple algebra. Once you have computed the parameters, you can use your model to make accurate predictions; given any point x, you can predict exactly what y will be.

However, financial models are not deterministic but probabilistic. For instance, if you were to plot a company's stock price returns on the y-axis and the growth rate of its quarterly earnings on the x-axis, you would see stock returns generally increase with earnings growth of a company. If you assume the relationship between stock price returns and quarterly earnings growth is *approximately* linear, you can use an analytical statistical technique to solve for the model's parameters m and b that gives you the line that best fits the company's sample data. If the linear approximation persists in the future, your model's predictions are not going to be precise, but they are going to be better than making random guesses or relying on luck.

Alternatively, you could use ML software to do similar calculations for you. In ML systems, the independent variable x is called a feature or predictor, and the dependent variable y is called the target or response variable. Feeding sample data to the ML system is referred to as training the system. When our linear ML system computes the values of the parameters m and b, we say that the ML system has learned the model from the in-sample data. The objective in ML is to predict the target values on out-of-sample data, which the system has not been trained on. This is where predictions become challenging.

We will get into the details of modeling, training, and testing probabilistic ML systems in the second half of the book. Here is a useful definition of ML from Tom Mitchell, an ML pioneer: "A computer program is said to learn from experience E with respect to some class of tasks T and performance measure P, if its performance at tasks in T, as measured by P, improves with experience E."[12] See Figure 1-5.

---

12 Aurélien Géron, "The Machine Learning Landscape," in *Hands-On Machine Learning with Scikit-Learn, Keras, and TensorFlow*, 3rd edition (O'Reilly Media, 2022), 1–34.

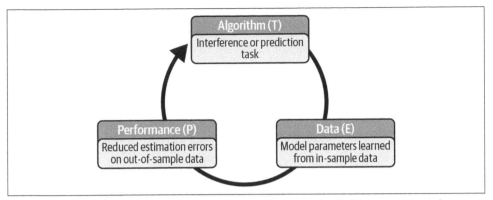

Figure 1-5. An ML model learns its parameters from in-sample data, but its performance is evaluated on out-of-sample data

Performance is measured against a prespecified objective function, such as maximizing annual stock price returns or lowering the mean absolute error of parameter estimates.

ML systems are usually classified into three types based on how much assistance they need from their human teachers or supervisors.

Supervised learning
   ML algorithms learn functional relationships from data, which are provided in pairs of inputs and desired outputs. This is the most prevalent form of ML used in research and industry. Some examples of ML systems include linear regression, logistic regression, random forests, gradient-boosted machines, and deep learning.

Unsupervised learning
   ML algorithms are only given input data and learn structural relationships in the data on their own. The K-means clustering algorithm is a commonly used data exploration algorithm used by investment analysts. Principal component analysis is a popular dimensionality reduction algorithm.

Reinforcement learning
   An ML algorithm continually updates a policy or set of actions based on feedback from its environment with the goal of maximizing the present value of cumulative rewards. It's different from supervised learning in that the feedback signal is not a desired output or class, but a reward or penalty. Examples of algorithms are Q-learning, deep Q-learning, and policy gradient methods. Reinforcement learning algorithms are being used in advanced trading applications.

In the 21st century, financial data scientists are training ML algorithms to discover complex functional relationships using data from multiple financial and nonfinancial sources. The newly discovered relationships may augment or replace the insights of finance and investment executives. ML programs are able to detect patterns in very high-dimensional datasets, a feat that is difficult if not impossible for humans. They are also able to reduce the dimensions to enable visualizations for humans.

AI is used in all aspects of the finance and investment process—from idea generation to analysis, execution, portfolio, and risk management. The leading AI-powered systems in finance and investing today use some combination of expert systems and ML-based systems by leveraging the advantages of both types of approaches and expertise. Furthermore, AI-powered financial systems continue to leverage human intelligence (HI) for research, development, and maintenance. Humans may also intervene in extreme market conditions, where it may be difficult for AI systems to learn from abrupt changes. So you can think of modern financial systems as a complex combination of SAI + ML + HI.

Probabilistic ML

Probabilistic ML is the next-generation ML framework and technology for AI-powered financial and investing systems. Leading technology companies clearly understand the limitations of conventional AI technologies and are developing their probabilistic versions to extend their applicability to more complex problems.

Google recently introduced TensorFlow Probability to extend its established TensorFlow platform. Similarly, Facebook and Uber have introduced Pyro to extend their PyTorch platform. Currently, the most popular open source probabilistic ML technologies are PyMC and Stan. PyMC is written in Python, and Stan is written in C++. In Chapter 7, we use the PyMC library because it's part of the Python ecosystem.

Probabilistic ML as discussed in this book is based on a generative model. It is categorically different from the conventional ML in use today, such as linear, nonlinear, and deep learning systems, even though these other systems compute probabilistic scores. Figure 1-6 shows the major differences between the two types of systems.

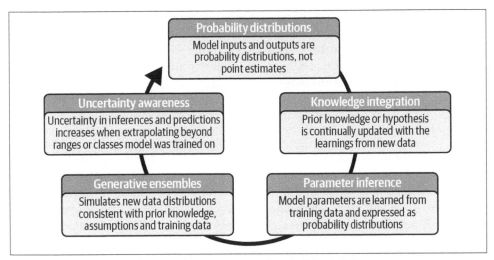

Figure 1-6. Summary of major characteristics of probabilistic ML systems

Probability Distributions

Even though conventional ML systems use calibrated probabilities, they only compute the most likely estimates and their associated probabilities as single-point values for inputs and outputs. This works well for domains, such as image recognition, where the data are plentiful and the signal-to-noise ratio is high. As was discussed and demonstrated in the previous sections, a point estimate is an inaccurate and misleading representation of financial reality, where uncertainty is very high. Furthermore, the calibrated probabilities may not be valid probabilities as the unconditional probability distribution of the data is almost never computed by MLE models. This can lead to poor quantification of uncertainty as will be explained in Chapter 6.

Probabilistic ML systems only deal in probability distributions in their computations of input parameters and model outputs. This is a realistic and honest representation of the uncertainty of a financial model's variables. Furthermore, probability distributions leave the user considerable flexibility in picking the appropriate point estimate, if required, based on their business objectives.

Knowledge Integration

Conventional ML systems do not have a theoretically sound framework for incorporating prior knowledge, whether it is well-established scientific knowledge, institutional knowledge, or personal insights. Later in the book, we will see that conventional statisticians sneak in prior knowledge using ad hoc statistical methods, such as null hypothesis, statistical significance levels, and L1 and L2 regularizations, while pounding the table about letting only "the data speak for themselves."

It is foolish not to integrate prior knowledge in our personal and professional lives. It is the antithesis of learning and vitiates against the nature of the scientific method. Yet this is the basis of null hypothesis significance testing (NHST), the prevailing statistical methodology in academia, research, and industry since the 1960s. NHST prohibits the inclusion of prior knowledge in experiments based on the bogus claim that objectivity demands that we only let the data speak for themselves. By following this specious claim, NHST ends up committing the prosecutor's fallacy, as we will show in Chapter 4.

NHST's definition of objectivity would require us to touch fire everywhere and every time we find it because we cannot incorporate our prior knowledge of what it felt like in similar situations in the past. That is the definition of foolishness, not objectivity. In Chapter 4, we will discuss how and why several metastudies have shown that the majority of published medical research findings based on NHST are false. Yes, you read that right, and it has been an open secret since a seminal paper published in 2005.[13]

Fortunately, in this book we don't have to waste much ink or pixels on this specious argument about objectivity or the proliferation of junk science produced by NHST. Probabilistic ML systems provide a mathematically rigorous framework for incorporating prior knowledge and updating it appropriately with learnings from new information. Representation of prior knowledge is done explicitly so that anyone can challenge it or change it. This is the essence of learning and the basis of the scientific method.

One of the important implications of the no free lunch (NFL) theorems is that prior domain knowledge is necessary to optimize an algorithm's performance for a specific problem domain. If we don't apply our prior domain knowledge, the performance of our unbiased algorithm will be no better than random guessing when averaged across all problem domains. There is no such thing as a free lunch, especially in finance and investing. We will discuss the NFL theorems in detail in the next chapter.

It is common knowledge that integration of accumulated institutional knowledge into a company's organization, process, and systems leads to a sustainable competitive advantage in business. Moreover, personal insights and experience with markets can lead to "alpha," or the generation of exceptional returns in trading and investing, for the fund manager who arrives at a subjectively different viewpoint from the rest of the crowd. That's how Warren Buffet, one of the greatest investors of all time, made

---

13 The paper is John P. A. Ioannidis, "Why Most Published Research Findings Are False," *PLOS Medicine* 2, no. 8 (2005): e124, *https://doi.org/10.1371/journal.pmed.0020124*. See also Julia Belluz, "This Is Why You Shouldn't Believe That Exciting New Medical Study," *Vox*, February 27, 2017, *https://www.vox.com/2015/3/23/8264355/research-study-hype*.

his vast fortune. Markets mock dogmatic and unrealistic definitions of objectivity with lost profits and eventually with financial ruin.

Parameter Inference

Almost all conventional ML systems use equally conventional statistical methodologies, such as p-values and confidence intervals, to estimate the uncertainty of a model's parameters. As will be explained in Chapter 4, these are deeply flawed—almost scandalous—statistical methodologies that plague the social sciences, including finance and economics. These methodologies adhere to a pious pretense to objectivity and to implicit and unrealistic assumptions, obfuscated by inscrutable statistical jargon, in order to generate solutions that are analytically tractable for a small set of scenarios.

Probabilistic ML is based on a simple and intuitive definition of probability as logic, and the rigorous calculus of probability theory in general and the inverse probability rule in particular. In the next chapter, we show how the inverse probability rule—mistakenly and mortifyingly known as Bayes's theorem—is a trivial reformulation of the product rule. It is a logical tautology that is embarrassingly easy to prove. It doesn't deserve to be called a theorem, given how excruciatingly difficult it is to derive most mathematical theorems.

However, because of the normalizing constant in the inversion formula, it was previously impossible to invert probabilities analytically, except for simple problems. With the recent advancement of state-of-the-art numerical algorithms, such as Hamiltonian Monte Carlo and automatic differentiation variational inference, probabilistic ML systems are now able to invert probabilities to compute model parameter estimates from in-sample data for almost any real-world problem. More importantly, they are able to quantify parameter uncertainties with mathematically sound credible intervals for any level of confidence. This enables inverse uncertainty propagation.

Generative Ensembles

Almost all conventional ML systems are based on discriminative models. This type of statistical model only learns a decision boundary from the in-sample data, but not how the data are distributed statistically. Therefore, conventional discriminative ML systems cannot simulate new data and quantify total output uncertainty.

Probabilistic ML systems are based on generative models. This type of statistical model learns the statistical structure of the data distribution and so can easily and seamlessly simulate new data, including generating data that might be missing or corrupted. Furthermore, the distribution of parameters generates an ensemble of models. Most importantly, these systems are able to simulate two-dimensional output uncertainty based on data variability and input parameter uncertainty, the probability distributions of which they have learned previously from in-sample data. This seamlessly enables forward uncertainty propagation.

Uncertainty Awareness

When computing probabilities, a conventional ML system uses the maximum likelihood estimation (MLE) method. This technique optimizes the parameters of an assumed probability distribution such that the in-sample data are most likely to be observed, given the point estimates for the model's parameters. As we will see later in the book, MLE leads to wrong inferences and predictions when data are sparse, a common occurrence in finance and investing, especially when a market regime changes abruptly.

What makes it worse is that these MLE-based ML systems attach horrifyingly high probabilities to these wrong estimates. We are automating the overconfidence of powerful systems that lack basic common sense. This makes conventional ML systems potentially risky and dangerous, especially when used in mission-critical operations by personnel who either don't understand the fundamentals of these ML systems or have blind faith in them.

Probabilistic ML systems do not rely on a single-point estimate, no matter how likely or optimal, but a weighted average of every possible estimate of a parameter's entire probability distribution. Moreover, the uncertainty of these estimates increases appropriately when systems deal with classes of data they have never seen before in training, or are extrapolating beyond known data ranges. Unlike MLE-based systems, probabilistic ML systems know what they don't know. This keeps the quantification of uncertainty honest and prevents overconfidence in estimates and predictions.

Summary

Economics is not a precise predictive science like physics. Not even close. So let's not pretend otherwise and treat academic theories and models of economics as if they were models of quantum physics, the obfuscating math notwithstanding.

All financial models, whether based on academic theories or ML strategies, are at the mercy of the trifecta of modeling errors. While this trio of errors can be mitigated with appropriate tools, such as probabilistic ML systems, it cannot be eliminated. There will always be asymmetry of information and cognitive biases. Models of asset values and risks will change over time due to the dynamic nature of capitalism, human behavior, and technological innovation.

Probabilistic ML technologies are based on a simple and intuitive definition of probability as logic and the rigorous calculus of probability theory. They enable the explicit and systematic integration of prior knowledge that is updated continually with new learnings.

These systems treat uncertainties and errors in financial and investing systems as features, not bugs. They quantify uncertainty generated from inexact inputs, parameters and outputs of finance, and investing systems as probability distributions, not point estimates. This makes for realistic financial inferences and predictions that are useful for decision making and risk management. Most importantly, these systems become capable of forewarning us when their inferences and predictions are no longer useful in the current market environment.

There are several reasons why probabilistic ML is the next-generation ML framework and technology for AI-powered financial and investing systems. Its probabilistic framework moves away from flawed statistical methodologies (NHST, p-values, confidence intervals) and the restrictive conventional view of probability as a limiting frequency. It moves us toward an intuitive view of probability as logic and a mathematically rigorous statistical framework that quantifies uncertainty holistically and successfully. Therefore, it enables us to move away from the wrong, idealistic, analytical models of the past toward less wrong, more realistic, numerical models of the future.

The algorithms used in probabilistic programming are among the most sophisticated algorithms in the AI world, which we will delve into in the second half of the book. In the next three chapters, we will take a deeper dive into why it is very risky to deploy your capital using conventional ML systems, because they are based on orthodox probabilistic and statistical methods that are scandalously flawed.

References

Géron, Aurélien. "The Machine Learning Landscape." In *Hands-On Machine Learning with Scikit-Learn, Keras, and TensorFlow*, 1–34. 3rd ed. O'Reilly Media, 2022.

Hayek, Friedrich von. "Banquet Speech." Speech given at the Nobel Banquet, Stockholm, Sweden, December 10, 1974. Nobel Prize Outreach AB, 2023, *https://www.nobelprize.org/prizes/economic-sciences/1974/hayek/speech/*.

Ioannidis, John P. A. "Why Most Published Research Findings Are False." *PLOS Medicine* 2, no. 8 (2005): e124. *https://doi.org/10.1371/journal.pmed.0020124*.

Offer, Avner, and Gabriel Söderberg. *The Nobel Factor: The Prize in Economics, Social Democracy, and the Market Turn*. Princeton, NJ: Princeton University Press, 2016.

Orrell, David, and Paul Wilmott. *The Money Formula: Dodgy Finance, Pseudo Science, and How Mathematicians Took Over the Markets*. West Sussex, UK: Wiley, 2017.

Sekerke, Matt. *Bayesian Risk Management*. Wiley, 2015.

Simons, Katerina. "Model Error." *New England Economic Review* (November 1997): 17–28.

Thompson, J. R., L.S. Baggett, W. C. Wojciechowski, and E. E. Williams. "Nobels For Nonsense." *Journal of Post Keynesian Economics* 29, no. 1 (Autumn 2006): 3–18.

Further Reading

Jaynes, E. T. *Probability Theory: The Logic of Science*. New York: Cambridge University Press, 2003.

Lopez de Prado, Marcos. *Advances in Financial Machine Learning*. Hoboken, New Jersey: Wiley, 2018.

Taleb, Nassim Nicholas. *Fooled by Randomness: The Hidden Role of Chance in Life and in the Markets*. New York: Random House Trade, 2005.

## CHAPTER 2

Analyzing and Quantifying Uncertainty

There are known knowns. These are things we know that we know. There are known unknowns. That is to say, there are things that we know we don't know. But there are also unknown unknowns. There are things we don't know we don't know.

—Donald Rumsfeld, Former US Secretary of Defense

The Monty Hall problem, a famous probability brainteaser, is an entertaining way to explore the complex and profound nature of uncertainty that we face in our personal and professional lives. More pertinently, the solution to the Monty Hall problem is essentially a betting strategy. Throughout this chapter, we use it to explain many key concepts and pitfalls in probability, statistics, machine learning, game theory, finance, and investing.

In this chapter, we will solve the apparent paradox of the Monty Hall problem by developing two analytical solutions of differing complexity using the fundamental rules of probability theory. We also derive the inverse probability rule that is pivotal to probabilistic machine learning. Later in this chapter, we confirm these analytical solutions with a Monte Carlo simulation (MCS), one of the most powerful numerical techniques that is used extensively in finance and investing.

There are three types of uncertainty embedded in the Monty Hall problem that we examine. Aleatory uncertainty is the randomness in the observed data (the known knowns). Epistemic uncertainty arises from the lack of knowledge about the underlying phenomenon (the known unknowns). Ontological uncertainty evolves from the nature of human affairs and its inherently unpredictable dynamics (the unknown unknowns).

Probability is used to quantify and analyze uncertainty in a systematic manner. In doing so, we reject the vacuous distinction between risk and uncertainty. Probability is truly the logic of science. It might be surprising for you to know that we can agree on the axioms of probability theory, yet disagree on the meaning of probability. We explore the two main schools of thought, the frequentist and epistemic views of probability. We find the conventional view of probability, the frequentist version, to be a special case of epistemic probability at best and suited to simple games of chance. At worst, the frequentist view of probability is based on a facade of objective reality that shows an inexcusable ignorance of classical physics and common sense.

The no free lunch (NFL) theorems are a set of impossibility theorems that are an algorithmic restatement of the age-old problem of induction within a probabilistic framework. We explore how these epistemological concepts have important practical implications for probabilistic machine learning, finance, and investing.

The Monty Hall Problem

The famous Monty Hall problem was originally conceived and solved by an eminent statistician, Steve Selvin. The problem as we know it now is based on the popular 1970s game show *Let's Make a Deal* and named after its host, Monty Hall. Here are the rules of this brainteaser:

1. There is a car behind one of three doors and goats behind the other two.
2. The objective is to win the car (not a goat!).
3. Only Monty knows which door hides the car.
4. Monty allows you to choose any one of the three doors.
5. Depending on the door you choose, he opens one of the other two doors that has a goat behind it.

So let's play the game. It doesn't really matter which door you chose because the game plays out similarly regardless. Say you chose door 1. Based on your choice of door 1, Monty opens door 3 to show you a goat. See Figure 2-1.

Figure 2-1. The Monty Hall problem[1]

Now Monty offers you a deal: he gives you the option of sticking with your original choice of door 1 or switching to door 2. Do you switch to door 2 or stay with your original decision of door 1? Try to solve this problem before you read ahead—it will be worth the trouble.

I must admit that when I first came across this problem many years ago, my immediate response was that it doesn't matter whether you stay or switch doors, since now it is equally likely that the car is behind either door 1 or door 2. So I stayed with my original choice. Turns out that my choice was wrong.

The optimal strategy is to switch doors because, by opening one of the doors, Monty has given you valuable new information which you can use to increase the odds of winning the car. After I worked through the solution and realized I was wrong, I took comfort in the fact that this problem had stumped thousands of PhD statisticians. It had even baffled the great mathematician Paul Erdos, who was only convinced that switching doors was a winning strategy after seeing a simulation of the solution. The in-depth analysis of the Monty Hall problem in this chapter is my "revenge analysis."

As the following sidebar explains, there may be psychological reasons why people don't switch doors.

---

1 Adapted from an image on Wikimedia Commons.

The Psychology of Financial Decision Making[2]

If the car is equally likely to be behind either of the two remaining doors, don't you think it is odd that most people don't switch doors? Behavioral economics, which uses psychology to explain economic behavior, calls this the endowment effect. People tend to put a higher value on the things they own than they would if they did not possess them. They seem to form an emotional or irrational attachment to them. Since they had chosen door 1, they felt like they owned it and became attached to it.

There may be another psychological reason for the endowment effect: loss aversion. Losses cause investors more pain than gains give them pleasure. That might explain why investors are generally reluctant to cut their losses but are quick to take their profits. It would have hurt a lot more if I switched doors and lost, outweighing the pleasure I would have, if I switched doors and won.

Inertia also plays an important role in decision making. People would rather be wrong through inaction, an error of omission, than be wrong through action, an error of commission.

Before we do a simulation of this problem, let's try to figure out a solution logically by applying the axioms of probability.

Axioms of Probability

Here is a refresher on the axioms, or fundamental rules, of probability. It is simply astonishing that the calculus of probability can be derived entirely from the following three axioms and a few definitions.

Say S is any scenario (also known as an event). In general, we define S as the scenario in which there is a car behind a door. So, S_1 is the specific scenario that the car is behind door 1. We define S_2 and S_3 similarly. The complement of S is S′ (not S) and is the scenario in which there is a goat (not a car) behind the door.

Scenarios S and S′ are said to be mutually exclusive, since there is either a goat or a car, but not both, behind any given door. Since those are the only possible scenarios in this game, S and S′ are also said to be collectively exhaustive scenarios or events. The set of all possible scenarios is called the sample space. Let's see how we can apply the rules of probability to the Monty Hall game.

---

2 Richard Thaler, *Misbehaving: The Making of Behavioral Economics* (New York: W. W. Norton & Company, 2015); Daniel Kahneman, *Thinking, Fast and Slow* (New York: Farrar, Straus and Giroux, 2011).

Axiom 1: P(S) ≥ 0

  Probability of an event or scenario, $P(S)$, is always assigned a nonnegative real number. For instance, when Monty shows us that there is no car behind door 3, $P(S_3) = 0$. An event probability of 0 means the event is impossible or didn't occur.

Axiom 2: $P(S_1) + P(S_2) + P(S_3) = 1$

  What this axiom says is that we are absolutely certain that at least one of the scenarios in the sample space will occur. Note that this axiom implies that an event probability of 1 means the event will certainly occur or has already occurred. We know from the rules of the Monty Hall game that there is only one car and it is behind one of the three doors. This means that the scenarios S_1, S_2, and S_3 are mutually exclusive and collectively exhaustive. Therefore, $P(S_1) + P(S_2) + P(S_3) = 1$. Also note that axioms 1 and 2 ensure that probabilities always have a value between 0 and 1, inclusive. Furthermore, $P(S_1) + P(\text{not } S_1) = 1$ implies $P(S_1) = 1 - P(\text{not } S_1)$.

Axiom 3: $P(S_2 \text{ or } S_3) = P(S_2) + P(S_3)$

  This axiom is known as the sum rule and enables us to compute probabilities of two scenarios that are mutually exclusive. Say we want to know the probability that the car is either behind door 2 or door 3, i.e., we want to know $P(S_2 \text{ or } S_3)$. Since the car cannot be behind door 2 and door 3 simultaneously, S_2 and S_3 are mutually exclusive, i.e., $P(S_2 \text{ and } S_3) = 0$. Therefore, $P(S_2 \text{ or } S_3) = P(S_2) + P(S_3)$.

Probability Distributions Functions

A probability mass function (PMF) provides the probability that a discrete variable will have a particular value, such as those computed in the Monty Hall problem. A PMF only provides discrete and finite values. A cumulative distribution function (CDF) enumerates the probability that a variable is less than or equal to a particular value. The values of a CDF are always non-decreasing and between 0 and 1 inclusive.

A probability density function (PDF) provides the probability that a continuous variable will fall within a range of values. A PDF can assume infinitely many continuous values. However, a PDF assigns a zero probability to any specific point estimate. It might seem surprising that a PDF can be greater than 1 at different points in the distribution. That's because a PDF is the derivative or slope of the (CDF) and has no constraint on its value not exceeding 1.

We will apply the axioms of probability to solve the Monty Hall problem. It is very important to note that in this book, we don't make the conventional distinction between a deterministic variable and a random variable. This is because we interpret probability as a dynamic, extrinsic property of the information about an event, which may or may not be repeatable or random. The only distinction we make is a commonsensical one between a variable and a constant. Events for which we have complete information are treated as constants. All other events are treated as variables.

For instance, after Monty places a car behind one of the doors and goats behind the other two, there is no randomness associated with what entity lies behind which door. All such events are now static and nonrandom for both Monty and his audience. However, unlike his audience, Monty is certain where the car is placed. For Monty, the probability that the car is behind a specific door is a constant, namely 1 for the door he chose to place the car behind and 0 for the other two doors he chose to place the goats behind. Since we lack any information about the location of the car when the game begins, we can treat it as a variable whose value we can update dynamically based on new information. For us, these events are not deterministic or random. Our probabilities only reflect our lack of information. However, we can apply the calculus of probability theory to estimate and update our estimates of where the car has been placed. So let's try to figure that out, without further ado.

Since each scenario is mutually exclusive (there is either a goat or a car behind each door) and collectively exhaustive (those are all the possible scenarios), their probabilities must add up to 1, since at least one of the following scenarios must occur:

$$P(S_1) + P(S_2) + P(S_3) = 1 \qquad \text{(Equation 2.1)}$$

Before we make a choice, the most plausible assumption is that the car is equally likely to be behind any one of the three doors. There is nothing in the rules of the game to make us think otherwise, and Monty Hall hasn't given us any hints to the contrary. So it is reasonable to assume that $P(S_1)=P(S_2)=P(S_3)$. Using Equation 2.1, we get:

$$3 \times P(S_1) = 1 \text{ or } P(S_1) = \frac{1}{3} \qquad \text{(Equation 2.2)}$$

Since $P(S_1) = P(S_2) = P(S_3)$, Equation 2.2 implies that it is logical to assume that there is a $\frac{1}{3}$ probability that the car is behind one of the three doors.

By the sum rule, the probability that the car is behind either door 2 or door 3 is:

$$P(S_2 \text{ or } S_3) = P(S_2) + P(S_3) = \frac{1}{3} + \frac{1}{3} = \frac{2}{3} \qquad \text{(Equation 2.3)}$$

After you choose door 1 and Monty opens door 3, showing you a goat, $P(S_3) = 0$. Substituting this value in Equation 2.3 and solving for $P(S_2)$, we get:

$$P(S_2) = P(S_2 \text{ or } S_3) - P(S_3) = \frac{2}{3} - 0 = \frac{2}{3} \qquad \text{(Equation 2.4)}$$

So switching your choice from door 1 to door 2 doubles your chances of winning the car: it goes from ⅓ to ⅔. Switching doors is the optimal betting strategy in this game. See Figure 2-2.

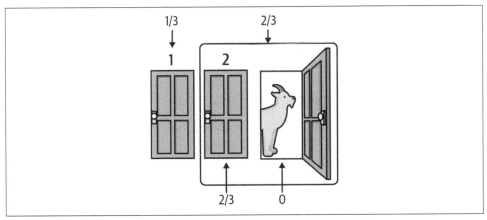

Figure 2-2. A simple logical solution to the Monty Hall problem[3]

It is important to note that because of uncertainty, there is still a ⅓ chance that you could lose if you switch doors. In general, randomness of results makes it hard and frustrating to determine if your investment or trading strategy is a winning one or a lucky one. It is much easier to determine a winning strategy in the Monty Hall problem because it can be determined analytically or by simulating the game many times, as we will do shortly.

Game Theory and the Monty Hall Problem

Game theory provides a mathematical framework for analyzing strategic decision making where the outcomes of any player are affected by the actions of other players in the game. It is a useful framework that is applied in finance and investing, among other disciplines.

The Monty Hall problem is a two-person, sequential, and competitive game (as opposed to a cooperative game). Monty is our worthy opponent and has only one strategy: after you have picked a door at random, he shows you another door with a goat behind it. You have two strategies: staying with your original choice of door, or switching doors. Essentially, we have already solved the Monty Hall problem using the basic principles of game theory. Your optimal strategy is switching doors since it maximizes your probability of winning the car, your payoff.

---

3 Adapted from an image on Wikimedia Commons.

Your switching strategy is also referred to as the game's Nash equilibrium. This concept is named after John Nash, an eminent mathematician who developed its theory. A Nash equilibrium is a point that players reach in any game in which no player can improve their payoffs by unilaterally changing their strategy, given the strategies of the other players. You can't do better than switching doors, given that Monty's strategy is to always show you a goat when you pick a door. He's not going to open the door with the car behind it—that defeats the purpose and profitability of the show.

Inverting Probabilities

Let's develop a more rigorous analytical solution to the Monty Hall problem. To do that, we need to understand conditional probabilities and how to invert them. This is the equivalent of understanding the rules of multiplication and division of ordinary numbers. Recall that when we condition a probability, we revise the plausibility of a scenario or event by incorporating new information from the conditioning data. The conditional probability of a scenario H given a conditioning dataset D is represented as $P(H|D)$, which reads as the probability of H given D and is defined as follows:

$P(H|D) = P(H \text{ and } D) / P(D)$ provided $P(D) \neq 0$ since division by 0 is undefined

The division by $P(D)$ ensures that probabilities of all scenarios conditioned on D will add up to 1. Recall that if two events are independent, their joint probabilities are the product of their individual probabilities. That is, $P(H \text{ and } D) = P(H) \times P(D)$ if knowledge of D does not improve our probability of H, and vice versa.

The definition of conditional probability of P given H also implies that $P(H \text{ and } D) = P(H|D) \times P(D)$. This is called the product rule. We can now derive the inverse probability rule from the product rule. We know from the symmetry of the joint probability of two events:

- $P(H \text{ and } D) = P(D \text{ and } H)$
- $P(H|D) \times P(D) = P(D|H) \times P(H)$
- $P(H|D) = P(D|H) \times P(H) / P(D)$

And that, ladies and gentlemen, is the proof of the famous and wrongly named "Bayes's theorem." If only all mathematical proofs were so easy! As you can see, this alleged theorem is a trivial reformulation of the product rule. It's as much a theorem as multiplying two numbers and solving for one of them in terms of their product (for example, $H = H \times D/D$). The hard part and the insightful bit is interpreting and applying the formula to invert probabilities and solve complex, real-world problems. Since the 1950s, the previously mentioned formula has also been wrongly known as Bayes's theorem. See the following sidebar.

Bayes Did Not Discover Bayes's Theorem and Was Not a Bayesian[4]

Thomas Bayes, an 18th-century theologian and amateur mathematician, would probably be rolling over in his grave if he knew that his name was being used in an intellectual war that has raged for almost a century over the meaning and application of probability theory. Bayes's surreal confusion would stem from the fact that he was not responsible for developing the inverse probability rule or the foundations of the statistical theory that wrongly bears his name. That distinction goes to the polymath Pierre-Simon Laplace, who built the foundations of this statistical school of thought in the late 1700s. It is shameful that Laplace doesn't get much of the credit for discovering it independently and writing down the general formula in its modern form.

Bayes's paper on inverse probability was published posthumously by his friend, Richard Price, who wrote about half of that paper and corrected several of Bayes's errors over two years before he sent it for publication. It is equally shameful that Price has been ignored for his contributions for completing Bayes's paper and actually submitting it for publication without adding his name to it. The Bayes-Price paper did not cause much of a stir among mathematicians when it was finally published. That's because Daniel Bernoulli and Abraham de Moivre had already worked on the inverse probability problem long before Bayes, and the paper was not really breaking new ground. In fact, Bayes had read de Moivre's book *The Doctrine of Chances* (Woodfall, 1718) and used it to try to solve his specific problem on inverting probabilities. Moreover, he never generalized the rule from his specific problem—a requirement for all rules and theorems, especially the eponymous ones.

In this book we will correct this blatant injustice and egregious misnomer by referring to the rule by its original name, the inverse probability rule. This is what the rule was called for over two centuries before R. A. Fisher referred to it pejoratively as Bayes's rule in the middle of the 20th century. I suspect that by attaching the name of an amateur mathematician to an incontrovertible mathematical rule, Fisher was able to undermine the inverse probability rule so that he could commit the prosecutor's fallacy with impunity under the pious pretense of only "letting the data speak for themselves." Fisher's "worse than useless" statistical inference methodology will be discussed further in Chapter 4. Also, in this book, we revert to the original name of the rule since it has a longer, authenitic tradition, and the alternative of calling the inverse probability rule the Laplace-Bernoulli-Moivre-Bayes-Price rule is way too long.

---

4 Stephen M. Stigler, "Who Discovered Bayes's Theorem?" *The American Statistician* 37, no. 4a (1983): 290–96; E. T. Jaynes, "Historical Digression," in *Probability Theory: The Logic of Science*, ed. G. Larry Bretthorst (New York: Cambridge University Press, 2003), 112–14; A. I. Dale, "Inverse Probability," in *A History of Inverse Probability: From Thomas Bayes to Karl Pearson* (New York: Springer, 1999), 1–16.

Furthermore, we will refer to Bayesian statistics as epistemic statistics and Bayesian inference as probabilistic inference. Just as frequentist statistics interprets probability as the relative limiting frequency of an event, epistemic statistics interprets probability as a property of information about an event. Hopefully, this will move us away from wrongly attributing this important scientific endeavor and body of knowledge to one person whose contributions to this effort may be dubious. In fact, there is no evidence to suggest that Bayes was even a Bayesian as the term is used today.

Epistemic statistics in general and the inverse probability rule in particular are the foundation of probabilistic machine learning, and we will discuss it in depth in the second half of this book. For now, let's apply it to the Monty Hall problem and continue with the same definitions of S_1, S_2, and S_3 and their related probabilities. Now we define our dataset D, which includes two observations: you choose door 1; and based on your choice of door 1, Monty opens door 3 to show you a goat. We want to solve for $P(S_2|D)$, i.e., the probability that the car is behind door 2, given dataset D.

We know from the inverse probability rule that this equals $P(D|S_2) \times P(S_2)/P(D)$. The challenging computation is $P(D)$, which is the unconditional or marginal probability of seeing the dataset D regardless of which door the car is behind. The rule of total probability allows us to compute marginal probabilities from conditional probabilities. Specifically, the rule states that the marginal probability of D, $P(D)$, is the weighted average probability of realizing D under different scenarios, with $P(S)$ giving us the specific probabilities or weights for each scenario in the sample space of S:

$$P(D) = P(D|S_1) \times P(S_1) + P(D|S_2) \times P(S_2) + P(D|S_3) \times P(S_3)$$

We have estimated the probabilities of the three scenarios at the beginning of the Monty Hall game, namely $P(S_1) = P(S_2) = P(S_3) = \frac{1}{3}$. These are going to be the weights for each possible scenario. Let's compute the conditional probabilities of observing our dataset D. Note that by $P(D|S_1)$ we mean the probability of seeing the dataset D, given that the car is actually behind door 1 and so on.

If the car is behind door 1 and you pick door 1, there are goats behind the other two doors. So Monty can open either door 2 or door 3 to show you a goat. Thus, the probability of Monty opening door 3 to show you a goat, given that you chose door 1, is $\frac{1}{2}$, or $P(D|S_1) = \frac{1}{2}$.

If the car is behind door 2 and you have chosen door 1, Monty has no choice but to open door 3 to show you a goat. So $P(D|S_2) = 1$.

If the car is behind door 3, the probability of Monty opening door 3 is zero, since he would ruin the game and you would get the car just for showing up. Therefore, $P(D|S_3) = 0$.

We plug the numbers into the rule of total probability to calculate the marginal or unconditional probability of observing the dataset D in the game:

$P(D) = P(D|S_1) \times P(S_1) + P(D|S_2) \times P(S_2) + P(D|S_3) \times P(S_3)$
$P(D) = [½ \times ⅓] + [1 \times ⅓] + [0 \times ⅓] = ½$

Now we have all the probabilities we need to use in the inverse probability rule to calculate the probability that the car is behind door 2, given our dataset D:

$P(S_2|D) = P(D|S_2) \times P(S_2) / P(D)$
$P(S_2|D) = [1 \times ⅓] / ½ = ⅔$

We can similarly compute the probability that the car is behind door 1, given our dataset D:

$P(S_1|D) = P(D|S_1) \times P(S_1) / P(D)$
$P(S_1|D) = [½ \times ⅓] / ½ = ⅓$

Clearly, we double our chances by switching, since $P(S_2|D) = 2P(S_1|D) = ⅔$. Note that there is still a ⅓ chance that you can win by not switching. But like trading and investing, your betting strategy should always put the odds in your favor.

Simulating the Solution

Still not convinced? Let's solve the Monty Hall problem by using a powerful numerical method called Monte Carlo simulation (MCS), which we mentioned in the previous chapter. This powerful computational method is applied by theoreticians and practitioners in almost every field, including business and finance. Recall that MCS samples randomly from probability distributions to generate numerous probable scenarios of a system whose outcomes are uncertain. It is generally used to quantify the uncertainty of model outputs. The following MCS code shows how switching doors is the optimal betting strategy for this game if played many times:

```
import random
import matplotlib.pyplot as plt

# Number of iterations in the simulation
number_of_iterations = [10, 100, 1000, 10000]

fig, axs = plt.subplots(nrows=2, ncols=2, figsize=(8, 6))

for i, number_of_iterations in enumerate(number_of_iterations):
    # List to store results of all iterations
    stay_results = []
    switch_results = []

    # For loop for collecting results
```

```
    for j in range(number_of_iterations):
        doors = ['door 1', 'door 2', 'door 3']

        # Random selection of door to place the car
        car_door = random.choice(doors)
        # You select a door at random
        your_door = random.choice(doors)

        # Monty can only select the door that does not have the car and one
        # that you have not chosen
        monty_door = list(set(doors) - set([car_door, your_door]))[0]
        # The door that Monty does not open and the one you have
        # not chosen initially
        switch_door = list(set(doors) - set([monty_door, your_door]))[0]

        # Result if you stay with your original choice and it has the
        # car behind it
        stay_results.append(your_door == car_door)
        # Result if you switch doors and it has the car behind it
        switch_results.append(switch_door == car_door)

    # Probability of winning the car if you stay with your original
    # choice of door
    probability_staying = sum(stay_results) / number_of_iterations
    # Probability of winning the car if you switch doors
    probability_switching = sum(switch_results) / number_of_iterations

    ax = axs[i // 2, i % 2]

    # Plot the probabilities as a bar graph
    ax.bar(['stay', 'switch'], [probability_staying, probability_switching],
    color=['blue', 'green'], alpha=0.7)
    ax.set_xlabel('Strategy')
    ax.set_ylabel('Probability of Winning')
    ax.set_title('After {} Simulations'.format(number_of_iterations))
    ax.set_ylim([0, 1])

    # Add probability values on the bars
    ax.text(-0.05, probability_staying + 0.05, '{:.2f}'
    .format(probability_staying), ha='left', va='center', fontsize=10)
    ax.text(0.95, probability_switching + 0.05, '{:.2f}'
    .format(probability_switching), ha='right', va='center', fontsize=10)

plt.tight_layout()
plt.show()
```

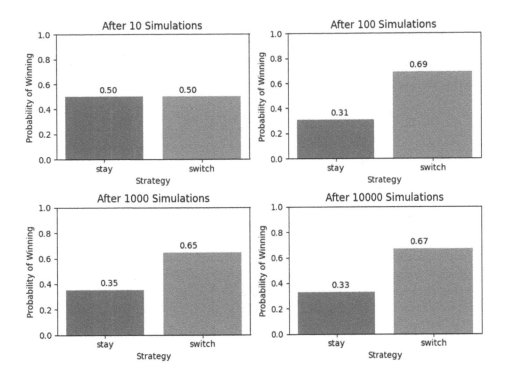

As you can see from the results of the simulations, switching doors is the winning strategy over the long term. The probabilities are approximately the same as in the analytical solution if you play the game ten thousand times. The probabilities become almost exactly the same as the analytical solution if you play the game over a hundred thousand times. We will explore the theoretical reasons for these results in particular, and MCS in general, in the next chapter.

However, it is not clear from the simulation if switching doors is the right strategy in the short term (10 trials), especially if the game is played only once. We know that Monty is not going to invite us back to play the game again regardless of whether we win or lose the car. So can we even talk about probabilities for one-off events? But what do we mean by probabilities anyway? Does everyone agree on what it means? Let's explore that now.

Meaning of Probability

Two major schools of thought have been sparring over the fundamental meaning of probability—the very soul of statistical inference—for about a century. The two camps disagree on not only the fundamental meaning of probability in those axioms we enumerated, but also the methods for applying the axioms consistently to make inferences. These core differences have led to the development of divergent theories of statistical inference and their implementations in practice.

Frequentist Probability

Statisticians who believe that probability is a natural, immutable property of an event or physical object, and that it is measured empirically as a long-run relative frequency, are called frequentists. Frequentism is the dominant school of the statistics of modern times, in both academic research and industrial applications. It is also known as orthodox, classical, or conventional statistics.

Orthodox statisticians claim that probability is a naturally occurring attribute of an event or physical phenomenon. The probability of an event should be measured empirically by repeating similar experiments ad nauseam—either in reality or hypothetically, using one's imagination or using computer simulations. For instance, if an experiment is conducted N times and an event E occurs with a frequency of M times, the relative frequency M/N approximates the probability of E. As the number of experimental trials N approaches infinity, the probability of E equals M/N. Figure 2-3 shows a histogram of the long-run relative frequencies of the sum of two fair dice rolled many times.

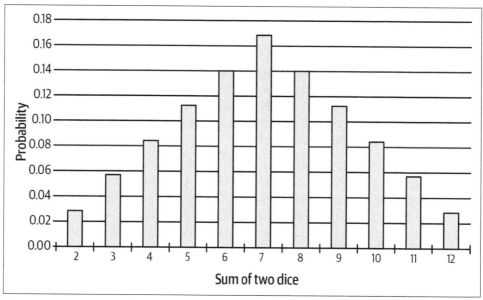

Figure 2-3. Long-run relative frequencies of the sum of two fair dice[5]

---

5 Adapted from an image on Wikimedia Commons.

Frequentists consider any alternative interpretation of probability as anathema, almost blasphemous. However, their definition of probability is ideological and not based on scientific experiments. As will be discussed later in the chapter, dice and coins don't have any static, intrinsic, "true" probabilities. For instance, coin tosses are not random but based on the laws of physics and can be predicted with 100% accuracy using a mechanical coin flipper. These experiments make a mockery of the frequentist definition of probability, which shows an egregious ignorance of basic physics. In Chapter 4, we will examine how the frequentist approach to probability and statistics has had a profoundly damaging impact on the theory and practice of social sciences in general and economic finance in particular, where the majority of the published research using their methods is false.

Epistemic Probability

The other important school of thought is popularly and mistakenly known as Bayesian statistics. As mentioned earlier, this is an egregious misnomer, and in this book we will refer to this interpretation as epistemic probability. Probability has a simpler, more intuitive meaning in the epistemic school: it is an extension of logic and quantifies the degree of plausibility of the event occurring based on the current state of knowledge or ignorance. Epistemic probabilities are dynamic, mental constructs that are a function of information about events that may or may not be random or repeatable.

Probabilities are updated as more information is acquired using the inverse probability rule. Most importantly, the plausibility of an event is expressed as a probability distribution as opposed to a point estimate. This quantifies the degree of plausibility of various outcomes that can occur given the current state of knowledge. Point estimates are avoided as much as possible, given the uncertainties endemic in life and business. Also, recall that the probability of a point estimate is zero for probability density functions. Probabilistic ML is based on this school of thought.

It is important to note that the epistemic interpretation of probability is broad and encompasses the frequentist interpretation of probability as a special limiting case. For instance, in the Monty Hall problem, we assumed that it is equally likely that a car is behind one of three doors; the epistemic and frequentist probabilities are both ⅓. Furthermore, both schools of thought would come to the same conclusion that switching doors doubles your probability and is a winning strategy. However, the epistemic approach did not need any independent and identically distributed trials of the game to estimate the probabilities of the two strategies. Similarly, for simple games of chance such as dice and cards, both schools of probability give you the same results, but frequentists need to imagine resampling the data, or actually conduct simulations.

Over the last century, frequentist ideologues have disparaged and tried to destroy the epistemic school of thought in covert and overt ways. Amongst other things, they labeled epistemic probabilities subjective, which in science is often a pejorative term. All models, especially those in the social and economic sciences, have assumptions that are subjective by definition, as they involve making design choices among many available options.

In finance and investing, subjective probabilities are the norm and are desirable, as they may lead to a competitive advantage. Subjective probabilities prevent the herding and groupthink that occurs when everyone follows the same "objective" inference or prediction about an event. What epistemic statistics will ensure is that our subjective probabilities are coherent and consistent with probability theory. If we are irrational or incoherent about the subjective probabilities underlying our investment strategy, other market participants will exploit these inconsistencies and make a Dutch book of bets against us. This concept is the sports-betting equivalent of a riskless arbitrage opportunity where we lose money on our trades or investments to other market participants no matter what the outcomes are.

The frequentist theory of statistics has been sold to academia and industry as a scientifically rigorous, efficient, robust, and objective school of thought. Nothing could be further from the truth. Frequentists use the maximum likelihood estimation (MLE) method to learn the optimal values of their model parameters. In their fervor to "only let the data speak" and make their inferences bias-free, they don't explicitly apply any prior knowledge or base rates to their inferences. They then claim that they have bias-free algorithms that are optimal for any class of problems. But the NFL theorems clearly state that this is an impossibility.

The NFL theorems prove mathematically that the claim that an algorithm is both bias-free and optimal for all problem domains is false. That's a free lunch, and not allowed in ML, search, and optimization. If an algorithm is actually bias-free as claimed, the NFL theorems tell us that it will not be optimal for all problem domains. It will have high variance on different datasets, and its performance will be no better than random guessing when averaged across all target distributions. The risk is that it will be worse than random guessing, which is what has occurred in the social and economic sciences, where the majority of research findings are false (see Chapter 4 for references). If the frequentist's defense is that all target distributions are not equally likely in this world, they need to realize that any selection of a subset of target distributions is a foolish admission of bias, because that involves making a subjective choice.

But we don't even have to use the sophisticated mathematics and logic of the NFL theorems to expose the deep flaws of the frequentist framework. In Chapter 4, we will examine why frequentist inference methods are "worse than useless," because they violate the rules of multiplication and division of probabilities (the product and inverse probability rules) and use the statistical skullduggery of the prosecutor's fallacy in their hypothesis testing methodology.

Despite the vigorous efforts of frequentists, epistemic statistics has been proven to be theoretically sound and experimentally verified. As a matter of fact, it is actually the frequentist version of probability that fails miserably, exposing its frailties and ad hoceries when subjected to complex statistical phenomena. For instance, the frequentist approach cannot be logically applied to image processing and reconstruction, where the sampling distribution of any measurement is always constant. Probabilistic algorithms dominate the field of image processing, leveraging their broader, epistemic foundation.[6]

A summary of the differences between the frequentist and epistemic statistics have been outlined in Table 2-1. Each of the differences have been or will be explained in this book and supported by plenty of scholarly references.

Table 2-1. Summary of the differences between frequentist and epistemic statistics

Dimension	Frequentist statistics	Epistemic statistics
Probability	An intrinsic, static property of the long-run relative frequency of an event or object. Not supported by physics experiments.	A dynamic, extrinsic property of the information about any event, which may or may not be repeatable or random.
Data	Sources of variance that are treated as random variables. Inferences don't work on small datasets.	Known and treated as constants. Size of the dataset is irrelevant.
Parameters	Treated as unknown or unknowable constants.	Treated as unknown variables.
Models	There is one "true" model with optimal parameters that explain the data.	There are many explanatory models with varying plausibilities.
Model types	Discriminative models—only learn a decision boundary. Cannot generate new data.	Generative models—learn the underlying structure of the data. Simulates new data.
Model assumptions	Implicit in null hypotheses, significance levels, regularizations, and asymptotic limits.	Most important model assumptions are explicitly stated and quantified as prior probabilities.
Inference method	Maximum likelihood estimation.	Inverse probability rule / product rule.
Hypothesis testing	Null hypothesis significance testing is binary and is guilty of the prosecutor's fallacy.	Degrees of plausibility assigned to many different hypotheses.
Uncertainty types	Only deals with aleatory uncertainty.	Deals with aleatory and epistemic uncertainties.
Uncertainty quantification	Confidence intervals are epistemologically incoherent and mathematically flawed. P-values are guilty of the inverse fallacy.	Credible intervals based on logic and common sense. Epistemologically coherent and mathematically sound.
Computational complexity	Low.	Medium to high.

---

6 Richard McElreath, "The Golem of Prague," in *Statistical Rethinking: A Bayesian Course with Examples in R and Stan* (Boca Raton, FL: Chapman and Hall/CRC, 2016), 1–18.

Dimension	Frequentist statistics	Epistemic statistics
No free lunch (NFL) theorems	Violates the NFL theorems. Doesn't include prior knowledge, so algorithms have high variance. When averaged across all possible problems, their performance is no better than random guessing.	Consistent with NFL theorems. Prior knowledge lowers the variance of algorithms, making them optimal for specific problem domains.
Scientific methodology	Ideological, unscientific, ad hoc methods under a facade of objectivity. Denies the validity of the inverse probability rule / product rule. Main cause of false findings in social and economic sciences.	Logical and scientific view that systematically integrates prior knowledge based on the inverse probability rule / product rule. Explicitly states and quantifies all objective and subjective assumptions.

Relative Probability

Are there any objective probabilities in the Monty Hall problem? The car is behind door 2, so isn't the "true" and objective probability of $S_2 = 1$ a constant? Yes, any host in the same position as Monty will assign $S_2 = 1$, just as any participant would assign $S_2 = \frac{1}{3}$. However, there is no static, immutable, "true" probability of any event in the sense that it has an ontological existence in this game independent of the actions of humans. If Monty has the car placed behind door 1, $S_2 = 0$ for him but remains constant at $\frac{1}{3}$ for any participant.

Probabilities depend on the model used, the phase of the game, and the information available to the participant or the host. As noted previously, probabilities for any participant or host are not subjective but a function of the information they have, since any host and any reasonable participant would arrive at the same probabilities using basic probability theory or common sense. Probability is a mental construct used to quantify uncertainties dynamically.

It is analogous to the physics of special relativity, which have been experimentally verified since Albert Einstein published his monumental paper in 1905. The principle of relativity states that the laws of physics are invariant across all frames of reference that are not accelerating relative to one another. Two observers sharing the same frame of reference will always agree on fundamental measurements of mass, length, and time. However, they will have different measurements of these quantities depending on how their frames of reference are moving relative to one another and compared to the speed of light. The principle of relativity has many important implications, including the fact that there is no such thing as absolute motion. Motion is always relative to a frame of reference.

Figure 2-4 shows two frames of reference, with the primed coordinate system moving at a constant velocity relative to the unprimed coordinate system. Observers O and O′ will agree that the same laws of physics apply in their worlds. However, observers O will claim that they are stationary and that observers O′ are moving forward along the x-axis at a constant velocity (+v). But observers O′ will claim that they are stationary and it is observers O that are moving backward along the x'-axis at a constant velocity (–v). This means that there is no way to say definitively whether O or O ' is really moving. They are both moving relative to each other, but neither one is moving in an absolute sense.

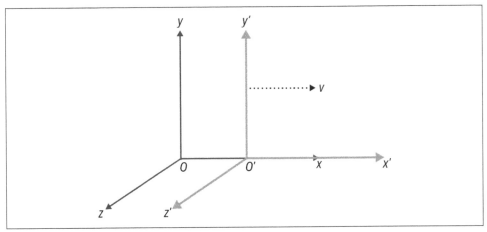

Figure 2-4. The principle of relativity using two frames of reference moving at a constant velocity relative to each other[7]

I find it useful to think in terms of relative probabilities based on an observer's frame of reference or access to information as opposed to objective or subjective probabilities. Regardless, probability theory works in all frames of reference we are concerned with. We need it to quantify the profound uncertainties that we have to deal with in our daily personal and professional lives. But before we quantify uncertainty, we need to understand it in some depth.

Risk Versus Uncertainty: A Useless Distinction

In conventional statistics and economics literature, a vacuous distinction is generally made between risk and uncertainty. Supposedly, risk can only be estimated for events that are known and have objective probability distributions and parameters associated with them. Probabilities and payoffs can be estimated accurately, and risk is computed using various metrics. When there are no objective probability distributions or if events are unknown or unknowable, the event is described as uncertain and the claim is made that risks cannot be estimated.

---

7 Adapted from an image on Wikimedia Commons.

In finance and investing, we are not dealing with simple games of chance, such as casino games, where the players, rules, and probability distributions are fixed and known. Both product and financial markets are quite different from such simple games of chance, where event risks can be estimated accurately. As was discussed in the previous chapter, unknown market participants may use different probability distributions in their models based on their own strategies and assumptions. Even for popular, consensus statistical distributions, there is no agreement about parameter estimates. Furthermore, because markets are not stationary ergodic, these probability distributions and their parameters are continually changing, sometimes abruptly, making a mockery of everyone's estimates and predictions.

So, based on the conventional definition of risk and uncertainty, almost all investing and finance is uncertain. In practice, this is a useless distinction and stems from useless frequentist statistics and neoclassical economics ideologies about objective, academic models, not from the realities of market participants. As practitioners, we develop our own subjective models based on our experience, expertise, institutional knowledge, and judgment. As a matter of fact, we protect our proprietary, subjective models assiduously, since sharing them with the public would undermine our competitive advantages.

Edward Thorp, the greatest quantitative gambler and trader of all time, invented an options pricing model much before Fischer Black and Myron Scholes published their famous "objective" model in 1973. Since Thorp's model was a trade secret of his hedge fund, he owed it to his investors not to share his model with the general public and fritter away his company's competitive advantage. Thorp applied his subjective, numerical, proprietary options model to generate one of the best risk-adjusted returns in history. Black and Scholes applied their "objective," analytical options pricing model to real markets only to experience near financial ruin and make a hasty retreat to the refuge of the ivory towers of academia.[8]

Options market makers and derivatives traders like me generally modify the "objective" Black-Scholes pricing model in different ways to correct for its many deep flaws. In doing so, we make our options trading models subjective and proprietary. Most importantly, we make it useful for successfully trading these complex markets.

The real value of the "objective" Black-Scholes options pricing model is clearly not in its accurate pricing of options. It's common knowledge among academics and practitioners alike that it's not accurate, especially since it erroneously treats volatility of the underlying asset as a constant. A classic joke about the Black-Scholes model is that you have to put "the wrong number in the wrong formula to get the right price."

---

8 Scott Patterson, *The Quants: How a New Breed of Math Whizzes Conquered Wall Street and Nearly Destroyed It* (New York: Crown Business, 2010).

The real value-add of the Black-Scholes model, explaining its enduring popularity among practitioners, is in its enabling communication among market participants who are generally using their own disparate, proprietary options pricing models. It is ironic that despite the Black-Scholes model's fictitious assumptions and market fantasies, it has contributed significantly to the rapid growth of real-world options markets. Humans are suckers for good works of fiction in any format. Perhaps Black and Scholes should have been awarded a real Nobel Prize in literature.

In epistemic statistics, probabilities are an extension of logic and can be assigned to any uncertain event—known, unknown, and unknowable. We do this by rejecting point estimates and setting the bar extremely high for assuming any event to be a certainty (probability = 1) or an impossibility (probability = 0). That's why in epistemic statistics we deal only with probability distributions. Unknowable events are acknowledged by using fat-tailed probability distributions like the Cauchy distribution, which has no defined mean or variance, reflecting the fact that almost anything is possible during the holding periods of our trades and investments.

Probability estimates are based on our prior knowledge, observed data, and expertise in making such estimates. But most importantly, they depend on human judgment, common sense, and an understanding of causation, which AI systems are incapable of processing. The degree of confidence we have in our estimates and forecasts will vary depending on many factors, including the nature of the event, the sources of uncertainty, our resources, and our abilities to perform such tasks.

In finance and investing, we don't have the luxury of not undertaking such imperfect, messy statistical endeavors. We do it knowing full well that these difficult exercises are rife with approximations, riddled with potential errors, and susceptible to the ravages and ridicule of markets. Dwight Eisenhower, former US general and president, explained the value of such exercises when he said, "In preparing for battle I have always found that plans are useless, but planning is indispensable."[9] The alternative of forsaking such statistical exercises by taking comfort in some useless definition of risk and uncertainty is even worse. The worst course of action is to be lulled into a false sense of security by some economic ideology of objective statistical models or normative theory of human behavior and rationality that have no basis in data and the experienced realities of the world.

We reject such useless distinctions between risk and uncertainty. All uncertain events are logically and realistically plausible based on an appropriate probability distribution and boundary conditions. We know that all models are wrong, including the useful ones, and do not pledge any fealty to these shadows of reality.

---

9 Quoted in "Quotation 64: Dwight D. Eisenhower on Why Plans Are Useless but Planning Is Essential," in *The Little Book of Big Management Wisdom* by Dr. James McGrath (O'Reilly Media, 2017), *https://www.oreilly.com/ library/view/the-little-book/9781292148458/html/chapter-079.html*.

The Trinity of Uncertainty

Uncertainty is generally classified into three types based on the source from which it arises: aleatory, epistemic, and ontological. These are complex concepts that philosophers and scientists worldwide have endeavored to understand and apply for millennia. Let's see how we can use the Monty Hall problem to understand the complexities of this trinity of uncertainty. Later, we apply each type of uncertainty to various aspects of machine learning that we are faced with in practice.

Aleatory Uncertainty

Aleatory means "of dice" in Latin. Fundamentally, aleatory uncertainty is the irreducible randomness of outcomes. Both the analytical and simulated solutions to the Monty Hall problem demonstrated that your strategy of staying or switching doors in this game does not guarantee you a win during a single play, or even multiple plays, of the game. You could stay with your original choice of door 1 and have a ⅓ chance of winning the car. You could switch to door 2 and have a ⅓ chance of losing the car. Whenever you play the game, you are indeed rolling the proverbial dice, since the outcome is uncertain.

Actually, it's more uncertain than rolling dice or tossing a coin, since they both have no aleatory uncertainty, only epistemic uncertainty, as explained in the next section. Tossing a coin is a canonical example of aleatory uncertainty in the current literature on probability and statistics. However, this shows an inexcusable ignorance of the laws of classical physics. It has been experimentally verified that if you know the initial conditions and other parameters of a coin toss, you can predict its outcome with 100% accuracy. That's because coin tossing is physics, not randomness.[10]

Statistician and former magician Persi Diaconis had engineers build him a mechanical coin flipper so that he could experiment and study coin tossing. Indeed, he and his colleagues verified that there is no randomness in a coin toss with the mechanical coin flipper.[11] The randomness of a coin toss arises from the inconsistency of initial conditions of human coin flipping and from the coin rolling on the ground.

---

10 Jaynes, "How to Cheat at Coin or Die Tossing," in *Probability Theory*, 317–20.

11 Persi Diaconis, Susan Holmes, and Richard Montgomery, "Dynamical Bias in the Coin Toss," *Society for Industrial and Applied Mathematics (SIAM) Review* 49, no. 2 (2007): 211–35.

The uncertainty we observe stems from our lack of precise information or knowledge of the physics of the tosses. It is a bad example of aleatory uncertainty. It also demonstrates that coins don't have any intrinsic, immutable, limiting frequency, as frequentists will have us believe. You can use the physics of the coin toss to make a biased coin honest and vice versa with some practice.[12]

Tossing coins and rolling dice are examples of epistemic uncertainty, which we will discuss in the next subsection. In contrast to coins or dice, no amount of information about the physical characteristics of the doors or their motion will reduce the aleatory uncertainty of where the car is in the Monty Hall problem. It is a great example of aleatory uncertainty, and why social systems are fundamentally different and much harder to predict than physical systems.

In machine learning (ML), aleatory uncertainty is the source of irreducible error and is generated because of data. It sets the lower bound on the generalization error that can be achieved by any ML model. This endemic noise is generated in two distinct ways:

Measurement uncertainty
> It is not always possible to measure data with complete accuracy. For instance, when there is high market volatility due to an event, such as the release of an economic report, it is almost impossible to capture every transaction or tick in real time, leading to missing or delayed tick data. Similarly, data transmission errors can lead to missing or corrupt tick data.

Sampling uncertainty
> Every time we take a random data sample from across a population at a particular time, or sample a stochastic process at different times, the sample statistics, such as mean and variance, will vary from sample to sample. This type of aleatory uncertainty is due to the inherent randomness of the sampling process itself and the variability of the underlying statistical distribution. For example, consumer sentiment surveys taken by different companies result in different statistical estimates. Also, the variance of a stock's price returns also changes over time. Figure 2-5 shows how a specific random data sample is taken from the population to estimate the population mean and variance.

---

12 Matthew P. A. Clark and Brian D. Westerberg, "How Random Is the Toss of a Coin?" *Canadian Medical Association Journal* 181, no. 12 (December 8, 2009): E306–E308.

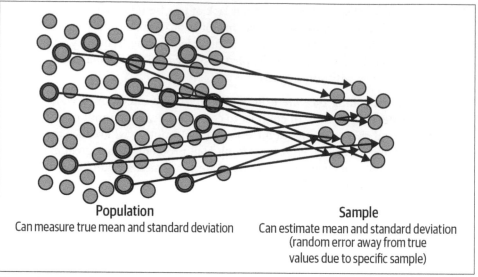

Population
Can measure true mean and standard deviation

Sample
Can estimate mean and standard deviation
(random error away from true
values due to specific sample)

Figure 2-5. Sampling uncertainty because a random sample is drawn to estimate the statistical properties of its population[13]

Epistemic Uncertainty

Episteme means "knowledge" in Greek. The epistemic uncertainty of any scenario depends on the state of knowledge or ignorance of the person confronting it. Unlike aleatory uncertainty, you can reduce epistemic uncertainty by acquiring more knowledge and understanding. When Monty opens a door to show you a goat, he is providing you with very valuable new information that reduces your epistemic uncertainty. Based on this information from Monty's response to your choice, the probability of door 1 having a car behind it remained unchanged at ⅓, but the probability for door 2 changed from ⅓ to ⅔, and the probability for door 3 changed from ⅓ to 0.

However, there is no uncertainty for Monty regarding which door the car is behind: his probability for each door is either 1 or 0 at all times. He is only uncertain about which door you are going to pick. Also, once you pick any door, he is certain what he is going to do next. But he is uncertain what you will do when offered the deal. Will you stay with your original choice of door 1 or switch to door 2, and most likely win the car? Monty's uncertainties are not epistemic but ontological, a fundamentally different nature of uncertainty, which we will discuss in the next subsection.

---

13 Adapted from an image on Wikimedia Commons.

So we can see from this game that the uncertainty of picking the right door for you is a function of one's state of knowledge or "episteme." It is important to note that this is not a subjective belief but a function of information or lack of it. Any participant and any host would have the same uncertainties calculated earlier in this chapter, and switching doors would still be the winning strategy.

 This game is also an example of the *asymmetry of information* that characterizes financial deals and markets. Generally speaking, parties to a deal always have access to differing amounts of information about various aspects of a deal or asset, which leads to uncertainty in their price estimates and deal outcomes. Different information processing capabilities and speeds further exacerbate those uncertainties.

There are many sources of epistemic uncertainty in ML arising from a lack of access to knowledge and understanding of the underlying phenomenon.

They can be categorized in the following ways:

Data uncertainty

To make valid inferences, we want our data sample to represent the underlying population or data-generating process. For instance, auditors sample a subset of a company's transactions or financial records during a particular time period to check for compliance with accounting standards. The auditor may fail to detect errors or fraud if the sample is unrepresentative of the population of transactions.

Model uncertainty

There is always uncertainty about which model to choose to make inferences and predictions. For example, when making financial forecasts, should we use linear regression or nonlinear regression models? Or a neural network? Or some other model?

Feature uncertainty

Assume we pick a linear model as our first approximation and baseline model for financial forecasting. What features are we going to select to make our inferences and forecasts? Why did we select those features and leave out others? How many are required?

Algorithmic uncertainty

Now that we have selected features for our linear model, what linear algorithm should we use to train the model and learn its parameters? Will it be ridge regression, lasso regression, support vector machines, or a probabilistic linear regression algorithm?

Parameter uncertainty

Say we decide to use a market model and a probabilistic linear regression algorithm as our baseline model. What probability distributions are we going to assign each parameter? Or are the parameters going to be point estimates? What about the hyperparameters—that is, parameters of the probability distributions of parameters? Are they going to be probability distributions or point estimates?

Method uncertainty

What numerical method are we going to use in our model to learn its parameters from in-sample data? Will we use the Markov chain Monte Carlo (MCMC) method or variational inference? A Metropolis sampling method or Hamiltonian Monte Carlo sampling method? What values are we going to use for the parameters of the chosen numerical methods? How do we justify those parameter values?

Implementation uncertainty

Assume we decide on using the MCMC method. Which software should we use to implement it? PyMC, Pyro, TensorFlow Probability, or Stan? Or are we going to build everything from scratch using Python? What about R or C++?

As the previous discussion shows, designing ML models involves making choices about the objective function, data sample, model, algorithm, and computational resources, among many others. As was mentioned in the previous chapter, our goal is to train our ML system so that it minimizes out-of-sample generalization errors that are reducible.

If we have prior knowledge about the problem domain, we might develop a simple system with few parameters because of such knowledge and assumptions. This is referred to as bias in ML. The risk is that our prior assumptions of the model may be erroneous, leading it to underfit the training data systematically and learn no new patterns or signals from it. Consequently, the model is exposed to bias errors and performs poorly on unseen test data. On the other hand, if we don't have prior knowledge about the problem domain, we might build a complex model with many parameters to adapt and learn as much as possible from the training data. The risk there is that the model overfits the training data and learns the spurious correlations (noise) as well. This result is that the model introduces errors in its predictions and inferences due to minor variations in the data. These errors are referred to as variance errors and the model performs poorly on unseen test data. Figure 2-6 shows the bias-variance trade-off that needs to made in developing models that minimize reducible generalization errors. This trade-off is made more difficult and dynamic when the underlying data distributions are not stationary ergodic, as they are in finance and investing problems.

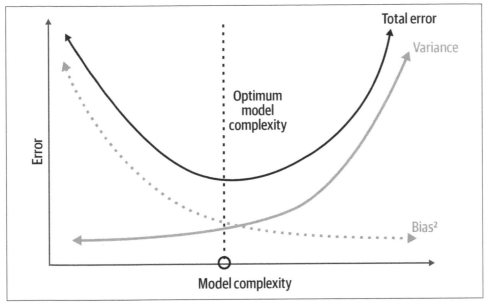

Figure 2-6. The bias-variance trade-off that needs to be made when developing ML models[14]

Ontological Uncertainty

Ontology is the philosophical study of the nature of being and reality. Ontological uncertainty generally arises from the future of human affairs being essentially unknowable.[15]

To make the Monty Hall game resemble a real-world business deal or a trade, we have to dive deeper into the objective of the game, namely winning the car. From Monty's perspective, winning means keeping the car so he can reduce the costs of the show while still attracting a large audience. When the game is viewed in this way, Monty's knowledge of the car's placement behind any one of the doors does not decrease his ontological uncertainty about winning the game. This is because he doesn't know which door you're going to pick and whether you will stay or switch doors when given the choice to do so. Since his probabilities are the complement of your probabilities, he has a ⅔ chance of keeping the car if you don't switch doors and ⅓ chance of losing the car to you if you do switch doors.

14 Adapted from an image on Wikimedia Commons.

15 Ove Njå, Øivind Solberg, and Geir Sverre Braut, "Uncertainty—Its Ontological Status and Relation to Safety," in *The Illusion of Risk Control: What Does It Take to Live with Uncertainty?*, ed. Gilles Motet and Corinne Bieder (Cham, Switzerland: SpringerOpen, 2017), 5–21.

There are other possible ontological uncertainties for you. Say you show up to play the game a second time armed with the analysis of the game and the door-switching strategy. Monty surprises you by changing the rules and does not open another door to show you a goat. Instead he asks you to observe his body language and tone of voice for clues to help you make your decision. However, Monty has no intention of giving you any helpful clues and wants to reduce your probability of winning to ⅓ regardless of your decision to stay or switch doors. Monty does this because earlier in the week his producer had threatened to cancel the show, since its ratings were falling and it was not making enough money to cover Monty's hefty salary.

Unexpected changes in business and financial markets are the rule, not the exception. Markets don't send out a memo to participants when undergoing structural changes. Companies, deals, and trading strategies fail regularly and spectacularly because of these types of changes. It is similar to the way one of Hemingway's characters described how he went bankrupt: "Two ways…Gradually and then suddenly."[16]

In ML, ontological uncertainty occurs when there is a structural discontinuity in the underlying population or data-generating process, as was discussed in Chapter 1, where we had to change the model from a binomial to a trinomial one. In finance and investing, the source of ontological uncertainty is the complexity of human activities, such as political elections, monetary and fiscal policy changes, company bankruptcies, and technological breakthroughs, to name just a few. Only humans can understand causality underlying these changes and use common sense to redesign the ML models from scratch to adapt to a new regime. Figure 2-7 shows the types of intelligent systems that are used in practice to navigate aleatory, epistemic, and ontological uncertainties of finance and investing.

As you can see, designing models involves understanding different types of uncertainties, with each entailing a decision among various design options. Answers to these questions require prior knowledge of the problem domain and experience experimenting with many different models and algorithms. They cannot be derived from first principles of deductive logic or learned only from sample data that are not stationary ergodic. This seems obvious to practitioners like me. What might surprise most practitioners, as it did me, is that there is a set of mathematical theorems called the no free lunch (NFL) theorems that prove the validity of our various approaches.

---

16 Ernest Hemingway, *The Sun Also Rises* (New York: Charles Scribner's Sons, 1954), 136.

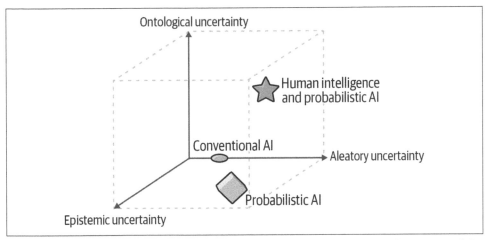

Figure 2-7. Human intelligence supported by probabilistic AI systems is the most useful model for navigating the three-dimensional uncertainties of finance and investing

The No Free Lunch Theorems

In 1891, Rudyard Kipling, a Nobel laureate in literature and an English imperialist from the province of Bombay, recounted a visit to a saloon in his travel journal *American Notes*: "It was the institution of the 'free lunch' that I had struck. You paid for a drink and got as much as you wanted to eat. For something less than a rupee a day a man can feed himself sumptuously in San Francisco, even though he be a bankrupt. Remember this if ever you are stranded in these parts."[17]

Fortuitously, I have been "stranded" in these parts for some time now and have a few rupees left over from my recent visit to the former province of Bombay. Unfortunately, this once popular American tradition of the "free lunch" is no longer common and has certainly disappeared from the bars in San Francisco, where a couple of hundred rupees might get you some peanuts and a glass of tap water. However, the idea that lunch is never free and we eventually pay for it with a drink—or personal data, or something else—has persisted and is commonly applied in many disciplines, especially economics, finance, and investing.

David Wolpert, an eminent computer scientist and physicist, discovered that this idea also applied to machine learning and statistical inference. In 1996 he shocked both these communities by publishing a paper that proved mathematically the impossibility of the existence of a superior ML learning algorithm that can solve all problems optimally. Prior knowledge of the problem domain is required to select the appropri-

---

17 Rudyard Kipling, *From Sea to Sea: Letters of Travel, Part II* (New York: Charles Scribner's Sons, 1899), 39.

ate learning algorithm and improve its performance.[18] Wolpert, who was a postdoctoral student at the time of the publication, was subjected to ad hominem attacks by industry executives and derision by academics who felt threatened by these theorems because they were debunking their specious claims of discovering such optimal, bias-free, general purpose ML learning algorithms.

Wolpert subsequently published another paper with William Macready in 1997 that provided a similar proof for search and optimization algorithms.[19] These theorems are collectively known as the no free lunch (NFL) theorems.Please note that prior knowledge and assumptions about the problem domain that is used in the selection and design of the learning algorithm is also referred to as bias. Furthermore, a problem is defined by a data generating target distribution that the algorithm is trying to learn from training data. A cost function is used to measure the performance of the learning algorithm on out-of-sample test data. These theorems have many important implications for ML that are critical for us to understand.

One important implication is that the performance of all learning algorithms when averaged across all problem domains will be the same. As shown in Figure 2-8, each data scientist has a different learning algorithm (A, B, C) whose performance is measured on unseen data of four different problem domains (apples, pears, tools, and shoes). On the apple problem domain, all three learning algorithms perform optimally. So we don't have a unique optimal learning algorithm for the apple domain or any other problem domain for that matter. However, the learning algorithms have varying performance measures on each of the other three problem domains. None of the learning algorithms performs optimally on all four problem domains. Regardless, the performance of all three learning algorithms when considered independently and averaged across the four problem domains is the same at $32 / 4 = 8$.

---

18 David Wolpert, "The Lack of A Priori Distinctions between Learning Algorithms," *Neural Computation* 8, no. 7 (1996): 1341–90.

19 David H. Wolpert and William G. Macready, "No Free Lunch Theorems for Optimization," *IEEE Transactions on Evolutionary Computation* 1, no. 1 (1997): 67.

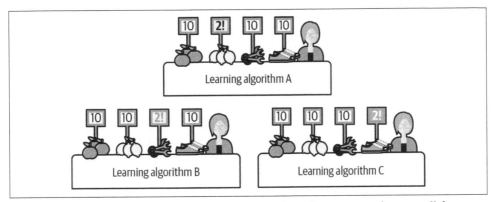

Figure 2-8. The performance of all three learning algorithms averaged across all four problem domains is the same, with a score of 8.[20]

This example illustrates the central idea in the NFL theorems that there are no mathematical reasons to prefer one learning algorithm over another based on expected performance across all problem domains. Since learning algorithms have varying performances on different problem domains, we must use our empirical knowledge of a specific problem domain to select a learning algorithm that is best aligned with the domain's target function. So how well the learning algorithm performs is contingent on the validity of our domain knowledge and assumptions. There are no free lunches in ML.

If we don't make the payment of prior knowledge to align our learning algorithm with the underlying target function of the problem domain, like the freeloading frequentists claim we must do to remain unbiased, the learning algorithm's predictions based on unseen data will be no better than random guessing when averaged over all possible target distributions. In fact, the risk is that it might be worse than random guessing. So we can't have our lunch and not pay for it in ML. If we bolt for the exit without paying for our lunch, we'll realize later that what we wolfed down was junk food and not a real meal.

The most common criticism of NFL theorems is that all target distributions are not equally likely in the real world. This criticism is spurious and misses the point of using such a mathematical technique. The reason is that in the bias-free world that frequentists fantasize about, we are required to assign equal probability to all possible target distributions *by definition*. Any selection of a single target distribution from a finite set of all possible target distributions *must necessarily* involve making a subjective choice, which, *by definition* of an unbiased world, is not allowed. Because we are forbidden in a bias-free world from using our prior knowledge of the problem

20 Adapted from an image on Wikimedia Commons.

domain to pick a single target distribution, the performance of an unbiased algorithm must be averaged over all possible, equally likely target distributions. The result is that the unbiased algorithm's average performance on unseen data is reduced to being no better than random guessing. The frequentist trick of implicitly selecting a target function while obfuscating their biased choice with statistical jargon and a sham ideology of objectivity doesn't stand up to scrutiny.

The most important practical implication of the NFL theorems is that good generalization performance of any learning algorithm is always context and usage dependent. If we have sound prior knowledge and valid assumptions about our problem domain, we should use it to select and align the learning algorithm with the underlying structure of our specific problem and the nature of its target function. While this may introduce biases into the learning algorithm, it is a payment worth making, as it will lead to better performance on our specific problem domain.

But remember that this optimality of performance is because of our "payment" of prior knowledge. Since our learning algorithm will be biased toward our problem domain, we should expect that it will almost surely perform poorly on other problem domains that have divergent underlying target functions, such that its average performance across all problem domains will be no better than the performance of another learning algorithm.

But the performance of our learning algorithms on other problem domains is not our concern. We are not touting our biased learning algorithms and models as a panacea for all problem domains. That would be a violation of the NFL theorems. In this book, we are concerned primarily with optimizing our probabilistic machine learning algorithms and models for finance and investing.

Most importantly, the NFL theorems are yet another mathematical proof of the sham objectivity and deeply flawed foundations of frequentist/conventional statistics. The frequentists' pious pretense of not using prior domain knowledge explicitly and making statistical inferences based solely on in-sample data is simply wrong and has had serious consequences for all the social sciences. It has led to base rate fallacies and a proliferation of junk studies whose results are no better than random guessing. We will discuss this further in Chapter 4.

Investing and the Problem of Induction

Inductive reasoning synthesizes information from past observations to formulate general hypotheses that will continue to be plausible in the future. Simply put, induction makes inferences about the general population distribution based on an analysis of a random data sample. Figure 2-9 shows how deductive and inductive reasoning are used in the scientific method.

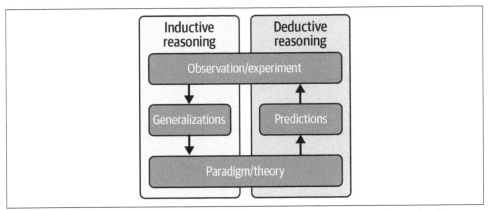

Figure 2-9. The use of inductive and deductive reasoning in the scientific method[21]

This is generally what we do in finance and investing. We analyze past data to detect patterns (such as trends) or formulate causal relationships between variables (such as earnings and price returns) or human behavior (such as fear and greed). We try to come up with a cogent thesis as to why these historical patterns and causal relationships will most likely persist in the future. Such financial analysis is generally divided into two types:

Technical analysis

This is the study of historical patterns of an asset's price and volume data during any time period based on its market dynamics of supply and demand. Patterns and statistical indicators are correlated with the asset's future uptrends, downtrends, or trendless (sideways) price movements. See Figure 2-10 for a technical pattern called a double bottom, which is a signal that indicates the asset will rally in the future after it is confirmed that it has found support at the second bottom price.

Generally speaking, technical analysts are not concerned with the nature of the asset or what is causing its prices to change at any given time. This is because all necessary information is assumed to be reflected in the price and volume data of the asset. Technical analysts are only concerned with detecting patterns in historical prices and volumes, computing statistical indicators, and using their correlations to predict future price changes of the asset. Technical investing and trading strategies assume that historical price and volume patterns and their related price correlations will repeat in the future because human behavior and the market dynamics of supply and demand on which they are based don't essentially change.

---

21 Adapted from an image on Wikimedia Commons.

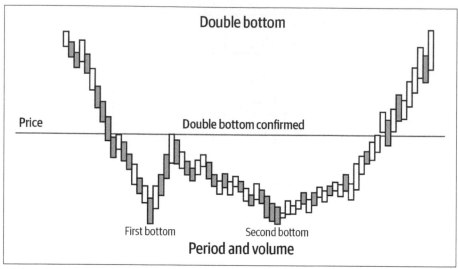

Figure 2-10. A double bottom technical pattern predicts that the price of the asset will rise in the future.

Fundamental analysis

This is the study of financial, economic, and human behavior. Analysts study historical company financial statements and economic, industry, and consumer reports. Using past empirical data, statistical analysis, or academic financial theories, analysts formulate causal mechanisms between features (or risk factors) and the fundamental value of an asset. Fundamental analysts are mainly concerned with the nature of the asset that they analyze and the underlying causal mechanisms that determine its valuation.

For instance, the discounted cash flow (DCF) model is used extensively for valuing assets, such as the equity and debt of a company or the value of its factory. Fundamental analysts forecast the cash flows that a company or capital project is expected to generate in the future (typically three to five years) and discount them back to the present using an interest rate to account for the opportunity cost of the company's capital. They also forecast macroeconomic variables like tax rates, inflation rates, gross domestic product, and currency exchange rates, among others. The fundamental principle of the DCF model is that cash tomorrow is worth less than cash today and must be discounted accordingly. This assumes that interest rates are always positive and cash can be lent out to earn interest at the appropriate rate. By forgoing the opportunity to lend out their cash at the appropriate rate, an investor incurs an opportunity cost that is reflected in the discount rate. See Figure 2-11.

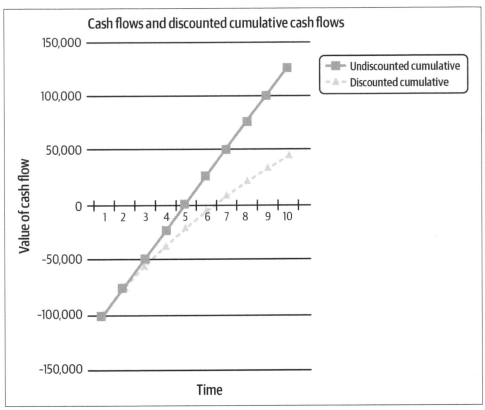

Figure 2-11. Cash flows need to be discounted because cash tomorrow is worth less than cash today, assuming interest rates are positive

The DCF model is very sensitive to minor changes in the discount rate and the projected growth rate of its cash flows. This is why the interest rate set by central bankers is pivotal to the valuation of all assets, as it directly impacts an investor's cost of capital. Fundamental trading and investing strategies assume that the formulated causal mechanisms between features (risk factors) and asset valuation will persist into the future.

All other methods, such as quantitative analysis or machine learning, use some combination of technical and fundamental analysis. Regardless, how do we know that the patterns of technical analysis and causal relationships of fundamental analysis that have been observed thus far will continue to persist in the future? Well, because the past has resembled the future so far. But that is exactly what we are trying to prove in the first place! This circular reasoning is generally referred to as the problem of induction.

This is a confounding metaphysical problem that has been investigated by the Carvaka school of Indian philosophy, at least 2,400 years before David Hume articulated the problem in the 18th century for a Western audience.[22] We can ignore the problem of induction in physics (see Sidebar). However, we cannot do that in the social sciences, especially finance and investing, where it is a clear and present danger to any extrapolation of the past into the future. That's because human beings have free will, emotions, and creativity, and they react to one another's actions in unpredictable ways. Sometimes history repeats itself, sometimes it rhymes, and sometimes it makes no sense at all. That's why Securities and Exchange Commission (SEC) in the United States mandates all marketing materials in the investment management industry to have a disclaimer that states past returns are no guarantee of future results. This trite but true statement is merely echoing the age-old problem of induction. Unlike the physical universe, social systems don't need infinite time and space to generate seemingly impossible events. An average lifetime is more than enough to witness a few of these mind-boggling events. For instance, in the last decade, over 15 trillion dollars' worth of bonds were issued with negative interest rates in Japan and Europe! Negative interest rates contradict common sense, fundamental principles of finance, and the foundation of the DCF model.

Physics and the Problem of Induction

The problem of induction has proven to be a tough nut to crack without a satisfactory logical solution. It compels us to acknowledge the fact that we make implicit assumptions about reality so that we can carry on with our daily lives. For instance, physics assumes the principle of uniformity of nature, which states that the laws of physics are invariant in space and time throughout the universe. This epistemologically unjustifiable assumption has served humanity spectacularly for millennia on our planet. The technological wonders of the modern world are proof of the astonishing power and accuracy of inductive reasoning and the persistence of the underlying unity of natural phenomena.

Despite the ontological debates about quantum mechanics, it is the most accurate and experimentally verified scientific theory of all time. One of the most precise tests of quantum mechanics is through measurements of a quantity called the electromagnetic fine-structure constant. These tests have shown that the predictions of quantum mechanics are extremely accurate to within 10 parts in a billion! Just take a moment to reflect on this incredible achievement. These are awe-inspiringly accurate out-of-sample predictions that other natural sciences can only dream about and economics can only fantasize about. That is why the philosopher C. D. Broad has aptly called inductive inference "the glory of science and the scandal of philosophy."

---

22 Roy W. Perrett, "The Problem of Induction in Indian Philosophy," *Philosophy East and West* 34, no. 2 (1984): 161–74.

While the stellar success of physics does not invalidate the problem of induction, we can ignore it for natural phenomena for the foreseeable future because physics has delivered it a knockout punch in this eon. However, while the count is still on, the laws of physics could change in the very distant future, and the problem of induction could rise again and have the last laugh.

Anything is theoretically possible in infinite time and space. For instance, our current astrophysical theory about the universe does not preclude the possibility that the universe may stop expanding many, many billion years from now and then start contracting, reversing the laws of physics. But don't worry about that fate, because the current laws of physics also predict that in about five billion years, the sun will become a red giant that expands in size so much that it will swallow the earth. In the meantime, rest assured that the sun will rise tomorrow.

The Problem of Induction, NFL Theorems, and Probabilistic Machine Learning

Inductive inference is foundational to ML All ML models are built on the assumption that patterns discovered in past training data will persist in future unseen data. It is important to note that the NFL theorems are a brilliant algorithmic restatement of the problem of induction within a probabilistic framework. In both frameworks, we have to use prior knowledge or assumptions about the problem domain to make predictions that are better than chance on unseen data. More importantly, this knowledge cannot be acquired from in-sample data alone or from principles of deductive logic or theorems of mathematics. Prior knowledge based on past empirical observations and assumptions about the underlying structural unity of the observed phenomenon or data-generating target function are required. It is only when we apply our prior knowledge about a problem domain can we expect to optimize our learning algorithm for making predictions on unseen data that will be much better than random guessing.

Most importantly, epistemic statistics embraces the problem of induction zealously and directly answers its central question: can we ever be sure that the knowledge that we have acquired from past observations is valid and will continue to be valid in the future? Of course not—the resounding answer is, we can almost never be sure. Learning continually from uncertain and incomplete information is the foundation on which epistemic statistics and probabilistic inference is built.

Consequently, as we will see in Chapter 5, epistemic statistics provides a probabilistic framework for machine learning that systematically integrates prior knowledge and keeps updating it with new observations because we can never be certain that the validity of our knowledge will continue to persist into the future. Almost all knowledge is uncertain to a greater or lesser degree and is best represented as a probability distribution, not a point estimate. Forecasts about the future (predictions) and the past (retrodictions) are also generated from these models as predictive probability distributions. Its biggest challenge, however, is dealing with ontological uncertainty, for which human intelligence is crucial.

Summary

In this chapter, we used the famous Monty Hall problem to review the fundamental rules of probability theory and apply them to solve the Monty Hall problem. We also realized how embarassingly easy it is to derive the inverse probability rule that is pivotal to epistemic statistics and probabilistic machine learning. Furthermore, we used the Monty Hall game to explore the profound complexities of aleatory, epistemic, and ontological uncertainty that pervade our lives and businesses. A better understanding of the three types of uncertainty and the meaning of probability will enable us to analyze and develop appropriate models for our probabilistic ML systems to solve the difficult problems we face in finance and investing.

We know for a fact that even a physical object like a coin has no intrinsic probability based on long-term frequencies. It depends on initial conditions and the physics of the toss. Probabilities are epistemic, not ontological—they are a map, not the terrain. It's about time frequentists stop fooling themselves and others with their mind-projection fallacies and give up their pious pretense of objectivity and scientific rigor.

The NFL theorems can be interpreted as restating the problem of induction for machine learning in general and finance and investing in particular. Past performance of an algorithm or investment strategy is no guarantee of its future performance. The target distribution of the problem domain or the out-of-sample dataset may change enough to degrade the performance of the algorithm and investment strategy. In other words, it is impossible to have a unique learning algorithm or investment strategy that is both bias-free and optimal for all problem domains or market environments. If we want an optimal algorithm for our specific problem domain, we have to pay for it with assumptions and prior domain knowledge.

Probabilistic machine learning incorporates the fundamental concepts of the problem of induction and NFL theorems within its framework. It systematically incorporates prior domain knowledge and continually updates it with new information while always expressing the uncertainty about its prior knowledge, inferences, retrodictions, and predictions. We will examine this epistemologically sound, mathematically rigorous, and commonsensical machine learning framework in Chapter 5. In the next chapter, we dive deeper into basic Monte Carlo methods and their applications to quantify aleatory and epistemic uncertainty using independent sampling.

References

Clark, Matthew P. A., and Brian D. Westerberg. "How Random Is the Toss of a Coin?" *Canadian Medical Association Journal* 181, no. 12 (December 8, 2009): E306–E308.

Dale, A. I. *A History of Inverse Probability: From Thomas Bayes to Karl Pearson*. New York: Springer, 1999.

Diaconis, Persi, Susan Holmes, and Richard Montgomery. "Dynamical Bias in the Coin Toss." *Society for Industrial and Applied Mathematics (SIAM) Review* 49, no.2 (2007): 211–235.

Hemingway, Ernest. *The Sun Also Rises*. New York: Charles Scribner's Sons, 1954.

Jaynes, E. T. *Probability Theory: The Logic of Science*. Edited by G. Larry Bretthorst, New York: Cambridge University Press, 2003.

Kahneman, Daniel. *Thinking, Fast and Slow*. New York: Farrar, Straus and Giroux, 2011.

Kipling, Rudyard. *From Sea to Sea: Letters of Travel, Part II*. New York: Charles Scribner's Sons, 1899.

McElreath, Richard. *Statistical Rethinking: A Bayesian Course with Examples in R and Stan*. Boca Raton, FL: Chapman and Hall/CRC, 2016.

McGrath, James. *The Little Book of Big Management Wisdom*. O'Reilly Media, 2017. Accessed June 23, 2023. *https://www.oreilly.com/library/view/the-little-book/ 9781292148458/html/chapter-079.html*.

Njå, Ove, Øivind Solberg, and Geir Sverre Braut. "Uncertainty—Its Ontological Status and Relation to Safety." In *The Illusion of Risk Control: What Does It Take to Live with Uncertainty?* edited by Gilles Motet and Corinne Bieder, 5–21. Cham, Switzerland: SpringerOpen, 2017.

Patterson, Scott. *The Quants: How a New Breed of Math Whizzes Conquered Wall Street and Nearly Destroyed It*. New York: Crown Business, 2010.

Perrett, Roy W. "The Problem of Induction in Indian Philosophy." *Philosophy East and West* 34, no. 2 (1984): 161–74.

Stigler, Stephen M. "Who Discovered Bayes's Theorem?" *The American Statistician* 37, no. 4a (1983): 290–296.

Thaler, Richard. *Misbehaving: The Making of Behavioral Economics.* New York: W. W. Norton & Company, 2015.

Wolpert, David. "The Lack of A Priori Distinctions between Learning Algorithms." *Neural Computation* 8, no. 7 (1996): 1341–90.

Wolpert, David H., and William G. Macready. "No Free Lunch Theorems for Optimization." *IEEE Transactions on Evolutionary Computation* 1, no. 1 (1997): 67.

## CHAPTER 3

Quantifying Output Uncertainty with Monte Carlo Simulation

I of dice possess the science and in numbers thus am skilled.

—*King Rituparna of the Mahabharata (circa 900 BCE), on estimating the leaves on a tree from a randomly selected branch*

The importance of Monte Carlo simulation (MCS), also known as the Monte Carlo method, cannot be overstated. In finance and investing, MCS is used to value all types of assets, optimize diverse portfolios, estimate risks, and evaluate complex trading strategies. MCS is especially used to solve problems that don't have an analytical solution.[1] Indeed, there are many types of financial derivatives—such as lookback options and Asian options—that cannot be valued using any other technique. While the mathematics underpinning MCS is not simple, applying the method is actually quite easy, especially once you understand the key statistical concepts on which it is based.

MCS also pervades machine learning algorithms in general and probabilistic machine learning in particular. As discussed in Chapter 1 and demonstrated in the simulated solution to the Monte Hall problem in Chapter 2, MCS enables you to quantify the uncertainty of a model's outputs in a process called forward propagation. It takes the traditional scenario and sensitivity analysis used by financial analysts to a completely different level.

You might be wondering how a method that uses random sampling can lead to a stable solution. Isn't that a contradiction in terms? In a sense it is. However, when you understand a couple of statistical theorems, you will see that repetition of trials under

---

1 Paolo Brandimarte, "Introduction to Monte Carlo Methods," in *Handbook in Monte Carlo Simulation: Applications in Financial Engineering, Risk Management, and Economics* (Hoboken, NJ: John Wiley & Sons, 2014).

certain circumstances tames randomness and makes it converge toward a stable solution. This is what we observed in the simulated solution to the Monty Hall problem, where the solution converged on the theoretical values after about 1000 trials. In this chapter, we use MCS to provide a refresher on key statistical concepts and show you how to apply this powerful tool to solve real-world problems in finance and investing. In particular, we apply MCS to a capital budgeting project, in this case a software development project, and estimate the uncertainty in its value and duration.

Monte Carlo Simulation: Proof of Concept

Monte Carlo Simulation: A Weapon of Mass Construction

MCS was developed during the Second World War by some of the best mathematicians and physicists working on the nuclear weapons program in the US. Stanisław Ulam, collaborating with Nicholas Metropolis and John von Neumann, invented the modern version of MCS and implemented it using the ENIAC, the first programmable, electronic, general-purpose digital computer. Given the secretive nature of the weapons program, Metropolis code named the method Monte Carlo after the famous casino in Monaco where Ulam's uncle would gamble away borrowed money. Comte de Buffon had used a similar method in the 18th century, as did the physicist Enrico Fermi in the 1930s.

Before we begin going down this path, how do we know that MCS actually works as described? Let's do a simple proof-of-concept of MCS by computing the value of pi, a known constant. Figure 3-1 shows how we set up the simulation to estimate pi.

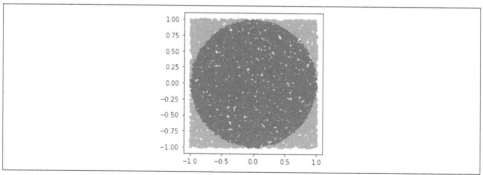

Figure 3-1. The blue circle of unit length in a red square with sides of two unit lengths is simulated to estimate the value of pi using MCS

As the Python code shows, you simulate the random spraying of N points to fill up the entire square. Next we count M points in the circle of unit length R. The area of the circle is pi × R^2 = M. The length of the square is 2R, so its area is 2R × 2R = 4 × R^2 = N. This implies that the ratio of the area of the circle to the area of the square is pi/4 = M/N. So pi = 4 × M/N:

```python
# Import modules
import numpy as np
from numpy import random as npr
import matplotlib.pyplot as plt

# Number of iterations in the simulation
n = 100000

# Draw random points from a uniform distribution in the X-Y plane to fill
#the area of a square that has a side of 2 units
x = npr.uniform(low=-1, high=1, size=n)
y = npr.uniform(low=-1, high=1, size=n)

# Points with a distance less than or equal to one unit from the origin will
# be inside the area of the unit circle.
# Using Pythagoras's theorem c^2 = a^2 + b^2
inside = np.sqrt(x**2 + y**2) <=1

# We generate N random points within our square and count the number of points
# that fall within the circle. Summing the points inside the circle is equivalent
# to integrating over the area of the circle.

# Note that the ratio of the area of the circle to the area of the square is
# pi*r^2/(2*r)^2 = pi/4. So if we can calculate the areas of the circle
# and the square, we can solve for pi
pi = 4.0*sum(inside)/n

# Estimate percentage error using the theoretical value of Pi
error = abs((pi-np.pi)/np.pi)*100

print("After {0} simulations, our estimate of Pi is {1} with an error of {2}%"
.format(n, pi, round(error,2)))

# Points outside the circle are the negation of the boolean array inside
outside = np.invert(inside)

# Plot the graph
plt.plot(x[inside], y[inside], 'b.')
plt.plot(x[outside], y[outside], 'r.')
plt.axis('square');
```

As in the Monty Hall simulation, you can see from the results of this simulation that the MCS approximation of pi is close to the theoretical value. Moreover, the difference between the estimate and the theoretical value gets closer to 0 as you increase the number of points N sprayed on the square. This makes the ratio of areas of the square and circle more accurate, giving you a better estimate of pi. Let's now explore the key statistical concepts that enable MCS to harness randomness to solve complex problems with or without analytical solutions.

Key Statistical Concepts

Here are some very important statistical concepts that you need to understand so that you will have deeper insights into why MCS works and how to apply it to solve complex problems in finance and investing. These are also the concepts that provide the theoretical foundation of financial, statistical, and machine learning models in general.

Mean and Variance

Figure 3-2 should refresh your memory of the basic descriptive statistical concepts you learned in high school.

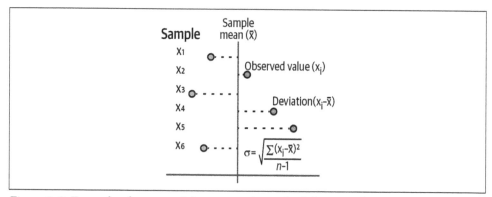

Figure 3-2. Formulas for a sample's mean and standard deviation[2]

---

2 Adapted from an image on Wikimedia Commons.

The arithmetic mean is a measure of the central tendency of a sample of data points. It is simple to calculate: add up all the point values in a sample and divide the sum by the total number of points. Other measures of central tendencies of a dataset are the median and the mode. Recall that the median is the value in the dataset that divides it into an upper and lower half. While the arithmetic mean is sensitive to outliers, the median does not change regardless of how extreme the outliers are. The mode is the most frequent value observed in a data. It is also unaffected by outliers. Sometimes there may be many modes in a sample, and other times a mode may not even exist.

It is important to note that the sum of all deviations from the arithmetic mean of the values always equals zero. That is what makes the arithmetic mean a good measure of the central tendency of a sample. It is also why you have to square the deviations from the mean to make them positive, so they do not cancel one another out. The average deviation from the mean gives you a sense of dispersion, or spread of the data sample, from its arithmetic mean.

Note that the variance of a sample is calculated by adding the sum of the squared deviations and dividing them by one less than the total number of points (n). The reason you use n-1 instead of n is that you have lost a degree of freedom by calculating the mean; i.e. the mean and n-1 points will give you the entire dataset. Standard deviation, which is in the units of the mean, is obtained by taking the square root of variance.

Volatility of asset price returns is calculated using the standard deviation of sample returns. If the returns are compounded continuously in a financial model, such as is assumed in geometric Brownian motion (GBM), we use the natural logarithm of price returns to calculate volatility. This also has the added advantage of making analytical and numerical computations much easier, since the practice of multiplying numbers can be transformed into adding their logarithms. Moreover, when performing multiplications involving numerous values less than 1, the precision of the computation can be compromised due to the inherent numerical underflow limitations of computers.

Expected Value: Probability-Weighted Arithmetic Mean

An important type of arithmetic mean is the expected value of a trade or investment. Expected value is defined as a probability-weighted arithmetic mean of future payoffs:

$$E[S] = P(S_1) \times Payoff(S_1) + ... + P(S_n) \times Payoff(S_n)$$

In finance, you should use expected value to estimate the future returns of your trades and investments. Other measurements used for this purpose are incomplete or misleading. For instance, it is common to hear traders on financial news networks talk about the reward-to-risk ratio of their trades. That ratio is an incomplete metric to consider because it does not factor in the estimated probabilities of positive and negative payoffs. You can structure a trade to have any reward-to-risk ratio you want. It says nothing about how likely you think the payoffs are going to be. If the reward-to-risk ratio is the key metric you're going to consider in an opportunity, don't waste your time with investing. Just buy a lottery ticket. The reward-to-risk ratio can go over 100 million to 1.

Why Volatility Is a Nonsensical Measure of Risk

Suppose the price of stock A goes up 5% in one month, 10% the next, and 20% in the third month. The monthly compounded return of A, the geometric mean of the returns, would be about 11.49%, with a monthly standard deviation, or volatility, of 7.64%. Note that we have computed the monthly volatility using the formula in Figure 3-2 and using 2 in the denominator, since this estimate is based on a sample of three months. Compare this to stock B, which declines –10% three months in a row. The monthly compounded return would be –10%, but the monthly volatility would be zero. Which stock would you like in your portfolio?

Volatility is a nonsensical measure of risk because it treats profits that don't equal the arithmetic mean (a measure of expectation) as risky as losses that do the same. What is also absurd is that losses that meet expectations are not considered a risk. Clearly, a loss is a loss whether or not it equals the average loss of the sample of returns.

Volatility doesn't consider the direction of the dispersion of returns and treats positive and negative deviations from the mean equally. So, volatility misestimates asymmetric risk. The volatility that investors talk about and don't want is the semistandard deviation of losses. However, semistandard deviation is analytically intractable and doesn't lend itself to elegant formulas in financial theories.

This implies that any risk or performance measure that is based on the volatility of returns is inherently flawed. The Sharpe ratio measures asset price returns in excess of a benchmark return and divides that by the volatility of asset price returns. It is a standard investment performance metric popular in academia and industry. However, many value investors, like Warren Buffet, hedge fund managers, and commodity trading advisors reject the Sharpe ratio as a flawed measure of performance. Worse still, volatility underestimates financial risk, which we discuss shortly.

 If your investment's positive returns are not meeting your expectations and its resultant volatility is keeping you up at night, you may rest assured, as help is nigh. Now you can lower the volatility of your investment returns by transferring those risky, positive return deviations to me for free!

Skewness and Kurtosis

Skewness measures the asymmetry of a distribution about its arithmetic mean. The skewness of a normal distribution is zero. Skewness is computed in a manner similar to that of variance, but instead of squaring the deviation from the mean, you raise it to the third power. This keeps the positive or negative sign of the deviations and so gives you the direction of average deviation from the mean. Skewness tells you where the expected value (mean) of the distribution is with respect to the median and the mode. See Figure 3-3.

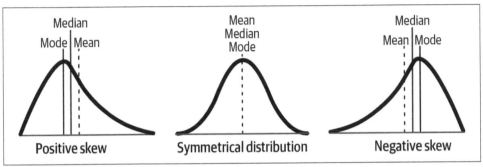

Figure 3-3. Skewed distributions compared to a symmetrical distribution such as the normal distribution[3]

As an investor or trader, you want your return distribution to be as positively skewed as possible. In a positively skewed distribution, the expected value is going to be greater than the median, and so it will be in the upper half of the distribution—positive returns are going to outweigh the negative returns on average. As discussed earlier, volatility is directionless and so will misestimate asymmetric risks of skewed distributions.

Kurtosis is a measure of how peaked the distribution is about the arithmetic mean and how fat its tails are compared to that of a normal distribution. Like skewness, kurtosis is computed in a manner similar to that of variance, but instead of squaring the deviation from the mean, you raise it to the fourth power. Fat-tailed distributions imply that low probability events are more likely than would be expected if the distribution were normal. A uniform distribution has no tails. In fact, a Cauchy (or Lorentzian) distribution looks deceptively similar to a normal distribution but has very fat tails because of its infinite mean and variance, as shown in Figure 3-4.

---

3 Adapted from an image on Wikimedia Commons.

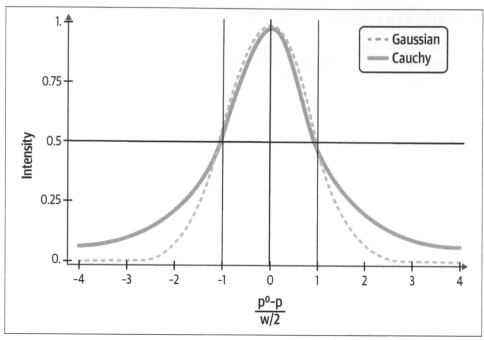

Figure 3-4. Compare the tails of the Cauchy distribution with the normal distribution[4]

The Gaussian or Normal Distribution

Gaussian distributions are found everywhere in nature and are used in all the sciences. It is quite common to see data distributed like a bell curve, as shown in Figure 3-5. That is why the Gaussian distribution is also called the normal distribution.

---

4 Adapted from an image on Wikimedia Commons.

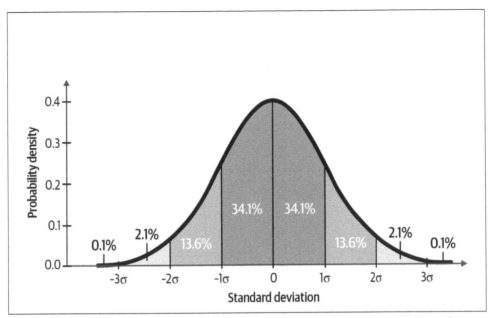

Figure 3-5. About 99.7% of the area of a Gaussian or normal distribution falls within 3 standard deviations from the mean[5]

Unfortunately, financial data and academic research show that normal distributions are not so common in all financial markets. But that hasn't stopped most academics and many practitioners from using them for their models. Why? Because Gaussian distributions are analytically tractable and lend themselves to elegant formulas that are solvable without using computers. If you know the mean and standard deviation of a Gaussian distribution, you know everything about the distribution. For instance, in Figure 3-3, you can see that about 68% of the data are within one standard deviation of the mean, 95% are within two standard deviations of the mean, and almost all the data are within three standard deviations of the mean.

Why Volatility Underestimates Financial Risk

The S&P 500 is a global market index and is used by market participants worldwide as a benchmark for the equity market. The index represents an equity portfolio composed of 500 of some of the best companies in the world at any time. Financial instruments based on the S&P 500 are the most liquid markets in the world and operate 24 hours a day for over 5 days of the week. I can attest to that, as I trade the ETF (exchange-traded fund) as well as options and futures based on this index.

---

5 Adapted from an image on Wikimedia Commons.

According to modern portfolio theory (MPT), asset price returns of the S&P 500 index should be approximately normally distributed. It also assumes that the mean and variance of this distribution are stationary ergodic. What this means is that these two parameters are time invariant, and we can estimate them from a reasonably large sample taken from any time period.

In the following Python code, we test the fundamental tenet of MPT that asset price returns are normally distributed. We import 30 years of S&P 500 price data and compute its daily returns, skewness, and kurtosis:

```python
# Import Python libraries
import pandas as pd
from datetime import datetime
import numpy as np

import matplotlib.pyplot as plt
plt.style.use('seaborn')

# Install web scraper for Yahoo Finance
!pip install yfinance
import yfinance as yf

# Import over 30 years of S&P 500 ('SPY') price data into a dataframe
# called equity
start = datetime(1993, 2, 1)
end = datetime(2022, 10, 15)
equity = yf.Ticker('SPY').history(start=start, end=end)

# Use SPY's closing prices to compute its daily returns.
# Remove NaNs from your dataframe.
equity['Returns'] = equity['Close'].pct_change(1)*100
equity = equity.dropna()

# Visualize and summarize SPY's daily price returns.
# Compute its skewness and kurtosis.
plt.hist(equity['Returns']), plt.title('Distribution of S&P 500 Daily Percentage
Returns Over the Past 30 Years'), plt.xlabel('Daily Percentage Returns'),
plt.ylabel('Frequency'), plt.show();
print("Descriptive statistics of S&P 500 percentage returns:\n{}"
.format(equity['Returns'].describe().round(2)))
print('The skewness of S&P 500 returns is: {0:.2f} and the kurtosis is: {1:.2f}.'
.format(equity['Returns'].skew(), equity['Returns'].kurtosis()))
```

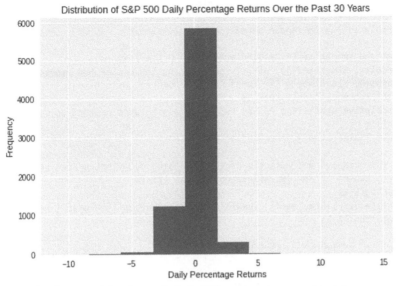

Distribution of S&P 500 Daily Percentage Returns Over the Past 30 Years

```
Descriptive statistics of S&P 500 percentage returns:
count    7481.00
mean        0.04
std         1.19
min       -10.94
25%        -0.44
50%         0.07
75%         0.59
max        14.52
Name: Returns, dtype: float64
The skewness of S&P 500 returns is: -0.07 and the kurtosis is: 11.43.
```

Clearly, the daily return distribution doesn't look anything close to normal. It has a negative skew of 0.07 and very fat tails with a kurtosis of 11.43. If S&P 500 daily returns were normally distributed, what would it look like? Let's simulate the world that theoretical finance claims we should be living in.

The time-invariant tenet of MPT implies that we can estimate its statistical moments using a sufficiently large sample from any time period. Thirty years' worth of data certainly qualifies. We use the mean and standard deviation from the previously mentioned historical data as our estimates for those parameters:

```
# Estimate the mean and standard deviation from SPY's 30 year historical data
mean = equity['Returns'].mean()
vol = equity['Returns'].std()
sample = equity['Returns'].count()

# Use NumPy's random number generator to sample from a normal distribution
# with the above estimates of its mean and standard deviation
# Create a new column called 'Simulated' and generate the same number of
```

```
# random samples from NumPy's normal distribution as the actual data sample
# you've imported above for SPY
equity['Simulated'] = np.random.normal(mean, vol, sample)

# Visualize and summarize SPY's simulated daily price returns.
plt.hist(equity['Simulated']), plt.title('Distribution of S&P 500 Simulated
Daily Returns'), plt.xlabel('Simulated Daily Percentage Returns'),
plt.ylabel('Frequency'), plt.show();
print("Descriptive statistics of S&P 500 stock's simulated percentage
returns:\n{}".
format(equity['Simulated'].describe()))

# Compute the skewness and kurtosis of the simulated daily price returns.
print('The skewness of S&P 500 simulated returns is: {0}
and the kurtosis is:
{1}.'.format(equity['Simulated'].skew().round(2), equity['Simulated']
.kurtosis().round(2)))
```

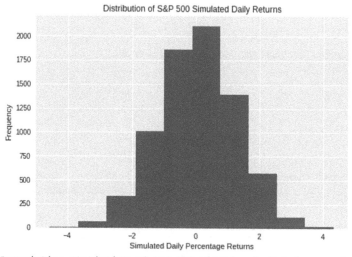

```
Descriptive statistics of S&P 500 stock's simulated percentage returns:
count    7481.000000
mean        0.066626
std         1.210278
min        -4.562200
25%        -0.736978
50%         0.075256
75%         0.880602
max         4.326674
Name: Simulated, dtype: float64
The skewness of S&P 500 simulated returns is: -0.02 and the kurtosis is: -0.0.
```

Since we are sampling randomly from a normal distribution, the values for both skewness and kurtosis have minor sampling errors around zero. Regardless, the two distributions look nothing like each other. The daily returns of the S&P 500 over the last 30 years are certainly not normally distributed.

Most financial time series are asymmetric and fat-tailed. These are not nice-to-know financial and statistical trivia. Asset price return distributions with negatively skewed, fat tails have the potential to bankrupt investors, corporations, and entire economies if their modelers ignore them, since they would be underestimating the probabilities of extreme events. The Great Financial Crisis is a recent reminder of the devastating consequences of building theoretical models using elegant mathematical equations that ignore the basic principles of the scientific method and the noisy, ugly, fat-tailed realities of real-world data.

The Law of Large Numbers

This is one of the most important statistical theorems. The law of large numbers (LLN) says that if samples are independent and drawn from the same distribution, the sample mean will almost surely converge to the theoretical mean as the sample size grows larger. In Figure 3-6, the value of the sum of all the numbers that appear on each throw of a die divided by the total number of throws or trials approaches 3.5 as the number of trials increases.

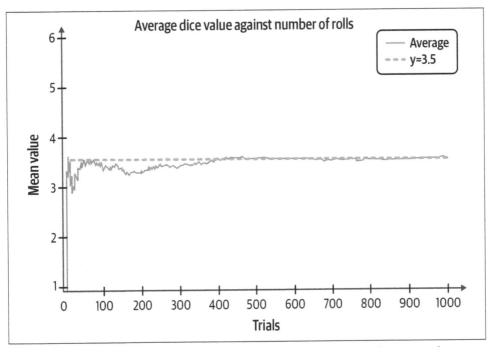

Figure 3-6. The sample mean of dice throws approaches its theoretical mean as the sample size gets larger[6]

---

6 Adapted from an image on Wikimedia Commons.

Note that the theoretical average does not have to be a physical outcome. There is no 3.5 on any fair die. Also, notice how the outcomes of the first few trials vary widely about the mean. However, in the long run, they converge inexorably to the theoretical mean. Of course, we assume that the die is fair and that we don't know the physics of the dice throws.

The Central Limit Theorem

The central limit theorem (CLT) says that if you keep taking samples from an unknown population of any shape and calculate the mean of each of the samples of size n, the distribution of these sample means will be normally distributed, as shown in Figure 3-7.

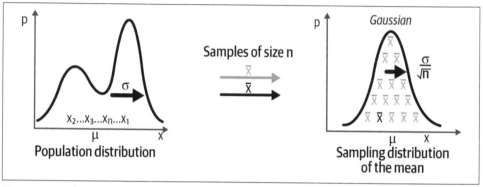

Figure 3-7. The sampling distribution of the sample mean is normally distributed[7]

This is one of the most amazing statistical phenomena. To appreciate the power of the CLT, consider a fair die that has a uniform distribution since each number on the die is equally likely at ⅙. Figure 3-8 shows what happens when you roll a fair die and add the numbers that show up on each throw and repeat the trials many times. Behold the magic of the CLT: horizontal lines are transformed into an approximate bell curve. If we increase the number of trials or tosses of the die, the curve will look like a bell curve.

---

7 Adapted from an image on Wikimedia Commons.

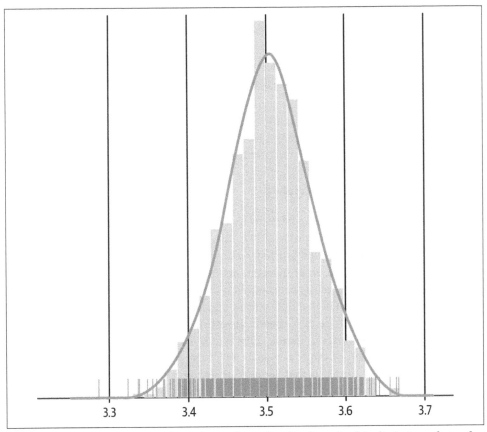

Figure 3-8. The CLT shows us how the uniform distribution of a fair die is transformed into an approximate Gaussian distribution[8]

Theoretical Underpinnings of MCS

MCS is based on the two most important theorems in statistics already mentioned: the law of large numbers (LLN) and the central limit theorem (CLT).[9] Recall that the LLN ensures that as the number of trials increases, the sample mean almost surely converges to the theoretical or population mean. The CLT ensures that the sampling errors or fluctuations of the sample averages from the theoretical mean become normally distributed as sample sizes get larger.

---

8 Adapted from an image on Wikimedia Commons.

9 A. Taylan Cemgil, "A Tutorial Introduction to Monte Carlo Methods, Markov Chain Monte Carlo and Particle Filtering," in *Academic Press Library in Signal Processing: Volume 1: Signal Processing Theory and Machine Learning*, ed. Paulo S. R. Diniz, Johan A. K. Suykens, Rama Chellappa, and Sergios Theodoridis (Oxford, UK: Elsevier, 2014), 1065–1114.

One of the reasons MCS works and is scalable to multidimensional problems is that the sampling error is independent of the dimension of the variable. This sampling error approaches zero asymptotically as the square root of the sample size and not the dimension of the variable. This is very important. It implies that a sampling error in an MCS is the same for a single variable as it is for a 100-dimensional variable.

However, the error decreases as the square root of the sample size n. So you have to increase the MCS iterations by a factor of 100 to increase the accuracy of its estimate by a single digit. But with computing power becoming cheaper by the day, this is not as big an issue now as it was in the last century.

Valuing a Software Project

Let's increase our understanding of MCS by applying it to a real-life financial problem such as valuing a capital project. The discounted cash flow (DCF) model discussed in the previous chapter is used extensively in corporations worldwide for valuing capital projects and other investments like bonds and equities. A discounted cash flow (DCF) model forecasts expected free cash flows (FCF) over N periods, typically measured in years. FCF in a time period equals cash from operations minus capital expenditures. The model also needs an estimate of the rate of return (R) per period required by the firm's investors. This rate is called the discount rate because it is used to discount each of the N period FCFs of the project to the present. The reason the FCFs are discounted is that we need to account for an investor's opportunity cost of capital for undertaking the project instead of another investment of similar risk. The model is set up in four steps:

1. Forecast the expected free cash flows (FCFs) of the project for each of the N periods.

2. Estimate the appropriate opportunity cost or discount rate (R) per period.

3. Discount each period's expected FCFs back to the present.

4. Add the discounted expected FCFs (previously described) to get the expected net present value (NPV):

   Expected NPV of project = $FCF_0 + FCF_1 / (1 + R) + FCF_2 / (1 + R)^2 + ...+ FCF_n / (1 + R)^N$

The NPV decision rule says that you should accept any investment whose expected NPV is greater than zero. This is because an investment with a positive expected NPV gives investors a higher rate of return than an alternative investment of similar risk, which is their opportunity cost.

To create our DCF model, we need to focus on the main drivers of costs and revenues for our software project. We also need to make sure that these variables are not strongly correlated with one another. Ideally, all FCFs of the model should be formulated using very few noncorrelated variables or risk factors.

As you know, software development is labor intensive, and so our main cost driver will be salaries and wages. Also, some developers will be working part time and some full time on the project. However, for developing the cost of labor, we only need the full-time equivalent (FTE) of the effort involved in producing the software, i.e., we estimate the effort as if all required developers were working full time. Scheduling is where we will figure out how much time to allot and when we will need each developer:

```python
# Import key Python libraries and packages that we need to process and analyze
# our data
import pandas as pd
from datetime import datetime
import numpy as np
from numpy import random as npr
import matplotlib.pyplot as plt
plt.style.use('seaborn')

# Specify model constants per full-time equivalent (fte)
daily_rate = 400
technology_charges = 500
overhead_charges = 200

# Specify other constants
tax_rate = 0.15

# Specify model risk factors that have little or no correlation among them.
# Number of trials/simulations
n = 10000
# Number of full-time equivalent persons on the team
fte = npr.uniform(low=1, high=5, size=n)
# In person days and driven independently by the scope of the project
effort = npr.uniform(low=240, high=480, size=n)
# Based on market research or expert judgment or both
price = npr.uniform(low=100, high=200, size=n)
# Independent of price in the price range considered
units = npr.normal(loc=1000, scale=500, size=n)
# Discount rate for the project period based on risk of similar efforts
discount_rate = npr.uniform(low=0.06, high=0.10, size=n)

# Specify how risk factors affect the project model
labor_costs = effort * daily_rate
technology_costs = fte * technology_charges
overhead_costs = fte * overhead_charges
revenues = price * units
# Duration determines the number of days the project will take to complete
# assuming no interruption. Different from the elapsed time of the project.
```

```python
duration = effort/fte

# Specify target_value
free_cash_flow = (revenues - labor_costs - technology_costs - overhead_costs)
                  * (1 - tax_rate)

# Simulate project NPV assuming initial FCF=0
npv = free_cash_flow/(1 + discount_rate)

# Convert numpy array to pandas DataFrame for easier analysis
NPV = pd.DataFrame(npv, columns=['NPV'])
# Estimate project duration in days
Duration = pd.DataFrame(duration, columns=['Days'])

# Plot histogram of NPV distribution
plt.hist(NPV['NPV'], bins=50), plt.title ('Distribution of Project NPV'),
plt.xlabel('Project NPV'),
plt.ylabel('Frequency'), plt.show();
print(NPV.describe().round())
success_probability = sum(NPV['NPV'] > 0)/n *100
print('There is a {0}% probability that the project will have a positive NPV.'
.format(round(success_probability)))
# Plot histogram of project duration distribution
plt.hist(Duration['Days'], bins=50),
plt.title ('Distribution of Project Duration'), plt.xlabel('Days'),
plt.ylabel('Frequency'), plt.show();
print(Duration.describe().round())
```

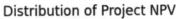

Distribution of Project NPV

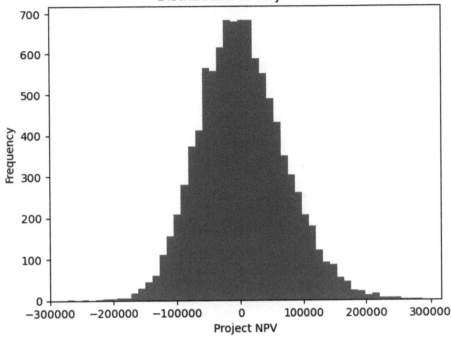

```
             NPV
count     10000.0
mean       3370.0
std       67024.0
min     -272139.0
25%      -42972.0
50%         -22.0
75%       45516.0
max      288188.0
```
There is a 50% probability that the project will have a positive NPV.

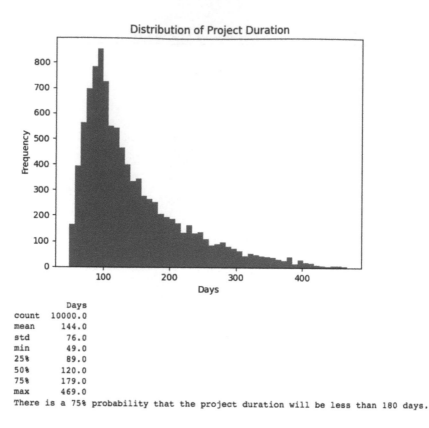

Distribution of Project Duration

```
                Days
count        10000.0
mean           144.0
std             76.0
min             49.0
25%             89.0
50%            120.0
75%            179.0
max            469.0
There is a 75% probability that the project duration will be less than 180 days.
```

Note that we did not discount the FCF distributions at the risk-free rate. The risk-free rate is the interest rate on a government security such as the US 10-year note. This is a common mistake in NPV simulations, but is incorrect, since each simulation is estimating the expected value of the FCF. Each FCF needs to be discounted at the risk-adjusted discount rate to account for the total risk of the project.

The distribution of risk-adjusted NPVs in the code output needs to be interpreted with caution. Using the dispersion of NPVs to make decisions would double count project risk. Using dispersion of NPVs adjusted at the risk-free rate to account for total risk has no sound theoretical basis in corporate finance.

Building a Sound MCS

To harness the power of MCS to solve complex financial and investment-related problems in the face of uncertainty, it is important that you follow a sound and replicable process. Here is a 10-step process for doing just that:

1. Formulate how target/dependent variables of your model are affected by features/independent variables, also called risk factors in finance.

2. Specify the probability distribution of each risk factor. Some common ones include Gaussian, Student's t-distribution, Cauchy, and binomial probability distributions.

3. Specify initial values and how time is discretized, such as in seconds, minutes, days, weeks, or years.

4. Specify how each risk factor changes over time, if at all.

5. Specify how each risk factor is affected by other risk factors. This is important since correlation among risk factors can incorrectly amplify or dampen effects. This phenomenon is also called multicollinearity.

6. Let the computer draw a random value from the probability distribution of each independent risk factor.

7. Compute the value of each risk factor based on that random value.

8. Compute target/dependent variables based on the computed value of all risk factors.

9. Iterate steps 6–8 as many times as necessary.

10. Record and analyze descriptive statistics of all iterations.

The power of MCS is that it transforms a complex, intractable problem that involves integral calculus into a simple one of descriptive statistics with its sampling algorithms. However, there are many challenges to building a sound MCS. Here are the most important ones:

- Specifying how each independent variable changes over time. Serial correlation (also known as autocorrelation) is the correlation of a variable with an instance of itself in the past. This correlation is not constant and usually changes over time, especially in financial markets.

- Specifying how each feature/independent variable is affected by other independent variables of the model. Correlations among independent variables/risk factors usually change over time.

- Fitting a theoretical probability distribution to the actual outcomes. Probability distributions of variables usually change over time.

- Convergence to the best estimate is nonlinear, making it slow and costly. It may not occur quickly enough to be of any practical value to trading or investing.

These challenges can be met as follows:

- Rigorous data analysis, domain knowledge, and industry expertise. You need to balance rigorous financial modeling with time, cost, and the effectiveness of the models that you produce.

- Treat all financial models as flawed and imperfect guides. Don't let the mathematical jargon intimidate or lull you into a false sense of security. Remember the adage "All models are wrong, but some are useful."

- Managing risk is of paramount importance. Always size capital positions appropriately, have wide error margins, and fallback plans if models fail.

- Clearly, there is no substitute for managerial experience and business judgment. Rely on your common sense, be skeptical, and ask difficult questions of a model's assumptions, inputs, and outputs.

Summary

Fundamentally, MCS is a set of numerical techniques that uses random sampling of probability distributions for computing approximate estimates or for simulating uncertainties of outcomes of a model. The central idea is to harness the statistical properties of randomness to develop approximate solutions to complex deterministic models and analytically intractable problems. MCS transforms a complex, often intractable, multidimensional problem in integral calculus into a much easier problem of descriptive statistics that any practitioner can use.

MCS is especially useful when there is no analytically tractable solution to a problem you are trying to solve. It enables you to quantify the probability and impact of all possible outcomes given your assumptions. It should be used when the traditional analysis of best-, worst-, and base-case scenarios may be inadequate for your decision making and risk management. MCS gives you a better understanding of the risk of complex financial models. Monte Carlo methods are one of the most powerful numerical tools and are pivotal to probabilistic machine learning.

In this chapter, we have applied MCS using independent random sampling. This involves randomly selecting samples from a probability distribution, with each sample being independent of any previous samples. This approach is efficient for simulating simple target probability distributions when samples are not correlated.

However, when dealing with complex target distributions and correlated samples, we have to use more advanced correlated random sampling methods. These dependent random sampling Monte Carlos are crucial to probabilistic machine learning. In Chapter 6, we will examine Markov chain Monte Carlo (MCMC) methods, which are powerful techniques for sampling from complex distributions with dependencies. In Chapter 7, we will apply these methods to financial modeling using the PMC library.

References

Brandimarte, Paolo. *Handbook in Monte Carlo Simulation: Applications in Financial Engineering, Risk Management, and Economics.* Hoboken, NJ: John Wiley & Sons, 2014.

Cemgil, A. Taylan. "A Tutorial Introduction to Monte Carlo Methods, Markov Chain Monte Carlo and Particle Filtering." In *Academic Press Library in Signal Processing: Volume 1: Signal Processing Theory and Machine Learning*, edited by Paulo S. R. Diniz, Johan A. K. Suykens, Rama Chellappa, and Sergios Theodoridis, 1065–1114. Oxford, UK: Elsevier, 2014.

## CHAPTER 4

The Dangers of Conventional Statistical Methodologies

Worse than useless.

—Jerzy Neyman, eminent mathematical statistician, referring to the statistical inference methodology of R. A. Fisher, the chief architect of conventional statistics

Recall from Chapter 1 that all financial models are at the mercy of the trifecta of errors, namely: errors in model specifications; errors in model parameter estimates; and errors resulting from the failure of a model to adapt to structural changes in its environment. Because of these errors, we need dynamic models that quantify the uncertainty inherent in our financial inferences and predictions.

A statistical inference methodology known as null hypothesis significance testing (NHST) almost completely dominates the research and practice of social and economic sciences. In this chapter, we examine how NHST and its p-value statistic is used for testing hypotheses and quantifying uncertainty of model parameters. The deep logical flaws of NHST methodology are primarily responsible for the reproducibility crisis in all the social and economic sciences, where the majority of published research findings are false.[1] In the next couple of sections, we expose the statistical skullduggery of NHST and its p-value statistic and show you how it is guilty of the prosecutor's fallacy. This fallacy is another version of the inverse fallacy, where a conditional statement is falsely equated with its inverse, thereby violating the inverse probability rule.

---

1 John P. A. Ioannidis, "Why Most Published Research Findings Are False," *PLOS Medicine* 2, no. 8 (2005), e124, *https://doi.org/10.1371/journal.pmed.0020124*; Campbell R. Harvey, Yan Liu, and Heqing Zhu, "…And the Cross-Section of Expected Returns," *The Review of Financial Studies* 29, no. 1 (January 2016): 5–68, *https://www.jstor.org/stable/43866011*.

Given the deep flaws and abuses of p-values for quantifying parameter uncertainty,[2] another methodology known as confidence intervals (CIs) is touted by orthodox statisticians as its mathematically rigorous replacement. Unfortunately, CIs are also the wrong tool for data analysis, since they were not designed to make statistical inferences from a single experiment.[3] Most importantly, the application of CIs in finance often violates the assumptions of the central limit theorem (CLT), making CIs invalid. In this chapter, we explore the trio of errors in applying CIs that are common in financial research and practice. We develop an ordinary least squares (OLS) linear regression model of equity returns using Statsmodels, a Python statistical package, to illustrate these three error types. We use the diagnostic test results of our regression model to support our reasons why CIs should not be used in data analyses in general and finance in particular.

The Inverse Fallacy

Recall the proof of the inverse probability rule, a trivial reformulation of the product rule. For any nonzero probability event H and D:

- *P(H and D) = P(D and H) (product of probabilities commute)*
- *P(H|D) × P(D) = P(D|H) × P(H) (applying product rule to both sides)*
- *P(H|D) = P(D|H) × P(H) / P(D) (the inverse probability rule)*

Note that joint probabilities, the product of two probabilities, commute—i.e., the order of the individual probabilities does not change the result of their product:

$P(H \text{ and } D) = P(D \text{ and } H)$

As you can see from the last equation, conditional probabilities do not commute:

$P(H|D) \neq P(D|H)$

This is a common logical mistake that people make in their thinking and scientists continue to make in their research when using NHST and p-values. This is called the inverse fallacy because you are incorrectly equating a conditional probability, P(D|H), with its inverse, P(H|D), and violating the inverse probability rule. The inverse fallacy

---

2 David Colquhoun, "An Investigation of the False Discovery Rate and the Misinterpretation of p-values," *Royal Society Open Science* (November 2014), *http://doi.org/10.1098/rsos.140216*; Charles Lambdin, "Significance Tests as Sorcery: Science Is Empirical—Significance Tests Are Not," *Theory & Psychology* 22, no. 1 (2012): 67–90, *https://doi.org/10.1177/0959354311429854*.

3 R. D. Morey, R. Hoekstra, J. N. Rouder, M. D. Lee, and E. J. Wagenmakers, "The Fallacy of Placing Confidence in Confidence Intervals," *Psychonomic Bulletin & Review* 23, no. 1 (2016): 103–123, *https://doi.org/10.3758/s13423-015-0947-8*.

---

is also known as transposed conditional fallacy. As a simple example, consider how the inverse fallacy incorrectly infers statement B from statement A:

- (A) Given that someone is a programmer, it is likely that they are analytical.
- (B) Given that someone is analytical, it is likely that they are a programmer.

But P(analytical | programmer) ≠ P(programmer | analytical). As you know, there are many, many analytical people who are not programmers, and such an inference seems absurd when framed in this manner. However, you will see that humans are generally not very good at processing conditional statements and their inverses, especially in complex situations. Indeed, prosecutors have ruined people's lives by using this flawed logic disguised in arguments that have led judges and juries to make terrible inferences and decisions.[4] A common example of the prosecutor's fallacy goes something like this:

- (A) Say about 0.1% of the 100,000 adults in your city have your blood type.
- (B) A blood stain with your blood type is found on the murder victim.
- (C) Therefore, claims the city prosecutor, there is a 99.9% probability that you are the murderer.

That's clearly absurd. What is truly horrifying—and we should all be screaming bloody murder—is that researchers and practitioners are unknowingly using the prosecutor's fallacious logic when applying NHST and p-values in their statistical inferences. More on NHST in the next section. Let's expose the prosecutor's flawed reasoning in this section so that you can see how it is used in the NHST methodology.

The probability of your guilt (G) before the blood stain evidence (E) was discovered to be P(G) = 1/100,000, since every adult in the city is an equally likely suspect. Therefore, the probability of your innocence (I) is P(I) = 99,999/100,000. The probability that the blood stain would match your blood type given you are actually guilty is a certainty, implying P(E | G) = 1. However, even if you are actually innocent, there is still a 0.1% probability that the blood stain would match your blood type merely by its prevalence in the city's adult population, implying P(E | I) = 0.001. The prosecutor needs to estimate P(G | E), the probability of your guilt given the evidence, with the previously mentioned probabilities. Instead of using the inverse probability rule, the prosecutor uses a fallacious argument as follows:

---

4 W. C. Thompson and E. L. Schumann, "Interpretation of Statistical Evidence in Criminal Trials: The Prosecutor's Fallacy and the Defense Attorney's Fallacy," *Law and Human Behavior* 11, no. 3 (1987): 167–187, *http://www.jstor.org/stable/1393631*.

- (A) Given the evidence, you can be either guilty or innocent, so $P(G \mid E) + P(I \mid E) = 1$
- (B) Now the prosecutor commits the inverse fallacy by making $P(I \mid E) = P(E \mid I)$
- (C) Thus the prosecutor's fallacy gives you $P(G \mid E) = 1 - P(I \mid E) = 1 - P(E \mid I)$
- (D) Plugging in the numbers, $P(G \mid E) = 1 - 0.001 = 0.999$ or 99.9%

Without explicitly using the inverse probability rule, your lawyer could use some common sense and correctly argue that there are 100 adults ($0.1\% \times 100,000$) in the city who have the same blood type as you do. Therefore, given evidence of the blood stain alone, there is only a 1 in 100 chance or 1% probability that you are guilty and 99% probability that you are innocent. This is approximately the same probability you would get when applying the inverse probability rule because it just formulates a commonsensical way of counting the possibilities. Let's do that now and calculate the probability of your innocence given the evidence, $P(I \mid E)$:

- (A) The inverse probability rule states $P(I \mid E) = P(E \mid I) \times P(I)/ P(E)$
- (B) We use the law of total probability to get $P(E) = P(E \mid I) \times P(I) + P(E \mid G) \times P(G)$
- (C) So $P(I \mid E) = 0.001 \times 0.99999 / [(0.001 \times 0.99999) + (1 \times 0.00001)] = 0.99$ or 99%

Before the prosecutor strikes you off the suspect list, it is important to note that it would also be fallacious for your lawyer to now ask the jury to disregard the blood stain as weak evidence of your guilt based on the 1% conditional probability just calculated. This flawed line of reasoning is called the defense attorney's fallacy and was used in the notorious O. J. Simpson murder trial. The evidence is not weak, because before the blood stain was found, you had a 1 in 100,000 chance of being the murderer. But after the blood stain was discovered, your chance of being guilty has gone up a thousand times to 1 in 100. That's very strong evidence indeed and nobody should disregard it. However, it is completely inadequate for a conviction if that is the only piece of evidence presented to the jury. The prosecutor will need additional incriminating evidence to make a valid case against you.

Now let's look at a realistic financial situation where the inverse fallacy might be harder to spot. Economic recessions are notoriously hard to recognize in the early stages of their development. As I write this chapter (in the fall of 2022), there is a debate raging among economists and investors about whether the US economy is currently in a recession or about to enter one. Economists at the National Bureau of Economic Research (NBER), the organization responsible for making the recession official, can only confirm the fact in retrospect. Sometimes the NBER takes over a year to declare when the recession actually started, as it did in the Great Recession of

2007–09. Of course, traders and investors cannot wait that long, and they develop their own indicators for predicting recessions in real time.

Assume that you have developed a proprietary economic indicator that crunches all kinds of data and correctly signals a recession 99% of the time when the US economy is actually in one or about to enter one. You also note that about 20% of the time your indicator signals a recession incorrectly even though the economy is not in one. Say you just found out that your proprietary indicator is flashing a recession signal. What is the probability that the US economy has actually entered into a recession? If you answered that the probability is 99%, as many people instinctively do, you would have committed the inverse fallacy since P(recession given signal) ≠ P(signal given recession).

Let's see why the probability of recession is not 99% but much lower. Assume R is the scenario that the US economy is in a recession and S is the event that your indicator signals that we are in a recession. You have the following conditional probabilities:

- The probability of your indicator giving you a recession signal given we actually are in one is $P(S|R) = 0.99$ or 99%. This is its true positive rate.

- This implies that the probability your indicator fails to detect a recession given we are actually in one, $P(\text{not } S|R) = 1 - P(S|R) = 0.01$ or 1%. This is its false negative rate.

- The probability your indicator incorrectly alerts you to a recession when there isn't one is $P(S|\text{not } R) = 0.20$ or 20%. This is its false positive rate.

- Similarly, the probability that your indicator successfully detects that the economy is not in a recession, $P(\text{not } S|\text{ not } R) = 1 - P(S|\text{not } R) = 0.80$ or 80%. This is its true negative rate.

These conditional probabilities are generally organized in a confusion matrix, as shown in Figure 4-1.

Your objective is to estimate $P(R|S)$, the conditional probability that the US economy is in a recession, given your indicator generates such a signal. To calculate this inverse probability $P(R|S)$, you can't only let the data speak about one specific scenario. Why? Because your economic indicator does not have 100% accuracy. It gives you a false recession signal 20% of the time when the economy is not in one. Could this scenario be 1 of the 5 when it is wrong about the economy being in a recession? Also, 1% of time it fails to detect a recession when the economy is actually in one. So maybe we have already been in a recession for many months, and it is 1 of the 100 instances when your indicator failed to flicker. How would you know just from the data about this particular scenario? You wouldn't, because you don't have a clue about the environment you are operating in. You need to leverage prior knowledge so that you can understand the context in which you are running your financial experiments.

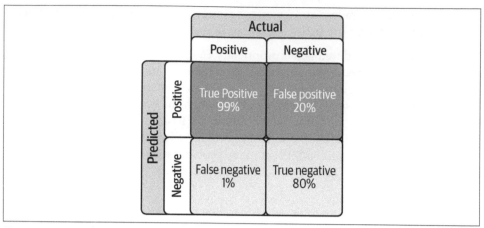

Figure 4-1. Confusion matrix of your proprietary recession indicator[5]

Your specific dataset is oblivious of how common or uncommon recessions are in the US. Why is that relevant? Because you don't know if your false positive rate is too high, or low enough, compared to the rate at which recessions tend to occur in the US for your indicator to be useful, despite its 99% true positive rate.

You will need to estimate the probability that the US could be in a recession in any given month $P(R)$ based on past occurrences; this is called the base rate of the particular event/scenario R. Ignoring the base rate leads to a violation of the inverse probability rule and invalid inferences, as we will demonstrate.

Let's compute the base rate from actual economic data. The NBER's time series for every month since 1982 that the US was in an economic recession can be downloaded from Federal Reserve Economic Data (FRED), a popular and free data source that has more than half a million economic and financial time series. Let's use the following Python code to calculate the monthly base rate of economic recessions in the US:

```
# Import libraries and FRED datareader
import numpy as np
import pandas as pd
import pandas_datareader.data as pdr
from datetime import datetime
start = datetime(1982, 1, 1)
end = datetime(2022, 9, 30)
# NBER business cycle classification
recession = pdr.DataReader('USREC', 'fred', start, end)
# Percentage of time the US economy was in recession since 1982
round(recession['USREC'].sum()/recession['USREC'].count()*100, 2)
```

---

5 Adapted from an image on Wikimedia Commons.

From this data, the US has been in an economic recession only 9.61% of the time in any given month from January 1982 to September 2022. Once you have estimated P(R), you can plug it into the law of total probability to get the unconditional probability, or marginal probability P(S), of getting a recession signal from your indicator regardless of the state of the economy. We then use P(R) in the inverse probability rule to calculate the probability the US economy is in recession, given that your proprietary indicator is signaling a recession:

$$P(S) = P(S|R) \times P(R) + P(S|not\ R) \times P(not\ R) = (0.99 \times 0.096) + (0.2 \times 0.904) = 0.276$$
$$P(R|S) = P(S|R) \times P(R) / P(S) = (0.99 \times 0.096) / 0.276 = 0.344$$

The calculation for P(S) says that you can expect your indicator to generate a signal 27.6% of the time regardless of whether the US economy is in a recession or not. Of the times you do see it flicker, P(R|S) says that in only 34.4% of those scenarios will the signal be correct about the economy being in a recession. Your signal will give you a false alarm P(not R|S) about 65.6% of the time. That's a very poor indicator—you're better off ignoring it.

This result seems counterintuitive since your indicator has a 99% true positive rate P(S|R). That's because you cannot shove your indicator's false positive rate under the rug and blithely ignore the base rate of US economic recessions with some ideological rubbish of being objective and letting only the data speak. That would be foolish because you would be denying the inverse probability rule and ignoring objective prior data about US economic cycles. Such fallacious inferences and decision making will almost surely see you go broke or be out of a job sooner rather than later.

In the real world of finance and investing, you will need a signal with a false positive rate lower than the base rate to give you a signal with a probability greater than 50% of being correct. To see this, let's redo the calculation with a revised false positive of 9%, which is slightly less than the 9.61% base rate at which the US economy has been in a recession in any given month since 1982:

$$P(S) = P(S|R) \times P(R) + P(S|not\ R) \times P(not\ R) = (0.99 \times 0.096) + (0.09 \times 0.904) = 0.176$$
$$P(R|S) = P(S|R) \times P(R) / P(S) = (0.95 \times 0.0967)/0.174 = 0.540$$

With a 54% probability of correctly calling a recession, your indicator will have an edge or positive expectation for better decision making and risk management.

To summarize, the true positive rate of your indicator is important. However, what is equally important is that the false positive rate of the indicator needs to be less than the base rate of the underlying feature in the population you are sampling from. So if you ignore the fact that your indicator is generating false positives P(S|not R) at a 20% rate while the US economy is generating a recessionary month at a 9.61% base rate, your false positives will overwhelm your true positives at a 2 to 1 ratio. It doesn't seem so far-fetched now to think that unscrupulous prosecutors, snake oil salesmen, and pseudoscientists could fool you (and themselves) with the inverse fallacy.

Since there is still a 34.4% chance that your indicator might be right, randomness could also fool you, too, by granting you a lucky guess, and the US economy could end up being in a recession. However, your probability estimate of 99% would be way off, and your reasoning would be fallacious. A trading or investing strategy based on luck, incorrect reasoning, and poor probability estimates will lead to financial ruin sooner rather than later. Far worse, a statistical methodology like NHST based on the inverse fallacy will overwhelm us with false positive studies, creating confusion and harm. This will ruin the scientific enterprise that we cherish and value so much.

NHST Is Guilty of the Prosecutor's Fallacy

Ronald Fisher, the head architect of modern statistics, introduced NHST in the 1920s. He also included Karl Pearson's p-value into his methodology for quantifying uncertainty. This was a postdata methodology and was meant to enable researchers to make statistical inferences from a single experiment based on a null hypothesis that is the negation of the hypothesis that the researcher is trying to prove.

In 1925, Fisher made the absurd and unsubstantiated claim that "the theory of inverse probability is founded upon error and must be wholly rejected."[6] Of course Fisher didn't and couldn't provide any proof for this claim. How could he? That would be akin to proving the rules of division are founded on error. As mentioned in the previous chapter, my suspicion is that by renaming the rule after an amateur mathematician, Thomas Bayes, he could cast aspersions on the rule. By rejecting the inverse probability rule, Fisher was able to use the prosecutor's fallacy to promote his flawed discriminatory ideas under the guise of objectivity and "letting the data speak for themselves."[7] Fisher's fawning cohorts in industry and slavish acolytes in academia merely repeated the lie about the inverse probability theory and banished it from their practice and curricula—a problem that continues to this day.

---

6 Quoted in John Aldrich, "R. A. Fisher on Bayes and Bayes' Theorem," *International Society for Bayesian Analysis* 3, no. 1 (2008): 163.

7 Francisco Louçã, "Emancipation Through Interaction—How Eugenics and Statistics Converged and Diverged," *Journal of the History of Biology* 42, no. 4 (2009): 649–684, *http://www.jstor.org/stable/25650625.*

NHST is built behind the facade of a valid form of propositional logic known as proof by contrapositive. The logic is as follows: suppose we have two propositions H and D such that if H is true, then D is true. Now if we can prove that D is false, then we can validly conclude that H must be false.

Following the latter logic, researchers using NHST formulate a hypothesis, called the null hypothesis (H_0), that they want to disprove before observing any data. H_0 is viewed as the negation of an alternative research hypothesis (H_1) that they want to establish but is not explicitly specified, i.e., H_1 = not H_0 and $P(H_1) + P(\text{not } H_0) = 1$. In this regard, they play the devil's advocate for the null hypothesis.

The null hypothesis is generally formulated as a summary statistic, such as the difference in the sample means of the data distribution of two groups that need to be compared. It is important to note that researchers do not predict the data that their research hypothesis H_1 is expected to generate, assuming that H_1 is true.

Before starting their experiment, researchers also choose a significance level, denoted by alpha, which works as a decision threshold to accept or reject the null hypothesis after observing the data. The convention is to set alpha to 5%. The alpha level is claimed to be the long-run probability that the researcher might incorrectly reject a true null hypothesis, thereby committing a type I error and generating false positive results (a result that is claimed to be true when it is actually false). The alpha level is the most critical element of the experiment, since it determines if the experiment is considered statistically significant or not.

It is important to note that any significance level is entirely subjective, as it is not based on the observed data or the null hypothesis or a scientific reason or any mathematical rule or theorem. The conventional use of the 5% alpha level is a totally arbitrary and self-fulling ritual. Since Fisher used a 5% alpha significance level, researchers and academics blindly follow his example. So much for the vaunted objectivity and scientific rigor of frequentists, not to mention letting the data speak for themselves.

Assuming the null hypothesis is true, the researcher computes a statistic called the p-value to quantify the probability of observing the summary statistic of the sample data (D) or something more extreme than it:

$$\text{p-value} = P(D|H_0)$$

If the p-value ≤ alpha, H_0 is rejected as false at the alpha significance level and the alternative hypothesis (H_1) is accepted as true.

But this logic of NHST is mind-bogglingly absurd. By rejecting the null hypothesis (H_0) given the p-value of the test statistic (D), the researcher is committing the inverse fallacy, because $P(H_0 \mid D) \neq P(D \mid H_0)$. See Figure 4-2.

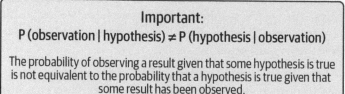

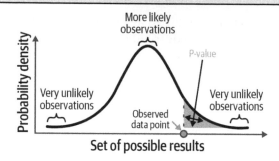

A P-value (shaded area) is the probability of an observed
(or more extreme) result, assuming that the null hypothesis is true.

Figure 4-2. How p-values are used in NHST[8]

NHST makes an even more absurd leap of logic. NHST commits the prosecutor's fallacy by allowing researchers to accept the unspecified, alternative research hypothesis,
which the data was not modeling in the first place. Go back to the previous section
and refresh your memory about how we disentangled the prosecutor's fallacy.

The researcher wants to determine $P(H_1|D)$, the probability the research hypothesis
(H_1) is true given the data. But NHST only computes $P(D|H_0)$, the probability of
observing the data assuming the null hypothesis (H_0) is true. It then uses the p-value
statistic to accept or reject the null hypothesis at the alpha significance level. So
researchers following the NHST methodology commit the prosecutor's fallacy as
follows:

- $P(H_1|D) = 1 - P(H_0|D)$ (true statement)
- $P(H_0|D) = P(D|H_0)$ (the inverse fallacy)
- $P(H_1|D) = 1 - P(D|H_0)$ (the prosecutor's fallacy)

---

8 Adapted from an image on Wikimedia Commons.

How should we validly calculate $P(H_1|D)$? The binary logic of proof by contrapositive in a deterministic world needs to be translated into the calculus of conditional probabilities in an uncertain world. This translation is enabled by the inverse probability rule and the law of total probability, as was applied in the previous section:

- $P(H_1|D) = 1 - P(H_0|D)$
- $P(H_1|D) = 1 - [P(D|H_0)P(H_0)/P(D)]$
- $\mathbf{P(H_1|D) = 1 - [P(D|H_0)P(H_0) / (P(D|H_0)P(H_0) + P(D|H_1)P(H_1))]}$

As this equation, which I have derived, shows, the researcher needs to estimate $P(D|H_1)$, the probability of observing the data assuming their research hypothesis H_1 is true. Most importantly, the researcher needs to estimate the prior probability or base rate of at least one of their complementary hypotheses, $P(H_0)$ or $P(H_1)$. That's because without the base rate, you cannot compute the evidence or the unconditional probability of observing the data. This fallacious logic is what makes statistical inferences about either the null hypothesis or the alternative research hypothesis invalid. It is for very good reasons that Jerzy Neyman, an eminent statistician and Fisher's peer, called Fisher's work on statistical inference "worse than useless."[9]

It is clear that NHST—the cornerstone of education, research, and practice of the social and economic sciences—is committing the prosecutor's fallacy. No wonder most of the published research findings using NHST are false. NHST has wasted billions of research dollars, defamed science, and done a great disservice to humanity with its false positive research studies. All this while professing the farce of rigor and objectivity. NHST continues to wreak havoc on the social and economic sciences, producing too many false research claims to this day despite many failed attempts to abolish it or reform it for over half a century.[10] It's about time we reject the NHST because it "is founded upon error and must be wholly rejected."[11]

Many in the social and economic sciences recommend replacing p-values with CI theory, which is touted as a mathematically more rigorous way of quantifying uncertainty. So let's examine CI theory to see if it is useful.

---

9 Johannes Lenhard, "Models and Statistical Inference: The Controversy Between Fisher and Neyman-Pearson," *The British Journal for the Philosophy of Science* 57, no. 1 (2006): 69–91, *http://www.jstor.org/stable/3541653*.

10 Dénes Szucs and John P. A. Ioannidis, "When Null Hypothesis Significance Testing Is Unsuitable for Research: A Reassessment," *Frontiers in Human Neuroscience* 11, no. 390 (August 2017), doi: 10.3389/fnhum. 2017.00390.

11 Aldrich, "R. A. Fisher on Bayes and Bayes' Theorem," 163.

The Confidence Game

As mentioned in the previous sidebar, Jerzy Neyman developed a statistical decision theory designed to support industrial quality control. His statistical theory provides a decision framework that seeks to control type I (false positive) and type II (false negative) errors to balance costs versus benefits over the long run based on many experiments. Neyman intentionally left out p-values because it was a nonsensical concept violating basic probabilistic logic.

---

12 Gerd Gigerenzer, "Statistical Rituals: The Replication Delusion and How We Got There," *Advances in Methods and Practices in Psychological Science* (June 2018): 198–218, *https://doi.org/10.1177/2515245918771329*.

In 1937, Neyman developed CI theory to be a *predata theory* of statistical inference, intended to inform statistical procedures that have long-run average properties *before* data are sampled from a population distribution. Neyman made it very clear that his CI theory was not intended to support inferences *after* data are sampled in a single scientific experiment. CI theory is not a *postdata theory of* statistical inference despite how it is applied today in research and practice in social and economic sciences.

CI theory quantifies uncertainty of population parameter estimates. For example, a 90% confidence interval (CI), as shown in Figure 4-3, is generally understood to imply that there is a 90% probability that the true value of a parameter of interest is in the interval [–a, a].

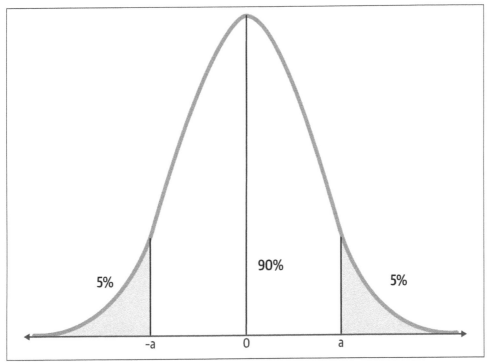

Figure 4-3. The interval [–a, a] is called a 90% confidence interval[13]

Fisher attacked Neyman's CI theory by claiming it did not serve the needs of scientists and potentially would lead to mutually contradictory inferences from data. Fisher's criticisms of CI theory have proven to be justified—but not because Neyman's CI theory is logically or mathematically flawed, as Fisher claimed.

---

13 Adapted from an image on Wikimedia Commons.

Let's examine the trio of errors that arise from the common practice of misusing Neyman's CI theory as a postdata theory—i.e., for making inferences about population parameters based on a specific data sample. The three types of errors using CIs are:

- Making probabilistic claims about population parameters
- Making probabilistic claims about a specific confidence interval
- Making probabilistic claims about sampling distributions

The frequentist philosophy of probability and statistical inference has had a profound impact on the theory and practice of financial economics in general and CIs in particular. To explore the implications of confidence intervals (CIs) for our purposes, we begin the next subsection by discussing the fundamental concepts of a simple market model and its relationship to financial theory. Afterward, we utilize Statsmodels, a statistical package in Python, to construct an ordinary least squares (OLS) linear regression model of equity returns to estimate the parameters of our market model. This real-world example allows us to illustrate how CIs are actually applied in financial data analysis. In the next sections, we examine why CIs are logically incoherent and practically useless.

Single-Factor Market Model for Equities

Modern portfolio theory assumes that rational, risk-averse investors demand a risk premium, a return in excess of a risk-free asset such as a treasury bill, for investing in risky assets such as equities. A stock's single-factor market model (MM) is basically a linear regression model of the realized excess returns of a stock (outcome or dependent variable) regressed against the realized excess returns of a single risk factor (predictor or independent variable) such as the overall market, as formulated here:

$$(R - F) = \alpha + \beta \times (M - F) + \epsilon$$

Where R is the realized return of a stock, F is the return on a risk-free asset such as a US Treasury security, M is the realized return of a market portfolio such as the S&P 500, α (alpha) is the expected stock-specific return, β (beta) is the level of systematic risk exposure to the market, and ε (epsilon) is the unexpected stock-specific return. The beta of a stock gives the average percentage return response to a 1% change in return of the overall market portfolio. For example, if a stock has a beta of 1.4 and the S&P 500 falls by 1%, the stock is expected to fall by –1.4% *on average*. See Figure 4-4.

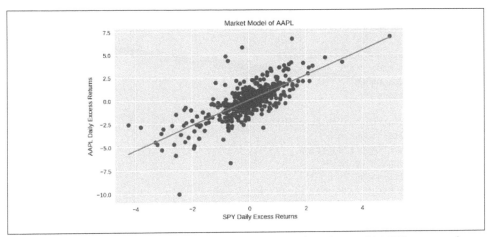

Figure 4-4. Market model showing the excess returns of Apple Inc. (AAPL) regressed against the excess returns of the S&P 500

Note that the MM of an asset is different from its capital asset pricing model (CAPM). The CAPM is the pivotal economic equilibrium model of modern finance that predicts expected returns of an asset based on its β or systematic risk exposure to the overall market. Unlike the CAPM, an asset's MM is a statistical model about realized returns that has both an idiosyncratic risk term a and an error term ε in its formulation.

According to the CAPM, the alpha of an asset's MM has an expected value of zero because market participants are assumed to hold efficient portfolios that diversify the idiosyncratic risks of any specific asset. Market participants are only rewarded for bearing systematic risk since it cannot be diversified away. In keeping with the general assumptions of an OLS regression model, both CAPM and MM assume that the expected value of the residuals ε will be normally distributed with a zero mean and a constant, finite variance.

A financial analyst, relying on modern portfolio theory and practice, assumes there is an underlying, time-invariant, stochastic process generating the price data of Apple Inc., which can be modeled as an OLS linear regression MM. This MM will have population parameters, alpha and beta, which have true, fixed values that can be estimated from reason random samples of Apple's closing price data.

Simple Linear Regression with Statsmodels

Let's run our Python code to estimate alpha and beta based on a sample of five years of daily closing prices of Apple. We can use any holding period return as long as it is used consistently throughout the formula. Using a daily holding period is convenient because it makes price return calculations much easier using pandas DataFrames:

```
# Install Yahoo finance package
!pip install yfinance

# Import relevant Python packages
import statsmodels.api as sm
import pandas as pd
import yfinance as yf

import matplotlib.pyplot as plt
plt.style.use('seaborn')
from datetime import datetime
#Import financial data
start = datetime(2017, 8, 3)
end = datetime(2022, 8, 6)

# S&P 500 index is a proxy for the market
market = yf.Ticker('SPY').history(start=start, end=end)
# Ticker symbol for Apple, the most liquid stock in the world
stock = yf.Ticker('AAPL').history(start=start, end=end)
# 10 year US treasury note is the proxy for risk free rate
riskfree_rate = yf.Ticker('^TNX').history(start=start, end=end)
# Create dataframe to hold daily returns of securities
daily_returns = pd.DataFrame()
daily_returns['market'] = market['Close'].pct_change(1)*100
daily_returns['stock'] = stock['Close'].pct_change(1)*100
# Compounded daily rate based on 360 days
# for the calendar year used in the bond market
daily_returns['riskfree'] = (1 + riskfree_rate['Close']) ** (1/360) - 1
# Plot and summarize the distribution of daily returns
plt.hist(daily_returns['market']), plt.title('Distribution of Market (SPY)
Daily Returns'), plt.xlabel('Daily Percentage Returns'),
plt.ylabel('Frequency'), plt.show()
# Analyze descriptive statistics
print("Descriptive Statistics of the Market's daily percentage returns:\n{}".
format(daily_returns['market'].describe()))

plt.hist(daily_returns['stock']),
plt.title('Distribution of Apple Inc. (AAPL) Daily Returns'),
plt.xlabel('Daily Percentage Returns'), plt.ylabel('Frequency'), plt.show()
# Analyze descriptive statistics
print("Descriptive Statistics of the Apple's daily percentage returns:\n{}"
.format(daily_returns['stock'].describe()))

plt.hist(daily_returns['riskfree']), plt.title('Distribution of the riskfree
rate (TNX) Daily Returns'), plt.xlabel('Daily Percentage Returns'),
plt.ylabel('Frequency'), plt.show()
# Analyze descriptive statistics
print("Descriptive Statistics of the 10 year note daily percentage returns:\n{}"
.format(daily_returns['riskfree'].describe()))
# Examine missing rows in the dataframe
market.index.difference(riskfree_rate.index)
# Fill rows with previous day's risk-free rate since daily rates
```

```
# are generally stable
daily_returns = daily_returns.ffill()
# Drop NaNs in first row because of percentage calculations
daily_returns = daily_returns.dropna()
# Check dataframe for null values
daily_returns.isnull().sum()
# Check first five rows of dataframe
daily_returns.head()
# AAPL's Market Model based on daily excess returns

# Daily excess returns of AAPL
y = daily_returns['stock'] - daily_returns['riskfree']
# Daily excess returns of the market
x = daily_returns['market'] - daily_returns['riskfree']

# Plot the data
plt.scatter(x,y)

# Add the constant vector to obtain the intecept
x = sm.add_constant(x)

# Use ordinary least squares algorithm to find the line of best fit
market_model = sm.OLS(y, x).fit()

# Plot the line of best fit
plt.plot(x, x*market_model.params[0]+market_model.params['const'])
plt.title('Market Model of AAPL'), plt.xlabel('SPY Daily Excess Returns'),
plt.ylabel('AAPL Daily Excess Returns'), plt.show();

# Display the values of alpha and beta of AAPL's market model
print("According to AAPL's Market Model, the security had a realized Alpha of
{0}% and Beta of {1}".format(round(market_model.params['const'],2),
round(market_model.params[0],2)))
# Summarize and analyze the statistics of your linear regression
print("The Market Model of AAPL is summarized below:\n{}"
.format(market_model.summary()));
```

After running our Python code, a financial analyst would estimate that alpha is 0.071% and beta is 1.2385, as shown in the Statsmodels summary output:

```
The Market Model of AAPL is summarized below:
OLS Regression Results
==============================================================================
Dep. Variable:         y                  R-squared:            0.624
Model:                 OLS                Adj. R-squared:       0.624
Method:                Least Squares      F-statistic:          2087.
Date:                  Sun, 07 Aug 2022   Prob (F-statistic):   2.02e-269
Time:                  06:28:33           Log-Likelihood:       -2059.8
No. Observations:      1260               AIC:                  4124.
Df Residuals:          1258               BIC:                  4134.
Df Model:              1
Covariance Type:       nonrobust
==============================================================================
```

```
             coef      std err       t       P>|t|     [0.025     0.975]
const       0.0710      0.035      2.028     0.043     0.002      0.140
0           1.2385      0.027     45.684     0.000     1.185      1.292
============================================================================
Omnibus:            202.982          Durbin-Watson:            1.848
Prob(Omnibus):        0.000          Jarque-Bera (JB):      1785.931
Skew:                 0.459          Prob(JB):                 0.00
Kurtosis:             8.760          Cond. No.                 1.30
============================================================================
Warnings:
[1] Standard Errors assume that the covariance matrix of the errors
is correctly specified.
```

Confidence Intervals for Alpha and Beta

Clearly, these point estimates of alpha and beta will vary depending on the sample size as well as start and end dates used in our random samples, with each estimate reflecting Apple's idiosyncratic price fluctuations during that specific time period. Even though the population parameters alpha and beta are unknown, and possibly unknowable, the financial analyst considers them to be true constants of a stochastic process. It is the random sampling of Apple's price data that introduces uncertainty in the estimates of constant population parameters. It is the data, and every statistic derived from the data, such as CIs, that are treated as random by frequentists. Financial analysts calculate CIs from random samples to express the uncertainty around point estimates of constant population parameters.

CIs provide a range of values with a probability value or significance level attached to that range. For instance, in Apple's MM, a financial analyst could calculate the 95% confidence interval by calculating the standard error (SE) of alpha and beta. Since the residuals ε are assumed to be normally distributed with an unknown, constant variance, the t-statistic would need to be used in computing CIs. However, because the sample size is greater than 30, the t-distribution converges to the standard normal distribution, and the t-statistic values are the same as the Z-scores of a standard normal distribution. So the analyst would multiply each SE by +/– the Z-score for a 95% CI and then add the result to the point estimate of alpha and beta to obtain its CI. From the previous Statsmodels regression results, the 95% CI for alpha and beta were computed as follows:

α+/– (SE × t-statistic / Z-score for 95% CI) = 0.0710 % +/– (0.035 % × 1.96) = [0.002%, 0.140%]
β+/- (SE × t-statistic / Z-score for 95% CI) = 1.2385 +/– (0.027 × 1.96) = [1.185, 1.292])

Unveiling the Confidence Game

To understand this trio of errors, we need to understand probability and statistical inference from the perspective of a modern statistician. As discussed in Chapter 2, frequentists, such as Fisher and Neyman, claim that probability is a natural, static property of an event and is measured empirically as its long-run relative frequency.

Frequentists postulate that the underlying stochastic process that generates data has statistical properties that do not change in the long run: the probability distribution is stationary ergodic. Even though the parameters of this underlying process may be unknown or unknowable, frequentists believe that these parameters are constant and have "true" values. Population parameters may be estimated from random samples of data. It is the randomness of data that creates uncertainty in the estimates of the true, fixed population parameters.

What most people think they are getting from a 95% CI is a 95% probability that the true population parameter is within the limits of the *specific* interval calculated from a specific data sample. For instance, based on the Statsmodels results, you would think there is a 95% probability that the true value of beta of Apple is in the range [1.185, 1.292]. Strictly speaking, your interpretation of such a CI would be wrong.

According to Neyman's CI theory, what a 95% CI actually means is that if we were to draw 100 random samples from Apple's underlying stock return distribution, we would end up with 100 different confidence intervals, and we can be confident that 95 of them will contain the true population parameter within their limits. However, we won't know which specific 95 CIs of the 100 CIs include the true value of the population parameter and which 5 CIs do not. We are assured that only the long-run ratio of the CIs that include the population parameter to the ones that do not will approach 95% as we draw random samples ad nauseam.

Winston Churchill could just as well have been talking about CIs instead of Russia's world war strategy when he said, "It is a riddle, wrapped in a mystery, inside an enigma; but perhaps there is a key." Indeed, we do present a key in this chapter. Let's investigate the triumvirate of fallacies that arise from misusing CI as a postdata theory in financial data analysis.

Errors in Making Probabilistic Claims About Population Parameters

Recall that a frequentist statistician considers a population parameter to be a constant with a "true" value. This value may be unknown or even unknowable. But that does not change the fact that its value is fixed. Therefore, a population parameter is either in a CI or it is not. For instance, if you believe the theory that capital markets are highly efficient, you would also believe that the true value of alpha is 0. Now 0 is definitely not in the interval [0.002%, 0.14%] calculated in the previous Statsmodels regression results. Therefore, the probability that alpha is in our CI is 0% and not 95% or any other value.

Because population parameters are believed to be constants by frequentists, there can be absolutely no ambiguity about them: the probability that the true value of a population parameter is within *any* CI is either 0% or 100%. So it is erroneous to make probabilistic claims about any population parameter under a frequentist interpretation of probability.

Errors in Making Probabilistic Claims About a Specific Confidence Interval

A more sophisticated interpretation of CIs found in the literature and textbooks goes as follows: hypothetically speaking, if we were to repeat our linear regression many times, the interval [1.185, 1.292] would contain the true value of beta within its limits about 95% of the time.

Recall that probabilities in the frequentist world apply only to long-run frequencies of *repeatable* events. By definition, the probability of a unique event, such as a specific CI, is undefined and makes no sense to a frequentist. Therefore, a frequentist cannot assign a 95% probability to either of the specific intervals for alpha and beta that we have calculated. In other words, we can't really infer much from a specific CI.

But that is the main objective of our exercise! This limitation of CIs makes it utterly useless for data scientists who want to make inferences about population parameters from their specific data samples: i.e., they want to make postdata inferences. But, as was mentioned earlier, Neyman intended his CI theory to be used for only predata inferences based on long-term frequencies.

Errors in Making Probabilistic Claims About Sampling Distributions

How do financial analysts justify making these probabilistic claims about CIs in research and practice? How do they square the circle? What is the key to applying CIs in a commonsensical way? Statisticians can, in theory or in practice, repeatedly sample data from a population distribution. The point estimates of sample means computed from many different random samples create a pattern called the sampling distribution of the sample mean. Sampling distributions enable frequentists to invoke the central limit theorem (CLT) in calculating the uncertainty around sample point estimates of population parameters. In particular, as was discussed in the previous chapter, the CLT states that if many samples are drawn randomly from a population with a finite mean and variance, the sampling distribution of the sample mean approaches a normal distribution asymptotically. The shape of the underlying population distribution is immaterial and can only affect the speed of this inexorable convergence to normality. See Figure 3-7 in the previous chapter.

The frequentist definition of probability as a long-run relative frequency of repeatable events resonates with the CLT's repeated drawing of random samples from a population distribution to generate its sampling distributions. So statisticians square the circle by invoking the CLT and claiming that their sampling distributions almost surely converge to a normal distribution, regardless of the shape of the underlying population distribution. This also enables them to compute CIs using the Z-scores of the standard normal distribution, as shown in the previous Statsmodels regression results. This is the key to the enigmatic use of CI as a postdata theory.

However, as financial executives and investors putting our capital at risk, we need to read the fine print of the CLT: specifically, we need to note its assumption that the underlying population distribution needs to have a finite mean and variance. While most distributions satisfy these two conditions, there are many that do not, especially in finance and economics. For these types of population distributions, the CLT cannot be invoked to save CIs. The key does not work on these doors—it is not a magic key. For instance, the Cauchy and Pareto distributions are fat-tailed distributions that do not have finite means or variances. As was mentioned in the previous chapter and is worth repeating, a Cauchy (or Lorentzian) distribution looks deceptively similar to a normal distribution, but has very fat tails because of its infinite variance. See Figure 4-5.

The diagnostic tests computed by Statsmodels in Figure 4-4 show us that the equity market has wrecked the key assumptions of our MM. Specifically, the Bera-Jarque and Omnibus normality tests show the probability that the residuals ε that are normally distributed are almost surely zero. This distribution is positively skewed and has very fat tails—a kurtosis that is about three times that of a standard normal distribution.

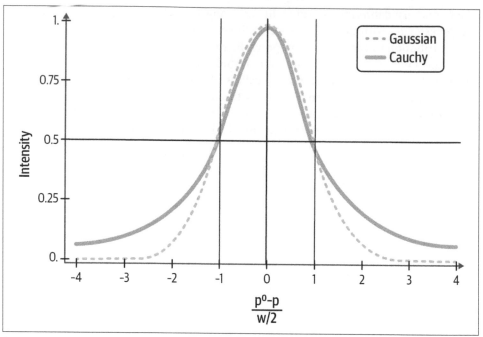

Figure 4-5. Compare Cauchy distribution with the normal distribution[14]

How about making the sample size even larger? Won't the distribution of the residuals get more normal with a much larger sample size, as claimed by financial theory? Let's run our MM using 25 years of Apple's daily closing prices—a quarter of a century's worth of data. Here are the results:

```
The Market Model of AAPL is summarized below:
OLS Regression Results
==========================================================================
Dep. Variable:        y                 R-squared:            0.270
Model:                OLS               Adj. R-squared:       0.270
Method:               Least Squares     F-statistic:          2331.
Date:                 Sun, 07 Aug 2022  Prob (F-statistic):   0.00
Time:                 07:03:34          Log-Likelihood:       -14187.
No. Observations:     6293              AIC:                  2.838e+04
Df Residuals:         6291              BIC:                  2.839e+04
Df Model:             1
Covariance Type:      nonrobust
==========================================================================
              coef      std err    t        P>|t|    [0.025    0.975]
const         0.1063    0.029      3.656    0.000    0.049     0.163
0             1.1208    0.023      48.281   0.000    1.075     1.166
```

---

14 Adapted from an image on Wikimedia Commons.

```
=========================================================================
Omnibus:          2566.940      Durbin-Watson:          2.020
Prob(Omnibus):    0.000         Jarque-Bera (JB):       66298.825
Skew:             -0.736        Prob(JB):               0.00
Kurtosis:         53.262        Cond. No.               1.25
=========================================================================
Warnings:
[1] Standard Errors assume that the covariance matrix of the errors
is correctly specified.
```

All the diagnostic test results make it clear that the equity market has savaged the "Nobel-prize-winning" CAPM (and related MM) theory. Even with a sample size that includes a quarter of a century of daily closing prices, the distribution of our model's residuals is grossly more non-normal than before. It is now very negatively skewed with an absurdly high kurtosis—almost 18 times that of a standard normal distribution. Most notably, the CI of our 25-year beta is [1.075, 1.166], which is outside the range of the CI of our 5-year beta [1.185,1.292]. In fact, the beta of AAPL seems to be regressing toward 1, the beta value of the S&P 500.

Invoking some version of the CLT and claiming asymptotic normality for the *sampling distributions* of the residuals or the coefficients of our regression model seem futile, if not invalid. There is a compelling body of economic research claiming that the underlying distributions of all financial asset price returns do not have finite variances. Financial analysts should not be so certain that they can summon the powers of the CLT and assert asymptotic normality in their CI computations. Furthermore, they need to be sure that convergence to asymptotic normality is reasonably fast because, as the eminent economist Maynard Keynes found out the hard way with his personal equity investments, "The market can stay irrational longer than you can stay solvent."[15] For an equity trade, a quarter of a century is an eternity.

Summary

Because of the errors detailed in this chapter with NHST, p-values, and CIs, I have no confidence in them (or the CAPM) and do not use them in my financial data analyses. I would not waste a penny trading or investing based on the estimated CIs of alpha and beta of any frequentist MM computed by Statsmodels or any other software application. I would also throw any social or economic study that uses NHST, p-values, or confidence intervals in the trash, where junk belongs and should not be recycled.

---

15 "Keynes the Speculator," John Maynard Keynes, accessed June 23, 2023, *https://www.maynardkeynes.org/keynes-the-speculator.html*.

Statistical hypothesis testing developed by Neyman and Pearson only makes sense as a predata decision theory for mechanical processes like industrial quality control. The mish-mash of the competing statistical theories of Fisher and Neyman was created by nonstatisticians (or incompetent statisticians) to please two bitter rivals, and they ended up creating a nonsensical, confusing blend of the two. Of course, this has not stopped data scientists from using NHST, p-values, and CIs blindly or academics from teaching it as a mathematically rigorous postdata theory of statistical inference.

CIs are not designed for making postdata inferences about population parameters from a single experiment. The use of CIs as a postdata theory is epistemologically flawed. It flagrantly violates the frail philosophical foundation of frequentist probability on which it rests. Yet, orthodox statisticians have concocted a mind-bending, spurious rationale for doing exactly that. You might get away with misusing Neyman's CI theory if the CLT applies to your data analysis—i.e., the underlying population distribution has a finite mean and variance resulting in asymptotic normality of its sampling distributions.

However, it is common knowledge among academics and practitioners that price returns of all financial assets are not normally distributed. It is likely that these fat tails are a consequence of infinite variances of their underlying population distributions. So the theoretical powers of the CLT cannot be utilized by analysts to rescue CIs from the non-normal, fat-tailed, ugly realities of financial markets. Even if asymptotic normality is theoretically possible in some situations, the desired convergence may not be quick enough for it to be of any practical value for trading and investing. Financial analysts should heed another of Keynes's warnings when hoping for asymptotic normality of their sampling distributions: "In the long run we are all dead."[16] And almost surely broke.

Regardless, financial data analysts using CIs as a postdata theory are making invalid inferences and grossly misestimating the uncertainties in their point estimates. Unorthodox statistical thinking, ground-breaking numerical algorithms, and modern computing technology make the use of "worse than useless" NHST, p-values, and CI theory in financial data analysis unnecessary. The second half of this book is dedicated to exploring and applying epistemic inference and probabilistic machine learning to finance and investing.

---

16 Paul Lay, "Keynes in the Long Run," History Today, accessed June 23, 2023, *https://www.historytoday.com/keynes-long-run*.

References

Aldrich, John. "R. A. Fisher on Bayes and Bayes' Theorem." *International Society for Bayesian Analysis* 3, no. 1 (2008): 161–70.

Colquhoun, David. "An Investigation of the False Discovery Rate and the Misinterpretation of p-values." *Royal Society Open Science* 1, no. 3 (November 2014). *http:// doi.org/10.1098/rsos.140216.*

Gigerenzer, Gerd. "Statistical Rituals: The Replication Delusion and How We Got There." *Advances in Methods and Practices in Psychological Science* (June 2018): 198–218. *https://doi.org/10.1177/2515245918771329.*

Harvey, Campbell R., Yan Liu, and Heqing Zhu. "…And the Cross-Section of Expected Returns." *The Review of Financial Studies* 29, no. 1 (January 2016): 5–68. *https://www.jstor.org/stable/43866011.*

Ioannidis, John P. A. "Why Most Published Research Findings Are False." *PLOS Medicine* 2, no. 8 (2005), e124. *https://doi.org/10.1371/journal.pmed.0020124.*

Lambdin, Charles. "Significance Tests as Sorcery: Science Is Empirical—Significance Tests Are Not." *Theory & Psychology* 22, no. 1 (2012): 67–90. *https://doi.org/ 10.1177/0959354311429854.*

Lenhard, Johannes. "Models and Statistical Inference: The Controversy Between Fisher and Neyman-Pearson." *The British Journal for the Philosophy of Science* 57, no. 1 (2006): 69–91. *http://www.jstor.org/stable/3541653.*

Louçã, Francisco. "Emancipation Through Interaction—How Eugenics and Statistics Converged and Diverged." *Journal of the History of Biology* 42, no. 4 (2009): 649–684. *http://www.jstor.org/stable/25650625.*

Morey, R. D., R. Hoekstra, J. N. Rouder, M. D. Lee, and E. J. Wagenmakers. "The Fallacy of Placing Confidence in Confidence Intervals." *Psychonomic Bulletin & Review* 23, no. 1 (2016): 103–123. *https://doi.org/10.3758/s13423-015-0947-8.*

Szucs, Dénes, and John P. A. Ioannidis. "When Null Hypothesis Significance Testing Is Unsuitable for Research: A Reassessment." *Frontiers in Human Neuroscience* 11, no. 390 (August 2017). doi: 10.3389/fnhum.2017.00390.

Thompson, W. C., and E. L. Schumann. "Interpretation of Statistical Evidence in Criminal Trials: The Prosecutor's Fallacy and the Defense Attorney's Fallacy." *Law and Human Behavior* 11, no. 3 (1987): 167–187. *http://www.jstor.org/stable/1393631.*

Further Reading

Jaynes, E. T. *Probability Theory: The Logic of Science*. Edited by G. Larry Bretthorst. New York: Cambridge University Press, 2003.

McElreath, Richard. *Statistical Rethinking: A Bayesian Course with Examples in R and Stan*. Boca Raton, FL: Chapman and Hall/CRC, 2016.

Leamer, Edward E. "Let's Take the Con Out of Econometrics," *The American Economic Review* 73, No. 1 (March 1983): 31-43

## CHAPTER 5

The Probabilistic Machine Learning Framework

Probability theory is nothing but common sense reduced to calculation.

—*Pierre-Simon Laplace, chief contributor to epistemic statistics and probabilistic inference*

Recall the inverse probability rule from Chapter 2, which states that given a hypothesis H about a model parameter and some observed dataset D:

$$P(H|D) = P(D|H) \times P(H) / P(D)$$

It is simply amazing that this trivial reformulation of the product rule is the foundation on which the complex structures of epistemic inference in general, and probabilistic machine learning (PML) in particular, are built. It is the fundamental reason why both these structures are mathematically sound and logically cohesive. On closer examination, we will see that the inverse probability rule combines conditional and unconditional probabilities in profound ways.

In this chapter, we will analyze and reflect on each term in the rule to gain a better understanding of it. We will also explore how these terms satisfy each of the requirements for the next generation of ML framework for finance and investing that we outlined in Chapter 1.

Applying the inverse probability rule to real-world problems is nontrivial for two reasons: logical and computational. As was explained in Chapter 4, our minds are not very good at processing probabilities, especially conditional ones. Also mentioned was the fact that P(D), the denominator in the inverse probability rule, is a normalizing constant that is analytically intractable for most real-world problems. The development of ground-breaking numerical algorithms and the ubiquity of cheap computing power in the 20th century has solved this problem for the most part.

We will address the computational challenges of applying the inverse probability rule in the next chapter. In this chapter, we address the logical challenges of applying the rule with a simple example from the world of high-yield bonds. All PML models, regardless of their complexity, follow the same process of applying the inverse probability rule.

Inferring a model's parameters is only half the solution. We want to use our model to make predictions and simulate data. Prior and posterior predictive distributions are data-generating distributions of our model that are related to and derived from the inverse probability rule. We also discuss how these predictive distributions enable forward uncertainty propagation of PML model outputs by generating new data based on the model assumptions and the observed data.

Investigating the Inverse Probability Rule

You might want to go back to the inverting probabilities section in Chapter 2 and refresh your memory about how the probabilities were analyzed and computed in the Monty Hall problem. Each term in the inverse probability rule that we calculated has a specific name, such as posterior probability distribution or the likelihood function, and serves a specific purpose in the mechanism of PML models. It is important that we understand these terms so that we can apply the PML mechanism to solve complex problems in finance and investing.

P(H) is the prior probability distribution that encodes our current state of knowledge about model parameters and quantifies their epistemic uncertainty before we observe any new data. This prior knowledge of parameters may be based on logic, prior empirical studies of a base rate, expert judgment, or institutional knowledge. It may also express our ignorance explicitly.

In the Monty Hall problem, our prior probability distribution of which door (S_1, S_2, S_3) the car was behind was $P(S_1, S_2, S_3) = (⅓, ⅓, ⅓)$. This is because before we made our choice of door or observed our dataset D, the most plausible hypothesis was that the car was equally likely to be behind any one of the three doors.

All models have implicit and explicit assumptions and constraints that require human judgment. Note that the prior probability distribution is an explicitly stated model assumption and expressed in a mathematically rigorous manner. It can always be challenged or changed. The frequentist complaint is that prior knowledge, in the form of a prior probability distribution, can be potentially misused to support specious inferences. That is indeed possible, and like all models, probabilistic models are not immune to the GIGO (garbage in, garbage out) virus. Epistemic inferences can be sensitive to the selection of prior probability distributions. However, disagreement about priors doesn't prove dishonesty or incoherent inference. More importantly, if someone wants to be dishonest, the explicitly stated prior probability distribution would be the last place to manipulate an inference. Furthermore, as the model ingests more data, the mechanism of epistemic inference automatically reduces the weight it assigns to the model's priors. This is an important self-correcting mechanism of probabilistic models, given their sensitivity to prior distributions.

Recall the no free lunch (NFL) theorems from Chapter 2 that say that if we want our algorithms to perform optimally, we have to "pay" for that outperformance with prior knowledge and assumptions about our specific problem domain and its underlying data distributions. Because of this crystal-clear transparency, the common objection to using prior probability distributions in making statistical inferences is just ideological grandstanding, if not downright foolishness. It is also dangerous and risky, according to NFL theorems. By not including prior knowledge about our problem domain, our algorithms could end up performing no better than random guessing. The risk is that the performance could be worse and cause irreparable harm.

It is imperative that your prior probability distribution avoid assigning a zero probability to any model parameter. That is because no amount of contradictory data observed afterward can change that zero value. Unless, of course, you are absolutely certain that the specific hypothesis about the zero-valued parameter is impossible to be realized within the age of the universe. That is the generally accepted definition of an impossible event in physics, because anything is possible in infinite space and time.

In finance, with creative, emotional, and free-willed human beings, you would be wise to place a much higher bar on what is considered impossible. For instance, nobody thought that negative nominal interest rates were possible or made any sense. Note that a nominal interest rate is approximately equal to the real interest rate plus the inflation rate. So a negative nominal interest rate means that you are paying somebody to borrow capital from you and are obligated to continue paying them an interest charge for the term of the loan. Absurd, right!? As was mentioned in Chapter 2, $15 trillion in European and Japanese government bonds were trading in the markets at negative nominal interest rates for over a decade!

P(D|H) is the likelihood function that gives us the conditional probability of observing the sample data D given a specific hypothesis H about a model parameter. It quantifies the aleatory uncertainty of sample-to-sample data for the specific hypothesis of parameter value H. It is the same likelihood function that is used in conventional statistics for sampling distributions.

In the Monty Hall problem, we computed three likelihood functions: $P(D \mid S_1)$, $P(D \mid S_2)$, $P(D \mid S_3)$. Recall that by $P(D|S_1)$ we mean the probability of observing the dataset D given that the car is actually behind door 1, and so on. These likelihood functions gave us the conditional probabilities of observing our dataset D under each of the parameters S_1, S_2, S_3.

Note that likelihood is a function and not a probability distribution since the area under its curve does not generally add up to 1. This is because the likelihood functions are conditioned on different hypotheses (S_1, S_2, S_3). The probabilities computed from our Monty Hall likelihood functions were $P(D \mid S_1) = \frac{1}{2}$, $P(D \mid S_2) = 1$, and $P(D \mid S_3) = 0$, which adds up to 1.5.

P(D) is the marginal likelihood function or the unconditional probability of observing the specific data sample D averaged over all plausible parameters or scenarios that could have generated it. It combines the aleatory uncertainty generated by our likelihood functions with our prior epistemic uncertainty about the parameter value that might have generated the data sample D.

The unconditional probability of observing our specific dataset D, which was Monty opening door 3 to show us a goat after we had chosen door 1, was calculated using the law of total probability in Chapter 2. This formula combined our prior probabilities and likelihood functions as follows:

$$P(D) = P(D|S_1) \times P(S_1) + P(D|S_2) \times P(S_2) + P(D|S_3) \times P(S_3)$$
$$P(D) = [\tfrac{1}{2} \times \tfrac{1}{3}] + [1 \times \tfrac{1}{3}] + [0 \times \tfrac{1}{3}] = \tfrac{1}{2}$$

In general, the marginal likelihood of observing data D is computed as a weighted average over all possible parameters that could have produced the observed data with the weights provided by the prior probability distribution. Using the law of total of probability, P(D) in general is computed as:

$$P(D) = \Sigma_i P(D|H_i) \times P(H_i) \text{ for discrete functions}$$
$$P(D) = \int P(D|H) \times P(H) dH \text{ for continuous functions}$$

Recall from Chapter 3 that a probability-weighted average sum is an arithmetic mean known as the expected value. So P(D) computes the expectation of observing the specific data sample D based on all our prior uncertain estimates of our model's parameters. This prior expected mean of the specific data sample we have observed acts as a normalizing constant that is generally hard to solve analytically for real-world problems.

P(H|D) is the posterior probability distribution and is the target of our inference. It updates our prior knowledge about model parameters based on the observed in-sample data D. It combines the prior epistemic uncertainty of our parameters and the aleatory uncertainty of our in-sample data. In the Monty Hall problem, we computed the posterior probability, $P(S_2 \mid D)$, that the car is behind door 2 given our dataset D as:

$$P(S_2|D) = P(D|S_2) \times P(S_2) / P(D)$$
$$P(S_2|D) = [1 \times \tfrac{1}{3}] / \tfrac{1}{2} = \tfrac{2}{3}$$

The posterior probability distribution can be viewed as a logical and dynamic integration of our prior knowledge with the observed sample data. When the data are sparse or noisy, the posterior probability distribution will be dominated by the prior probability distribution, and the influence of the likelihood function will be relatively small. This is useful in situations where we have confidence in our prior knowledge and want to use it to make inferences in the face of sparse or noisy data.

Conversely, as more data are accumulated, the posterior distribution will be increasingly influenced by the likelihood function. This is desirable learning behavior, as it means that our inference needs to reconcile observed data with our prior knowledge as we collect more information. It's possible that the data strengthens and refines our prior knowledge. Another possibility is that the data are too noisy or sparse and add no new knowledge. The learning opportunities occur when the data are irreconcilable and challenge our prior knowledge. Assuming there are no issues with the data in terms or quality and accuracy, we have to question all our model assumptions, starting with our priors. This generally occurs when market regimes change.

The balance between the prior distribution and the likelihood function in the posterior distribution can be adjusted by choosing an appropriate prior distribution and by collecting more or higher-quality data. Sensitivity analysis of the prior probability distribution can be used to assess the impact of different choices of the prior probability distribution on the posterior distribution and the final results. This involves thoughtful trial and error.

The posterior probability distribution also enables inverse uncertainty propagation of our model's parameters. Recall from Chapter 1 that inverse uncertainty propagation is the computation of uncertainty of a model's input parameters that is inferred from the observed data. The posterior probability distribution encodes the probabilistic learnings of our model. Not only does the posterior probability distribution learn our model's parameters from the observed data and our prior knowledge about them, but it also quantifies the epistemic and aleatory uncertainty of these estimates.

The posterior probability distribution does all of this in a transparent manner, and this is very important in the finance and investment management industries, which are heavily regulated. Contrast this with other traditional ML algorithms like random forests, gradient-boosted machines, and deep learning models, which are essentially black boxes because the underlying logic of their inferences are generally hard to decipher.

The posterior distribution $P(H \mid D)$ can also serve as the prior probability distribution $P(H)$ when a new data sample arrives in the next iteration of the learning cycle. This enables dynamic, iterative, and integrative PML models. This is a very powerful mechanism for finance and investment models and is summarized in Figure 5-1.

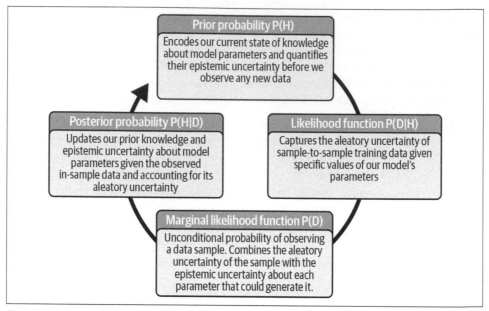

Figure 5-1. How the inverse probability rule builds upon knowledge with iterative probabilistic learning from data

Estimating the Probability of Debt Default

Let's apply the PML mechanism discussed in the previous section to the problem of estimating the probability that a company might default on its debt. Assume you are an analyst at a hedge fund that buys high-yielding debt of companies with risky credit in the public credit markets because they often offer attractive risk-adjusted returns. These bonds are also known pejoratively as junk bonds because of their risky nature and the real possibility that these companies may not be able to pay back their bond holders.

Your fund's analysts evaluate the credit risk of these companies using the company's proprietary knowledge, experience, and management methods. When a portfolio manager estimates that there is only a 10% chance that a company might default, they buy its bonds at market prices that compensate the fund for the risk it is taking.

Your fund also uses conventional ML algorithms to search various data sources for information relating to the companies in their portfolio. These data might include earnings releases, press releases, analyst reports, credit market analyses, investor sentiment surveys, and the like. As soon as the ML classification model receives each piece of information that might affect a portfolio company, it immediately classifies the information as either a positive or negative rating for the company.

Over the years, your fund's ML classification system has built a very valuable proprietary database of the vital information characteristics or features of these risky corporate borrowers. In particular, it has found that companies that eventually default on their debt accumulate 70% negative ratings. However, the companies that do not eventually default only accumulate 40% negative ratings.

Say you have been asked by your portfolio manager to develop a PML model that takes advantage of these proprietary resources to evaluate continually the probabilities of debt default as soon as new information about a company is processed by the ML classification system. If you are successful in developing this PML model, your fund will have an edge in the timing and direction of its high-yield debt trading strategies.

Now assume that your ML classification system has just alerted you of a negative rating it has assigned to XYZ, a new company in the funds' bond portfolio that you are charged with monitoring. How would you update the probability of default of XYZ company based on the new negative rating? Let's apply the PML model to this simple problem as a way to learn the PML process that you would apply to real, complex trades and investments.

- The probabilities of XYZ company defaulting—P(default)—and not defaulting—P(no default)—on its debt obligations are the model's parameters that you want to estimate.

- Negative and positive ratings about XYZ company comprise the data that will inform you and condition your parameter estimates.

- You assume that all ratings are independent of one another and also that all the ratings are being sampled from the same underlying statistical distribution.

- Since XYZ company is in your fund's portfolio, your prior probability of default before seeing any negative or positive ratings is P(default) = 10%.

- This implies that the prior probability that XYZ will not default on its debt is P(no default) = 90%.

- The likelihood that you would observe a negative rating from your ML classification system if XYZ were to default eventually is P(negative | default) = 70%.

- The likelihood of XYZ not defaulting eventually despite a negative rating is P(negative | no default) = 40%.

It might seem odd that P(negative | default) + P(negative | no default) = 0.7 + 0.4 = 1.1. These two probabilities don't add up to 1 because they are conditioned on two noncomplementary hypotheses about the portfolio company. It might be helpful to think of any portfolio company as being one of two types of weighted coins: a no-default coin and a default coin. No-default coins show their negative side 40% of the time. Default coins show their negative side 70% of the time. You are trying to figure out which one of the two types of weighted coins your portfolio manager has chosen from a bag filled with both two types of coins.

You want to estimate the posterior probability of default after observing a negative rating, P(default | negative), and in light of your institutional knowledge of credit risk management. You now have all the probabilities and information you need to create a PML model and apply the inverse probability rule. Let's encode the solution in Python:

```python
# Import Python libraries
import numpy as np
import pandas as pd

# Create a dataframe for your bond analysis
bonds = pd.DataFrame(index=['Default', 'No Default'])

# The prior probability of default
# P(Default) = 0.10 and P(No Default) = 0.90

bonds['Prior'] = 0.10, 0.90

# The likelihood functions for observing negative ratings
# P(Negative|Default) = 0.70 and P(Negative|No Default) = 0.40

bonds['Likeli_Neg'] = 0.70, 0.40

# Joint probabilities of seeing a negative rating depending on
# default or no default
# P(Negative|Default) * P(Default) and P(Negative|No Default) * P(No Default)

bonds['Joint1'] = bonds['Likeli_Neg'] * bonds['Prior']

# Add the joint probabilities to get the marginal likelihood or unconditional
# probability of observing a negative rating
# P(Negative) = P(Negative|Default) * P(Default) + P(Negative|No Default)
#             * P(No Default)

prob_neg_data = bonds['Joint1'].sum()

# Use the inverse probability rule to calculate the updated probability of
# default based on the new negative rating and then print the data table.

bonds['Posterior1'] = bonds['Likeli_Neg'] * bonds['Prior']/prob_neg_data
bonds.round(2)
```

	Prior	Likeli_Neg	Joint1	Posterior1
Default	0.1	0.7	0.07	0.16
No Default	0.9	0.4	0.36	0.84

Based on our code, you can see the posterior probability of default of company XYZ given it has just received a negative rating P(default | negative) = 16%. The probability of default has risen from our prior probability of 10%, as would be expected.

Say a few days later your ML classifier alerts you to another negative rating about XYZ company. How do you update the probability of default now? The PML process is exactly the same. But now our prior probability of default is our current posterior probability of default, calculated previously. This is one of the most powerful features of the PML model: it learns dynamically by continually integrating our prior knowledge with new data in a mathematically rigorous manner. Let's continue to code our solution to demonstrate this:

```
#Our new prior probability is our previous posterior probability, Posterior1.
#Compute and print the table.

bonds['Joint2'] = bonds['Likeli_Neg'] * bonds['Posterior1']
prob_neg_data = bonds['Joint2'].sum()
bonds['Posterior2'] = bonds['Likeli_Neg'] * bonds['Posterior1']/prob_neg_data
bonds.round(2)
```

	Prior	Likeli_Neg	Joint1	Posterior1	Joint2	Posterior2
Default	0.1	0.7	0.07	0.16	0.11	0.25
No Default	0.9	0.4	0.36	0.84	0.33	0.75

```
# Create a new table so that you can plot a graph with the appropriate information
table = bonds[['Prior', 'Posterior1', 'Posterior2']].round(2)

# Change columns so that x axis is the number of negative ratings
table.columns = ['0', '1', '2']

# Select the row to plot in the graph and print it.
default_row = table.iloc[0]
default_row.plot(figsize = (8,8), grid = True,
xlabel = 'Updates based on recent negative ratings',
ylabel = 'Probability of default', title = 'XYZ Bonds');
```

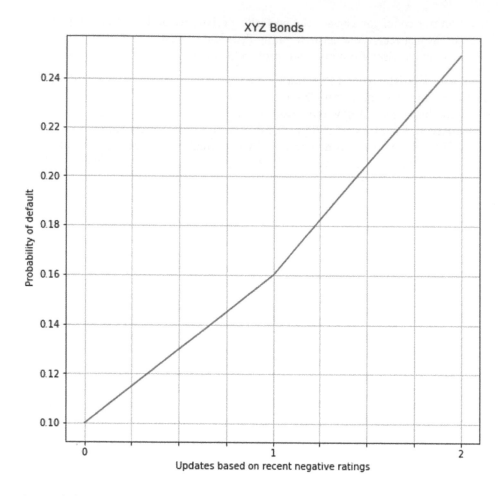

The probability of default given two negative ratings, P(default | 2 negatives), has gone up substantially to 25% in light of new information about the company, and its probability of default is approaching the fund's risk limit. You decide to bring these results to the attention of the portfolio manager, who can do a more in-depth, holistic analysis of XYZ company and the current market environment.

It is important to note that PML models can ingest data one point at a time or all at once. The resulting final posterior probability will be the same regardless of the order in which the data arrives. Let's verify this claim. Let's assume instead that the fund's ML classifier spat out two negative ratings of XYZ company within minutes.

- Assume again that the ratings of the ML classification system are independent and sampled from the same distribution as before.
- The probability of two consecutive negative ratings given that XYZ will default, P(2 negatives | default), is computed using the product rule for independent events:
  - P(2 negatives | default) = P(negative | default) × P(negative | default) = 0.70 × 0.70 = 0.49
- Similarly, probability of two negative ratings is computed given that XYZ will not default eventually: P(2 negatives | no default) = 0.40 × 0.40 = 0.16.
- The marginal likelihood or unconditional probability of observing two negative ratings for XYZ company is a weighted average over both possibilities of the company meeting its debt obligations:
  - P(2 negatives) = P(2 negatives | default) × P(default) + P(2 negatives | no default) × P(no default)
  - Plugging in the numbers for P(2 negatives) = (0.49 × 0.1) + (0.16 × 0.9) = 0.193
- Therefore, the posterior probability of XYZ company defaulting given two consecutive negative ratings is found:
  - P(default | 2 negatives) = P(2 negatives | default) × P(default) / P(2 negatives)
  - Plugging in the numbers for P(default | 2 negatives) = 0.049/0.193 = 0.25 or 25%

This is the same posterior probability we calculated for `posterior2` in the Python code.

Generating Data with Predictive Probability Distributions

As was mentioned in Chapter 1, PML models are generative models that learn the underlying statistical structure of the data. This enables them to simulate new data seamlessly, including generating data that might be missing or corrupted. Most importantly, a PML model enables forward uncertainty propagation of its model's outputs. It does this through its prior and posterior predictive distributions, which simulate potential data that a PML model could generate in the future and that are consistent with observed training data, model assumptions, and prior knowledge.

It is important to note that the prior and posterior distributions are probability distributions for inferring the distributions of our model's *parameters* before and after training, respectively. They enable inverse uncertainty propagation. In contrast, the prior and posterior predictive distributions are probability distributions of our model for *generating new data* before and after training, respectively. They enable forward uncertainty propagation.

The prior and posterior predictive distributions combine two types of uncertainty: the aleatory uncertainty of sample-to-sample data simulated from its likelihood function; and the epistemic uncertainty of its parameters encoded in its prior and posterior probability distributions. Let's continue to work on the example in the previous section to illustrate and explore these two predictive distributions.

The prior predictive distribution P(D′) is the prior probability distribution of simulated data (D′) we expect to observe in the training data (D) *before* we actually start training our model. The prior predictive distribution P(D′) does this by averaging the likelihood function P(D′ | H) over the prior probability distribution P(H) of the parameters.

Our PML model includes assumptions, constraints, likelihood functions, and prior probability distributions. The prior predictive distribution serves as a check on the appropriateness of our PML model before training begins. In essence, the prior predictive distribution P(D′) is retrodicting the training data (D) so that we can assess our model's readiness for training. See Figure 5-2.

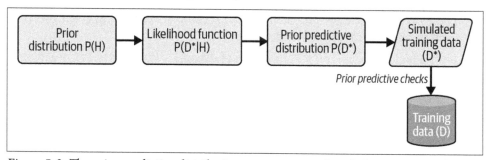

Figure 5-2. The prior predictive distribution generates new data before training. This simulated data is used to check if the model is ready for training.

If the actual training data (D) do not fall within a reasonable range of the simulated data (D′) generated by our prior predictive distribution, we should consider revising our model, starting with the prior probability distribution and then the likelihood function.

In the previous section, we already calculated the prior predictive mean of a negative rating, P(negative), as an expected value or weighted average mean when we calculated its marginal likelihood of observing a negative rating:

P(negative) = P(negative | default) × P(default) + P(negative | no default) × P(no default)
P(negative) = (0.70 × 0.10) + (0.40 × 0.90) = 0.43

We can similarly work out the prior predictive mean of a positive rating, P(positive), by using the complement of the negative likelihood functions.

P(positive | default) = 1 – P(negative | default) and
P(positive | no default) = 1 – P(negative | no default).
Using these probabilities to compute the marginal likelihood function and plugging in the numbers, we get:
P(positive) = P(positive | default) × P(default) + P(positive | no default) × P(no default)
P(positive) = (0.30 × 0.10) + (0.60 × 0.90) = 0.57

In general, the prior predictive distribution is computed as follows:

$P(D') = \Sigma_i P(D'|H_i) \times P(H_i)$ for discrete functions
$P(D') = \int P(D'|H) \times P(H)dH$ for continuous functions

Note that there is a difference between the marginal likelihood function and the prior predictive distribution, even though the formulas look the same. The marginal likelihood function is the expected value of observing a specific data sample (D), such as a negative rating. The prior predictive distribution is a probability distribution that gives you the unconditional probability of any possible data (D') within its sample space before any observations have actually been made. In our example, it gives you the unconditional probabilities of observing a negative and a positive rating for a portfolio company before you actually begin monitoring the company.

Posterior predictive distribution P(D″| D) simulates the posterior probability distribution of out-of-sample or test data (D″) we expect to observe in the future after we have trained our model on the training data (D). It simulates test data samples (D″) by averaging the likelihood function P(D″ | H) over the posterior probability distribution P(H|D). In essence, the trained posterior predictive distribution P(D″ | D) is predicting the unseen test data (D^) so that we can assess our model's readiness for testing. See Figure 5-3.

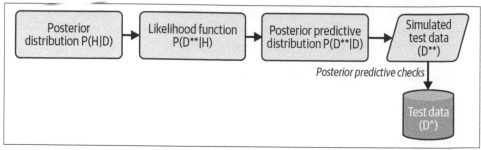

Figure 5-3. The posterior predictive distribution generates new data after training. This simulated data is used to check if the model is ready for testing.

Note that after we have trained our PML model on the in-sample data (D) and captured its aleatory uncertainty by using the likelihood function P(D|H), our posterior distribution P(H|D) gives us a better estimate of our parameter (H) and its epistemic uncertainty compared to our prior distribution P(H). Our likelihood function P(D″|H) continues to express the aleatory uncertainty of observing the out-of-sample data (D″).

The posterior predictive distribution serves as a final model check in the test environment. We can evaluate the usefulness of our model based on how closely the out-of-sample data distribution follows the data distribution predicted by the posterior predictive probability distribution.

In general, the posterior predictive distribution is given by the following formulas:

$P(D'' \mid D) = \Sigma_i P(D'' \mid H_i) \times P(H_i \mid D)$ for discrete functions

$P(D'' \mid D) = \int P(D'' \mid H) \times P(H \mid D) dH$ for continuous functions

The probability of observing another negative rating for XYZ company, given that we have already observed two negative ratings, needs to be updated. While it is still the expected value of generating another negative rating as before, the weights assigned to each parameter value are provided by the posterior probability distribution conditioned on observing two negative ratings. This is called the posterior predictive mean and is calculated as follows:

P(negative | 2 negatives) = P(negative | default) × P(default | 2 negatives) + P(negative | no default) × P(no default | 2 negatives) = (0.7 × 0.25) + (0.4 × 0.75) = 0.475 or 47.5%

What is the probability of observing a positive rating for XYZ company now that we have observed two negative ratings? Since the posterior predictive distribution is a probability distribution, it follows that P(positive | 2 negatives) = 1 − P(negative | 2 negatives) = 0.525 or 52.5%. You can check for yourself that this is true by working through the probabilities as we have done in the previous sections.

Summary

In this chapter, we investigated the specific terms of the inverse probability rule and how they support a comprehensive PML framework discussed in Chapter 1. Specifically, the following terms of the rule enable continual knowledge integration and inverse uncertainty propagation:

- The prior probability distribution P(H) encodes our current knowledge and epistemic uncertainty about our model's parameters before we observe any in-sample or training data.
- The likelihood function P(D|H) captures the data distribution and aleatory uncertainty of sample-to-sample training data we observe given a specific value of our model's parameters.
- The marginal likelihood function P(D) gives us the unconditional probability of observing a specific sample by averaging over all possible parameter values, weighted by their prior probabilities. It combines the aleatory uncertainty of the observed sample data with the epistemic uncertainty about each parameter that might have generated that sample. It is a generally intractable constant that normalizes the posterior probability distribution so that it integrates to 1.
- The posterior probability distribution P(H|D) updates the estimates of our model's parameters by integrating our prior knowledge about them with how plausible it is for each parameter to have generated the in-sample data that we actually observe. It is the target probability distribution that interests us most as it encodes the probabilistic learning of our model's parameters, including their aleatory and epistemic uncertainties.

The prior and posterior predictive distributions enable forward uncertainty propagation of our PML model. They also act as checks on the usefulness of our models:

- The prior predictive distribution P(D′) gives us the unconditional probabilities of observing hypothetical in-sample training data (D′) before we actually begin our experiment and observe them. Note that this is not the actually observed in-sample data D.
- The posterior predictive distribution P(D″|D) gives us the conditional probabilities of observing hypothetical out-of-sample test data (D″) after our PML model has learned its parameters from in-sample training data (D).

It is important to note that the prior P(H) and posterior distributions P(H | D) give us the probability distributions about our model's parameters before and after training our model on in-sample data D, respectively.

The prior predictive P(D′) and posterior predictive P(D″ | D) distributions give us the data-generating probability distributions of simulated in-sample (D′) and out-of-sample data (D″) before and after training our model on in-sample data D, respectively.

These powerful mechanisms enable dynamic, iterative, and integrative machine learning conditioned on data while quantifying both the aleatory and epistemic uncertainties of those learnings. The PML model enables both inference of model parameters and predictions based on those parameters conditioned on data. It seamlessly integrates inverse uncertainty propagation and forward uncertainty propagation in a logically consistent and mathematically rigorous manner while continually ingesting new data. This provides rock solid support for sound, dynamic, data-based decision making and risk management.

In the next chapter, we explore one of the most important features of PML models, especially for finance and investing. What puts PML models in a class of their own is that they know what they don't know and calibrate their epistemic uncertainty accordingly. This leads us away from potentially disastrous and ruinous consequences of traditional ML systems that are extremely confident regardless of their ignorance. Adapting a famous line from Detective "Dirty" Harry, an iconic movie cop: a model's got to know its limitations.

Further Reading

Downey, Allen B. "Bayes's Theorem." In *Think Bayes: Bayesian Statistics in Python*, 2nd ed. O'Reilly Media, 2021.

Jaynes, E. T. *Probability Theory: The Logic of Science*. Edited by G. Larry Bretthorst. New York: Cambridge University Press, 2003.

McElreath, Richard. "Small Worlds and Large Worlds." In *Statistical Rethinking: A Bayesian Course with Examples in R and Stan*, 19–48. Boca Raton, FL: Chapman and Hall/CRC, 2016.

Ross, Kevin. "Introduction to Prediction." In *An Introduction to Bayesian Reasoning and Methods*. Bookdown.org, 2022. *https://bookdown.org/kevin_davisross/bayesian-reasoning-and-methods/*.

## CHAPTER 6

The Dangers of Conventional AI Systems

A man's got to know his limitations.

—Detective "Dirty" Harry in the movie Magnum Force, as he watches an overconfident criminal mastermind's car explode

A model's got to know its limitations. This is worth emphasizing because of the importance of this characteristic for models in finance and investing. The corollary is that an AI's got to know its limitations. The most serious limitation of all AI systems is that they lack common sense. This stems from their inability to understand causal relationships. AI systems only learn statistical relationships during training that are hard to generalize to new situations without comprehending causality.

In Chapter 1, we examined the three ways in which financial markets can humble you even when you apply our best models cautiously and thoughtfully. Markets will almost surely humiliate you when your models are based on flawed financial and statistical theories such as those discussed in the first half of the book. That's actually not such a bad outcome, because a humiliating financial loss can often lead to personal insights and growth. A worse outcome is getting fired from your job or your career coming to an ignoble end. The worst outcome is personal financial ruin, where the wisdom gained from such an experience may not be timely enough to be useful.

When traditional ML models (such as deep learning networks and logistic regression) are trained, they generally use the maximum likelihood estimation (MLE) method to learn the model parameters from in-sample data. Consequently, these ML systems have three deep flaws that severely limit their use in finance and investing. First, the parameter estimates of their models are erroneous when used with small datasets, especially when they learn from noisy financial data. Second, these ML models are awful at extrapolating beyond the data ranges and classes on which they have been trained and tested. Third, the probability scores of MLE models have to be calibrated into valid probabilities by using a function such as a Sigmoid or Softmax function. However, these calibrations are not guaranteed to represent the underlying probabilities accurately leading to poor uncertainty quantifications.

What makes all these flaws egregious is that the conventional statistical models on which these ML systems are based make erroneous estimates and predictions with appallingly high confidence, making them very dangerous in an uncertain world. Just like in the movie *Magnum Force*, these overconfident AI models have the potential of blowing up investment accounts, companies, financial institutions, and economies if they are implemented without understanding their severe limitations.

In Chapter 4, we exposed the fallacious inferential reasoning of popular statistical methods such as NHST, p-values, and confidence intervals. In this chapter, we examine the severe limitations and flaws of the popular MLE method and why it fails in finance and investing. We do this by examining a case where we want to project whether a newly listed public company we have invested in will beat its quarterly earnings expectations, based on a short track record. By comparing the results of a traditional MLE model with that of a probabilistic model, we demonstrate why probabilistic models are better suited for finance and investing in general, especially when datasets are sparse.

As discussed earlier, most real-world probabilistic inference problems cannot be solved analytically because of the intractable complexity of the summations/integrals in the marginal probability distribution. Instead of using flawed probability calibration methods used by MLE models, we settle for approximate numerical solutions to probabilistic inference problems. Even though the earnings expectation problem can be solved analytically using basic calculus, we apply grid approximation to solve it to show how this simple, powerful technique works and makes probabilistic inference much easier to understand.

Markov chain Monte Carlo (MCMC) simulation is a breakthrough numerical method that has transformed the usability of probabilistic inference by estimating analytically intractable, high dimensional posterior probability distributions. MCMC simulates complex probability distributions using dependent random sampling algorithms. We explore the fundamental concepts underlying this powerful, scalable simulation method. As a proof-of-concept of the MCMC method, we use the famous Metropolis sampling algorithm to simulate a Student's t-distribution with fat tails.

AI Systems: A Dangerous Lack of Common Sense

Humans are endowed with a very important quality that no AI has been able to learn so far: a commonsensical ability to generalize our learnings reasonably well to unseen, out-of-sample related classes or ranges, even if we have not been specifically trained on them. Unlike AI systems, almost all humans can easily deduce, infer, and adjust their knowledge to new circumstances based on common sense. For instance, a deep neural network trained to recognize live elephants in the wilderness was unable to recognize a taxidermy elephant on display in a museum.[1] Even a toddler could do this task easily by just using their common sense. As others have pointed out, the AI system literally could not see the elephant in the room!

The primary reason for such common failures is that AI models only compute correlations and don't have the tools to comprehend causation. Furthermore, humans are able to abstract concepts from specific examples and think in terms of generalization of objects and causal relationships among them, while AI systems are just unable to do that. This is a major problem when dealing with noisy, big datasets as they present abundant opportunities for correlating variables that have no plausible physical or causal relationship. With large datasets, spurious correlations among variables are the rule, not the exception.

For instance, Figure 6-1 shows that between 1999 and 2009, there was a 99.8% correlation between US spending on science, space and technology, and suicides by hanging, strangulation, and suffocation.[2]

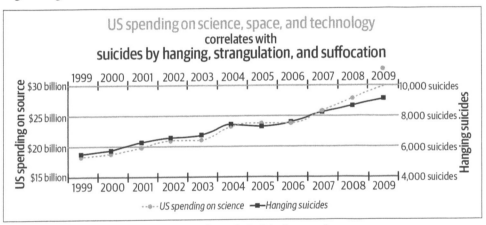

Figure 6-1. Spurious correlations are the rule in big datasets[3]

---

1 Oliver Dürr and Beate Sick, "Bayesian Learning," in *Probabilistic Deep Learning with Python, Keras, and TensorFlow Probability* (Manning Publications, 2020), 197–228.

2 Tyler Vigen, *Spurious Correlations* (New York: Hachette Books, 2015).

3 Adapted from an image on Wikimedia Commons.

Clearly this relationship is nonsensical and underscores the adage that correlation does not imply causation. Humans would understand the absurdity of such spurious correlations quite easily, but not AI systems. This also makes AI systems easy to fool by humans who understand such weaknesses and can exploit them.

While artificial neural networks were inspired by the structure and function of the human brain, our understanding of how human neurons learn and work is still incomplete. As a result, artificial neural networks are not exact replicas of biological neurons, and there are still many unsolved mysteries surrounding the workings of the human brain. The term "deep neural networks" is a misleading marketing term to describe artificial neural networks with more than two hidden layers between the input and output layers. There is nothing deep about a deep neural network that lacks the common sense of a toddler.[4]

Why MLE Models Fail in Finance

The MLE statistical method is used by all conventional parametric ML systems, from simple linear models to complex deep learning neural networks. The MLE method is used to compute the optimal parameters that best fit the data of an assumed statistical distribution. The MLE algorithm is useful when the model is dealing with only aleatory uncertainty of large datasets that have time-invariant statistical distributions where optimization makes sense.

Much valuable information and assessment of uncertainty are lost when a statistical distribution is summarized by a point estimate, even if it is an optimal estimate. By definition and design, a point estimate cannot capture the epistemic uncertainty of model parameters because they are not probability distributions. This has serious consequences in finance and investing, where we are dealing with complex, dynamic social systems that are steeped in all three dimensions of uncertainty: aleatory, epistemic, and ontological. In Chapter 1, we discussed why it is dangerous and foolish to use point estimates in finance and investing given that we are continually dealing with erroneous measurements, incomplete information, and three-dimensional uncertainty. In other words, MLE-based traditional ML systems operate only along one dimension in the three-dimensional space of uncertainty as illustrated in Figure 2-7. What is even more alarming is that many of these ML systems are generally black boxes operating confidently at high speeds with flawed probability calibrations.

---

4 Melanie Mitchell, "Knowledge, Abstraction, and Analogy in Artificial Intelligence," in *Artificial Intelligence: A Guide for Thinking Humans* (New York: Farrar, Straus and Giroux, 2019), 247–65.

Furthermore, MLE ignores prior domain knowledge in the form of base rates or prior probabilities, which can lead to base-rate fallacies, as discussed in Chapter 4. This is especially true when MLE is applied to small datasets. Let's actually see why this is indeed the case by applying the MLE method to a real-world problem of estimating the probability that a company will actually beat the market's expectation of its earnings estimates based on a short track record. This example has been inspired by the coin tossing example illustrated in the book referred to in the references.[5]

An MLE Model for Earnings Expectations

Assume you have changed jobs and are now working at a mutual fund as an equity analyst. Last year, your fund was allocated equity shares in the initial public offering (IPO) of ZYX, a high-growth technology company. Even though ZYX has never turned a profit in its entire nascent life, its brand is already a household name due in large part to its aggressive marketing campaigns that were supported by massive amounts of venture capital. Clearly, private and public equity investors bought into its compelling growth story, as narrated by its charismatic CEO.

In all the last three quarters since its IPO, the negative earnings of ZYX beat market expectations of even bigger losses. In financial markets, less bad is good. The stock price of ZYX has continued its relentless climb upward and is currently trading at all-time highs, enriching everyone in the process. Your portfolio manager (PM) has asked you to estimate the probability that ZYX's earnings will beat market expectations in the upcoming fourth quarter. Based on your probability estimate, your PM is going to increase or decrease the fund's equity investment in ZYX before their earnings announcement, which is due shortly.

Having been schooled in conventional statistical methods, we decide to build a standard MLE model to compute the required probability. The earnings announcement event has only two outcomes that interest us: either the earnings beat market expectations, or they fall short of them. We don't care about the outcome of earnings merely meeting market expectations. Like many other investors, your PM has decided that such an outcome is the equivalent of earnings falling short of market expectations. It is common knowledge that management of companies play a game with Wall Street analysts throughout the year, where they lower their earnings expectations so that it becomes easier to beat those expectations when the actual earnings are announced.

---

5 Dürr and Sick, "Bayesian Learning."

Let's design our quarterly earnings MLE model and specify the assumptions that underpin it:

- In a single event or trial, the model's output variable y can assume only one of two possible outcomes, y = 1 or y = 0.
- The two outcomes are mutually exclusive and collectively exhaustive.
- Assign y = 1 to the outcome that ZYX beats market expectations of its quarterly earnings.
- Assign y = 0 to the outcome that ZYX does not beat or only meets market expectations of its quarterly earnings.

We now have to select a statistical distribution for our likelihood function that best models the binary event of an earnings announcement. The Bernoulli distribution models a single event or trial that has binary outcomes. See Figure 6-2.

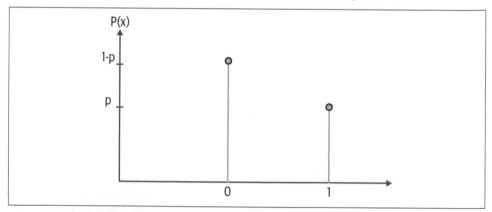

Figure 6-2. Bernoulli variable[6] with outcome x = 1 occurring with probability p and outcome x = 0 occurring with probability 1-p

---

6 Adapted from an image on Wikimedia Commons.

Recall that in Chapter 1, we used the binomial distribution to model the total number of interest rate increases by the Federal Reserve over several meetings or trials. The Bernoulli distribution is a special case of the binomial distribution since they both have the same probability distribution when used for a single trial.

- Assume that variable y follows a Bernoulli distribution with an unknown parameter p, which gives us the probability of an earnings beat (y = 1).
- Since both probabilities must add up to 1, this implies that the probability of not beating earnings expectations (y = 0) is its complement, 1-p.

Our objective is to find the MLE of the parameter p, the probability that ZYX beats the market expectations of its quarterly earnings based on ZYX's short track record of setting market expectations and then beating them.

A Bernoulli process of the variable y is a discrete time series of independent and identically distributed (i.i.d.) Bernoulli trials, denoted by y_i.

- The i.i.d. assumption means that each earnings announcement is independent of all the previous ones and is drawn from the same Bernoulli distribution with constant parameter p.
- In its last three quarters, ZYX beat earnings expectations, so our training data for parameter p is $D = (y_1 = 1, y_2 = 1, y_3 = 1)$.

Let's call p′ the MLE for the parameter p of the Bernoulli variable y. It can be shown mathematically that p′ is the expected value or arithmetic mean of the sample of time series data D. It is the optimal parameter that when inserted in a Bernoulli likelihood function best fits the time series data D. This implies p′ trained on dataset D is:

- $p'(D) = (y_1+y_2+y_3) / 3 = (1 + 1 + 1) / 3 = 3 / 3 = 1$
- Therefore, the probability that ZYX will beat market expectations of its earnings in its fourth quarter is $P(y_4 = 1 \mid p') = p' = 1$ or 100%.

Since MLE models only allow aleatory uncertainty caused by random sampling of data, let's compute the variance of y. The variance of a Bernoulli variable y with parameter p′ is given by:

- Aleatory uncertainty or variance $(y \mid p') = (p') \times (1 - p') = 1 \times (1 - 1) = 1 \times 0 = 0$.
- Epistemic uncertainty = 0 since p′ is a point estimate that is an optimum.
- Ontological uncertainty = 0 since p′ is considered a "true" constant and the Bernoulli distribution is assumed to be time invariant.

So our MLE model is assigning a 100% probability with a 0 sampling error that $y_4 = 1$. In other words, our model is absolutely certain that ZYX is going to beat market expectations of its earnings estimate in the upcoming fourth quarter. Our model's heroic prediction of ZYX's earnings beating market expectations is based on only three data points of a fledgling, loss-making technology company. Moreover, our current MLE model will continue to predict an earnings beat for every quarterly earnings event for the rest of ZYX's life. It's not just death and taxes that are certain. We need to add our MLE model's predictions to the list.

Any financial analyst with even a modicum of common sense would not present this MLE model and its predictions to their portfolio manager. However, it is very common to have sparse datasets in finance and investing. For instance, we have financial data for only two occurrences of global pandemics. Early stage technology startup companies or strategy/special projects have little or no relevant data for making specific decisions. Since the Great Depression ended in 1933, the US economy has experienced only 13 recessions. Since 1942, the S&P 500 has had three consecutive years of negative total returns only once (2000–2003). These are some of the obvious examples. The list of sparse datasets in finance and investing is quite long indeed.

Clearly, MLE models are dangerous when applied to sparse datasets common in finance and investing. They really don't know their limitations and unabashedly flaunt their ignorance. Building complex financial ML systems based on MLE models will only lead to financial disasters sooner rather than later.

A Probabilistic Model for Earnings Expectations

Now let's delete our useless MLE model and pause to reflect on the problem. With only three data points to work with, it would be foolhardy to be absolutely certain about any point estimate of the parameter p, the probability that ZYX's fourth quarter earnings will beat market expectations. Why is that? There are so many possible things that could have gone wrong in the past quarter that only some company insiders might be aware of. Given the persistent asymmetry of information between the company management and its shareholders, this is always possible. This is a major source of our epistemic uncertainty about parameter p.

Most importantly, there are so many things—company specific, political, regulatory, legal, monetary, and economic—that can go wrong in the immediate future and change the market's expectations before ZYX makes its earnings public. These are some of the sources of our ontological uncertainty. Of course, nobody knows what will happen in the future, but it is more likely that the future will reflect the recent past than not.

So based on our understanding of the three dimensions of uncertainty of the real world we live in and the information that we currently have, we can reasonably bet that it is very probable that ZYX will beat the market's expectations of its fourth quarter earnings. However, it's not a certainty. This implies that our model parameter p should be able to take any value between 0 and 1, with the ones closer to 1 being more probable. In other words, our estimate for p is better expressed by a probability distribution than as any particular point estimate. In particular, after seeing the dataset D, our estimate for p is best expressed as a positively skewed probability distribution.

Note that the MLE is the optimal value for p that best replicates the observed data. But there is no universal natural law that says that it is a certainty that the MLE is the value of p that produced the in-sample data. Other values of the parameter p could easily have generated the dataset D too. We are dealing with complex social systems with emotional beings that do suboptimal things all the time. Most importantly, we are not constrained by the problem to pick only one value for p.

Let's actually quantify and visualize the statistical distribution for p more precisely by building a probabilistic model. Recall that a probabilistic model requires us to specify two probability distributions:

- The first is a prior probability distribution $P(p)$ that encapsulates our knowledge or hypothesis about model parameters before we observe any data. Let's assume you have no prior knowledge about ZYX company or any idea of what the parameter p should be. This makes a uniform distribution, $U(0, 1)$, that we learned in the Monty Hall problem a good choice for our prior distribution. This distribution assigns equal probability to all values of p between 0 and 1. So $P(p)$ ~$U(0, 1)$, where the tilde sign (~) is shorthand for "is statistically distributed as."

- The second is a likelihood function $P(D \mid p)$ that gives us the plausibility of observing our in-sample data D assuming any value for our parameter p between 0 and 1. We will continue to use the Bernoulli probability distribution and its related process in our probabilistic model. So the likelihood function of our probabilistic model is $P(D \mid p)$ ~Bernoulli (p).

Our objective is to estimate the posterior probability distribution of our model parameter p given the in-sample data D and our prior knowledge or hypothesis of p. This will give us the probability distribution for the outcome $y = 1$, the probability of an earnings beat. As always, we will use the inverse probability rule to compute the probability distribution of p given the data D. Our probabilistic model can be specified as follows:

$P(p \mid D) = P(D \mid p) \times P(p) / P(D)$ where
$P(p)$ ~$U(0, 1)$
$P(D \mid p)$ ~ Bernoulli (p)
$D = (y_1 = 1, y_2 = 1, y_3 = 1)$

This posterior distribution is simple enough to be solved analytically using basic calculus.[7] However, this involves using integrals over probability density functions, which may not be accessible to many readers. Instead of doing that here, we will compute the posterior distribution using a simple numerical approach called grid approximation. This approach will convert our problem of integral calculus into a much simpler problem of descriptive statistics. This should help us to build our intuition for the underlying mechanism of our probabilistic model.

Since our prior distribution is discrete and uniformly distributed, we can split the interval between 0 and 1 into 9 equidistant points, 0.1 apart, as shown in Figure 6-3.

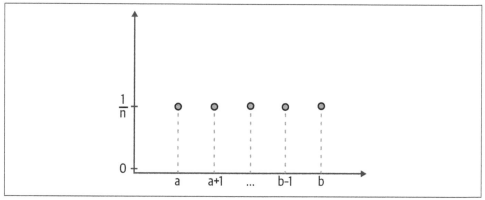

Figure 6-3. There are n number of grid points uniformly distributed between a and b, and each has a probability of $1/n$[8]

So our grid points are {p_1 = 0.1, p_2 = 0.2, .., p_9 = 0.9}. Since the n grid points are uniformly distributed, they all have the same probability, namely P(p) = 1/n, where n is the number of grid points. In our approximation, we have n = 9 grid points.

- The prior probability for every parameter p_1,...p_9 on our one-dimensional grid is P(p) = 1/9 = 0.111.

For every parameter p_i we sample from the set of nine grid points to simulate an earnings event with a value of p_i, the Bernoulli likelihood function generates y = 1 with probability pi or y = 0 with probability 1-p_i. The Bernoulli process for the last three quarters of ZYX's earnings event is given by our training data D = (y_1 = 1, y_2 = 1, y_3 = 1). So the likelihood of the Bernoulli process is:

$$P(D \mid p_i) = p_i \times p_i \times p_i = p_i^3$$

7 Dürr and Sick, "Bayesian Learning."

8 Adapted from an image on Wikimedia Commons.

For each parameter p_i, we use a grid point $\{p_1,...p_9\}$ to compute the unnormalized posterior distribution $P^*(p \mid D)$, using the inverse probability rule. To compute the normalized posterior $P(p \mid D)$, we first add up the all the unnormalized posterior values and then divide each unnormalized posterior by the sum as follows:

$$P^*\left(p_i \middle| D\right) \propto P\left(D \middle| p_i\right) P\left(p_i\right) = p_i^3 \times 0.111$$
$$P(p_i \mid D) = P^*\left(p_i \middle| D\right) / \Sigma_i P^*\left(p_i \middle| D\right)$$

Let's use Python code to develop a grid approximation of the solution:

```python
# Import the relevant Python libraries
import numpy as np
import pandas as pd
import matplotlib.pyplot as plt

# Create 9 grid points for the model parameter, from 0.1 to 0.9 spaced 0.1 apart
p = np.arange(0.1, 1, 0.1)

# Since all parameters are uniformly distributed and equally likely, the
# probability for each parameter = 1/n = 1/9
prior = 1/len(p)

# Create a pandas DataFrame with the relevant columns to store
# individual calculations
earnings_beat = pd.DataFrame(columns = ['parameter', 'prior', 'likelihood',
'posterior*', 'posterior'])

# Store each parameter value
earnings_beat['parameter'] = p

# Loop computes the unnormalized posterior probability distribution
# for each value of the parameter
for i in range(0,len(p)):
  earnings_beat.iloc[i,1] = prior
  # Since our training data has three earnings beats in a row,
  # each having a probability of p
  earnings_beat.iloc[i,2] = p[i]**3
  # Use the unnormalized inverse probability rule
  earnings_beat.iloc[i,3] = prior * (p[i]**3)

# Normalize the probability distribution so that all values add up to 1
earnings_beat['posterior'] = earnings_beat['posterior*']
                        /sum(earnings_beat['posterior*'])

# Display the data frame to show each calculation
earnings_beat
```

	parameter	prior	likelihood	posterior*	posterior
0	0.1	0.111111	0.001	0.000111	0.000494
1	0.2	0.111111	0.008	0.000889	0.003951
2	0.3	0.111111	0.027	0.003	0.013333
3	0.4	0.111111	0.064	0.007111	0.031605
4	0.5	0.111111	0.125	0.013889	0.061728
5	0.6	0.111111	0.216	0.024	0.106667
6	0.7	0.111111	0.343	0.038111	0.169383
7	0.8	0.111111	0.512	0.056889	0.25284
8	0.9	0.111111	0.729	0.081	0.36

```
# Plot the prior and posterior probability distribution for the model parameter
plt.figure(figsize=(16,6)), plt.subplot(1,2,1), plt.ylim([0,0.5])
plt.stem(earnings_beat['parameter'],earnings_beat['prior'],
use_line_collection=True)
plt.xlabel('Model parameter p'), plt.ylabel('Probability of parameter P(p)'),
plt.title('Prior distribution of our model parameter')

plt.subplot(1,2,2), plt.ylim([0,0.5])
plt.stem(earnings_beat['parameter'],earnings_beat['posterior'],
use_line_collection=True)
plt.xlabel('Model parameter p'), plt.ylabel('Probability of parameter P(p)'),
plt.title('Posterior distribution of our model parameter')
plt.show()
```

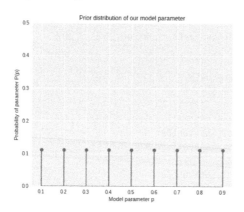
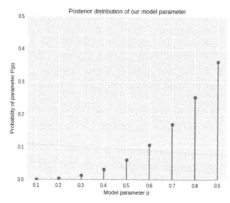

This figure clearly shows that our probabilistic model has computed a probability distribution for the model parameter p before and after training the model on in-sample data D. This is a much more realistic solution, given that we always have incomplete information about any event.

Our model has learned the parameter p from our prior knowledge and the data. This is only half the solution. We need to use our model to predict the probability that ZYX will beat the market's expectations of its fourth quarter earnings estimates. In other words, we need to develop the predictive distributions of our model. Let's continue coding that:

```
# Since P(yi=1|pi) = pi, we compute the probability weighted average of
# observing y=1 using our prior probabilities as the weights
# This probability weighted average gives us the prior predictive probability of
# observing y=1 before observing any data
prior_predictive_1=sum(earnings_beat['parameter']*earnings_beat['prior'])

# The prior predictive probability of observing outcome y=0 is the complement of
# P(y=1) calculated above
prior_predictive_0 = 1 - prior_predictive_1

# Since we have picked a uniform distribution for our parameter, our model
# predicts that both outcomes are equally likely prior to observing any data
print(prior_predictive_0, prior_predictive_1)
(0.5, 0.5)

# Since P(yi=1|pi) = pi, we compute the probability weighted average of
# observing y=1 but now we use the posterior probabilities as the weights
# This probability weighted average gives us the posterior predictive
# probability of observing y=1 after observing in-sample data
D={y1=1, y2=1, y3=1}
posterior_predictive_1 =
sum(earnings_beat['parameter'] * earnings_beat['posterior'])

# The posterior predictive probability of observing outcome y=0 is the
# complement of P(y=1|D) calculated above
posterior_predictive_0 = 1- posterior_predictive_1

# After observing data D, our model predicts that observing y=1 is
# about 3 times more likely than observing y=0
round(posterior_predictive_0,2), round(posterior_predictive_1,2)
(0.24, 0.76)

# Plot the prior and posterior predictive probability distribution
# for the event outcomes
plt.figure(figsize=(16,6)), plt.subplot(1,2,1), plt.ylim([0,1])
plt.stem([0,1],[prior_predictive_0, prior_predictive_1],

use_line_collection=True)
plt.xlabel('Binary outcome for variable y'), plt.ylabel('Probability P(y)'),
plt.title('Prior predictive distribution of an earnings beat')
```

```
plt.subplot(1,2,2), plt.ylim([0,1])
plt.stem([0,1],[posterior_predictive_0, posterior_predictive_1],

use_line_collection=True)
plt.xlabel('Binary outcome for variable y'), plt.ylabel('Probability P(y)'),
plt.title('Posterior predictive distribution of an earnings beat')
plt.show()
```

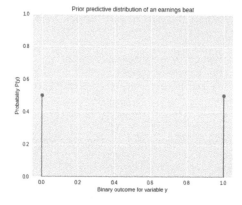
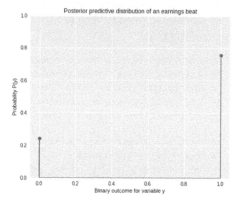

The expected value or posterior predictive mean is 76%, which is close to the theoretical value of 75%. Regardless, our probabilistic model is not 100% sure that ZYX will beat market expectations in the fourth quarter, even though it has successfully done so in the last three quarters. Our model predicts that it is about three times more likely to beat market expectations than not. This is a far more realistic probability distribution and something we can use to make our investment decisions.

Unfortunately, the numerical grid approximation technique we used to solve the earnings expectations problem does not scale if the model has more than a few parameters. So the most scalable and robust numerical methods that we are left with are random sampling methods for estimating approximate solutions for probabilistic inference problems.

Markov Chain Monte Carlo Simulations

Generally speaking, there are two types of random sampling methods: independent sampling, and dependent sampling. The standard Monte Carlo simulation (MCS) method that we learned in Chapter 3 is an independent random sampling method. However, random sampling does not work well when samples are dependent or correlated with one another.

Furthermore, these independent sampling algorithms are inefficient when the target probability distribution they are trying to simulate has many parameters or dimensions. We generally encounter these two issues when simulating complex posterior probability distributions. So we need random sampling algorithms which work with samples that are dependent or correlated with one another.[9] Markov chains are a popular way of generating dependent random samples. The most important aspect of a Markov chain is that the next sample generated is only dependent on the previous sample and independent of everything else.

Markov Chains

A Markov chain is used to model a stochastic process consisting of a series of discrete and dependent states linked together in a chain-like structure. It is a sequential process that transitions probabilistically in discrete time from state to state in the chain. The most important aspect of a Markov state is that it is memoryless. For any state, its future state only depends on the transition probabilities of the current state and is independent of all past states and the path it took to get to its current state. It's as if Markovian chains have encoded Master Oogway's Zen saying from the movie *Kung Fu Panda*: "Yesterday is history, tomorrow is a mystery, but today is a gift. That is why it is called the present."

Equally important, this simplifying memoryless property makes the Markovian chain easy to understand and implement. A random walk process, whether arithmetic or geometric, is a specific type of Markov chain and is used extensively to model asset prices, returns, interest rates, and volatility. A graphic representation of a Markov chain depicting the three basic and discrete states of the financial markets and their hypothetical transition probabilities is shown in Figure 6-4.

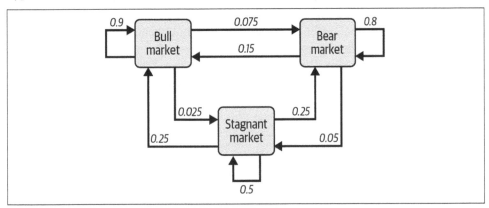

Figure 6-4. A Markov chain depicting the three basic states of the financial markets and their hypothetical transition probabilities[10]

---

9 Ben Lambert, "Leaving Conjugates Behind: Markov Chain Monte Carlo," in *A Student's Guide to Bayesian Statistics* (London, UK: Sage Publications, 2018), 263–90.

10 Adapted from an image on Wikimedia Commons.

According to this state transition diagram, if the financial market is currently in a bear market state, there is an 80% probability it will remain in a bear market state. However, there is a 15% probability that the market will transition to a bull market state and a 5% probability it will transition to a stagnant market state.

Say the market transitions from a bear market state to a stagnant market state and then to a bull market state over time. Once it is in the bull market state, it will have no dependence or memory of the stagnant market state or bear market state. Probabilities about its transition to its future state will be dependent only on its present bull market state. So, for example, there is a 90% probability that it will stay in a bull market state regardless of whether it came from a stagnant market state or a bear market state or some permutation of the two. In other words, the future state of any Markov chain is conditionally independent of all past states given the current state.

Despite the random walks a stochastic process takes in the state space of a Markov chain, if it can go from one state to every other state in a finite number of moves, the Markov chain is said to be stationary ergodic. Based on this definition, the Markov chain of the hypothetical financial market process depicted in Figure 6-3 is stationary ergodic because the market will eventually reach any state in the Markov chain given enough time. Such a hypothetical stationary ergodic financial market would imply that the ensemble average price returns of all investors is expected to equal the price returns of every single random trajectory taken by any single investor in the ensemble over a long enough time period.

However, as was discussed earlier, real financial markets are neither stationary nor ergodic. For instance, as an investor, you could suffer heavy losses in an unrelenting bear market state, or make foolish investments in a bubblicious bull market state, or be forced to liquidate your investments to pay for expensive divorce lawyers in a stagnant market state, and never be in another market state again. You would then be banished to a special Markovian state called an absorbing state from which there is no escape. This special state absorbs the essence of the lyric from the Eagles' song "Hotel California": "You can check out any time you like, but you can never leave." We will discuss the problem of ergodicity in finance and investing in Chapter 8.

The Metropolis MCMC Algorithm: A Transformational Team Effort

The idea of combining Monte Carlo methods with Markov chains to create a Markov chain Monte Carlo (MCMC) algorithm was first developed in the late 1940s by a team of brilliant physicists and mathematicians led by Nicholas Metropolis, for simulating the behavior of atoms in a lattice. The team included Arianna W. Rosenbluth, Marshall Rosenbluth, Augusta H. Teller, and Edward Teller, all of whom were instrumental in the development of the first MCMC algorithm. Arianna Rosenbluth wrote its first full implementation in machine language, the low-level computer language of 0's and 1's! The Metropolis algorithm was a groundbreaking MCMC algorithm and is ranked by many experts as one of the top 10 most important algorithms developed in the 20th century.

The Metropolis MCMC algorithm uses a symmetric normal proposal distribution to simulate any target distribution, and that is why it is also called the Random Walk Metropolis algorithm. The development of other MCMC algorithms and cheap computational resources made numerical approximations accessible to many scientists and practitioners in the 1990s, transforming the scope and usability of epistemic statistics and probabilistic inference.

Metropolis Sampling

The Metropolis algorithm generates a Markov chain to simulate any discrete or continuous target probability distribution. The Metropolis algorithm iteratively generates dependent random samples based on three key elements:

Proposal probability distribution
> This is a probability distribution that helps explore the target probability distribution efficiently by proposing the next state in the Markov chain based on the current state. Different proposal distributions can be used depending on the problem.

Proposal acceptance ratio
> This is a measure of the relative probability of the proposed move. In a probabilistic inference problem, the acceptance ratio is the ratio of the posterior probabilities of the target distribution evaluated at the proposed state to the current state in the Markov chain. Recall from the previous chapter that taking the ratio of the posterior probabilities at two different points gets rid of the analytically intractable marginal probability distribution.

Decision rules on the proposed state
> These are probabilistic decision rules that determine whether to accept or reject the proposed state in the chain. If the acceptance ratio is greater than or equal to 1, the proposed state is accepted and the Markov chain moves to the next state. If the acceptance ratio is less than 1, the algorithm generates a random number between 0 and 1. If the random number is less than the acceptance ratio, the proposed state is accepted. Otherwise it is rejected.

The Metropolis algorithm builds its Markov chain iteratively and stops when the required number of samples have been accepted. The accepted samples are then used to simulate the target probability distribution.

As a proof-of-concept of MCMC simulation, we will use the Metropolis algorithm to simulate a Student's t-distribution with six degrees of freedom. This distribution is widely used in finance and investing for modeling asset price return distributions with fat tails. The Student's t-distribution is a family of probability distributions, with each specific distribution controlled by its degrees of freedom parameter. The lower that value, the fatter the tails of the distribution. We will apply this distribution and discuss it further in the next chapter.

In the following Python code, we use the uniform distribution as the proposal distribution and the Student's t-distribution with six degrees of freedom as our target distribution to simulate. It initializes the Markov chain arbitrarily at x = 0 and runs the Metropolis sampling algorithm 10,000 times. The resulting samples are stored in a list, which is plotted to visualize the sample path of the Markov chain. Finally, the code plots a histogram of the samples to show its convergence to the actual target distribution:

```python
#Import Python libraries
import numpy as np
import scipy.stats as stats
import matplotlib.pyplot as plt

# Define the target distribution - Student's t-distribution
# with 6 degrees of freedom.
# Use location=0 and scale=1 parameters which are the default
# values of the Student's t-distribution
# x is any continuous variable
def target(x):
    return stats.t.pdf(x, df=6)

# Define the proposal distribution (uniform distribution)
def proposal(x):
    # Returns random sample between x-0.5 and x+0.5 of the current value
    return stats.uniform.rvs(loc=x-0.5, scale=1)

# Set the initial state arbitrarily at 0 and set the number of
# iterations to 10,000
x0 = 0
n_iter = 10000

# Initialize the Markov chain and the samples list
x = x0
samples = [x]

# Run the Metropolis algorithm to generate new samples and store them in
# the 'samples' list
for i in range(n_iter):
    # Generate a proposed state from the proposal distribution
    x_proposed = proposal(x)

    # Calculate the acceptance ratio
    acceptance_ratio = target(x_proposed) / target(x)

    # Accept or reject the proposed state
    if acceptance_ratio >= 1:
```

```
        # Accept new sample
        x = x_proposed
    else:
        u = np.random.rand()
        # Reject new sample
        if u < acceptance_ratio:
            x = x_proposed

    # Add the current state to the list of samples
    samples.append(x)

# Plot the sample path of the Markov chain
plt.plot(samples)
plt.xlabel('Sample Number')
plt.ylabel('Sample Value')
plt.title('Sample Path of the Markov Chain')
plt.show()

# Plot the histogram of the samples and compare it with the target distribution
plt.hist(samples, bins=50, density=True, alpha=0.5, label='MCMC Samples')
x_range = np.linspace(-5, 5, 1000)
plt.plot(x_range, target(x_range), 'r-', label='Target Distribution')
plt.xlabel('Sample Value')
plt.ylabel('Probability Density')
plt.title('MCMC Simulation of Students-T Distribution')
plt.legend()
plt.show()
```

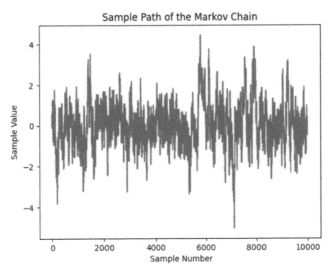

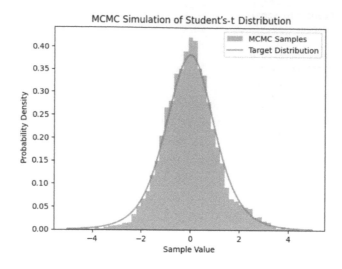

In 1970, William Hastings generalized the Metropolis sampling algorithm so that asymmetric proposal distributions and more flexible acceptance criteria could be applied. The resulting Metropolis-Hastings MCMC algorithm can simulate any target probability distribution asymptotically, i.e., given enough samples, the simulation will converge to the target probability distribution. However, this algorithm can be inefficient and costly for high-dimensional, complex target distributions.

The Metropolis-Hastings algorithm is dependent on the arbitrary initial starting value of the Markov chain. The initial samples gathered during this period, called the burn-in period, are generally discarded. The randomness of the walk-through state space can waste time due to the possibility of revisiting the same regions several times. Moreover, the algorithm can get stuck in narrow regions of multidimensional spaces.

Modern dependent sampling algorithms have been developed to address the shortcomings of this general-purpose MCMC sampling algorithm. The Hamiltonian Monte Carlo (HMC) algorithm uses the geometry of any continuous target distribution to move efficiently in high-dimensional space. It is the default MCMC sampling algorithm in the PyMC library, and we don't need any specialized knowledge to use it. In the next chapter, we will use these MCMC algorithms to simulate the posterior probability distributions of model parameters.

Summary

Traditional statistical MLE models on which most conventional ML systems are based are limited in their capabilities. They are designed to deal with only aleatory uncertainty and are unaware of their limitations. As we have demonstrated in this chapter, MLE-based models make silly predictions confidently. This makes them dangerous in our world of three-dimensional uncertainty. Poor predictive performance and disastrous risk management from such overconfident, simplistic, and hasty ML models are almost surely inevitable in the complex world of finance and investing.

In designing probabilistic models, we acknowledge the fact that only death is certain —everything else, including taxes, has a probability distribution. Probabilistic models are designed to manage uncertainties generated from noisy sample data and inexact model parameters. These models enable us to go from a one-dimensional world of aleatory uncertainty to a two-dimensional world with aleatory and epistemic uncertainties. This makes them more appropriate for the world of finance and investing. However, this comes at the cost of higher computational complexities.

To apply probabilistic machine learning to complex financial and investing problems, we have to use dependent random sampling because other numerical methods don't work or don't scale. MCMC simulation methods are transformative. They use dependent random sampling algorithms to simulate complex probability distributions that are difficult to sample from directly. We will apply MCMC methods in the next chapter, using a popular probabilistic ML Python library.

Ontological uncertainty emanates from complex social systems, which can be disruptive at times. Among other things, it involves rethinking and redesigning the probabilistic model from scratch and making it more appropriate for the new market environment. This is generally best managed by human beings with common sense, judgment, and experience. We are still very much relevant in the bold, new world of AI and have, indeed, the hardest job.

References

Dürr, Oliver, and Beate Sick. *Probabilistic Deep Learning with Python, Keras, and TensorFlow Probability*. Manning Publications, 2020.

Guo, Chuan, Geoff Pleiss, Yu Sun, and Kilian Q. Weinberger. "On Calibration of Modern Neural Networks." Last revised August 3, 2017. *https://arxiv.org/abs/1706.04599*.

Lambert, Ben. *A Student's Guide to Bayesian Statistics*. London, UK: Sage Publications, 2018.

Mitchell, Melanie. *Artificial Intelligence: A Guide for Thinking Humans*. New York: Farrar, Straus and Giroux, 2020.

Vigen, Tyler. *Spurious Correlations*. New York: Hachette Books, 2015.

## CHAPTER 7

Probabilistic Machine Learning with Generative Ensembles

Don't look for the needle in the haystack. Just buy the haystack!
— *John Bogle, inventor of the index fund and founder of the Vanguard Group*

Most of us probably didn't know we were learning one of the most powerful and robust ML algorithms in high school when we were finding the line of best fit to a scatter of data points. The ordinary least squares (OLS) algorithm that is used to estimate the parameters of linear regression models was developed by Adrien-Marie Legendre and Carl Gauss more than two hundred years ago. These types of models have the longest history and are viewed as the baseline machine learning models in general. Linear regression and classification models are considered to be the most basic artificial neural networks. It is for these reasons that linear models are considered to be the "mother of all parametric models."

Linear regression models play a pivotal role in modern financial practice, academia, and research. The two foundational models of financial theory are linear regression models: the capital asset pricing model (CAPM) is a simple linear regression model; and the model of arbitrage pricing theory (APT) is a multiple regression model. Factor models used extensively by investment managers are just multiple regression models with public and proprietary factors. A factor is a financial feature such as the inflation rate. Linear models are also the model of choice for many high-frequency traders (HFT), who are some of the most sophisticated algorithmic traders in the industry.

There are many reasons why linear regression models are so popular. These models have a sound mathematical foundation and have been applied extensively in various fields—from astronomy to medicine to economics—for over two centuries. They are viewed as base models and the first approximations for any solution. Linear regression models have a closed-form analytical solution that most people learn in high school. These models are easy to build and interpret. Most spreadsheet software packages have this algorithm already built in with associated statistical analysis. Linear regression models can be trained very quickly and handle noisy financial data well. They are highly scalable to large datasets and become even more powerful in higher-dimensional spaces.

In this chapter, we examine how a probabilistic linear regression model is fundamentally different from a conventional/frequentist linear regression model that is based on maximum likelihood estimates (MLE) of parameters. Probabilistic models are more useful than MLE models because they are less wrong in their modeling of financial realities. As usual, probabilistic models demonstrate this usefulness by including the additional dimension of epistemic uncertainty about the model's parameters and by explicitly including our prior knowledge or ignorance about them.

The inclusion of epistemic uncertainty in the model transforms probabilistic machine learning into a form of ensemble machine learning since each set of possible parameters generates a different regression model. This also has the desirable effect of increasing the uncertainty of the model's predictions when the ensemble has to extrapolate beyond the training or test data. As discussed in Chapter 6, we want our ML system to be aware of its ignorance. A model should know its limitations.

We demonstrate these fundamental differences in approach by developing a probabilistic market model (MM) that transforms the MLE-based MM that we worked on in Chapter 4. We also use credible intervals instead of flawed confidence intervals. Furthermore, our probabilistic models seamlessly simulate data before and after being trained on in-sample data.

Numerical computations of probabilistic models present a major challenge in applying probabilistic machine learning (PML) models to real-world problems. The grid approximation method that we used in the previous chapter does not scale as the number of parameters increases. In the previous chapter, we introduced the Markov chain Monte Carlo (MCMC) sampling methods. In this chapter, we will build our PML model using the PyMC library, the most popular open source probabilistic machine learning library in Python. PyMC has a syntax that is close to how probabilistic models are developed in practice. It has several advanced MCMC and other probabilistic algorithms, such as Hamiltonian Monte Carlo (HMC) and automatic differentiation variational inference (ADVI), which are arguably some of the most sophisticated algorithms in machine learning. These advanced MCMC sampling algorithms can be applied to problems with a basic understanding of the complex mathematics underpinning them, as discussed in Chapter 6.

MLE Regression Models

Deterministic linear models, such as those found in physics and engineering, make mind-blowingly precise estimates and predictions that market participants can only dream about for their financial models. On the other hand, all nondeterministic or statistical linear models include a random component that captures the difference between a model's prediction (Y) and its observed value (Y'). This difference is called the residual and is depicted in Figure 7-1 by the vertical lines that go from the line of best fit to the observed data points. The goal of training the model is to learn the optimal parameters that minimize some average of the residuals.

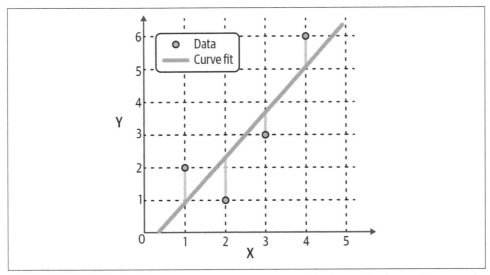

Figure 7-1. The line of best fit of a linear regression model. The residuals are the vertical lines between the observed data and the fitted line.[1]

As shown in Figure 7-1, the target (Y) of a simple linear regression model has only one feature (X) and is expressed as:

Y = a + b × X + e, where a and b are constants to be learned from training data by minimizing the residual, e = Y − Y'.

A multiple linear regression model uses a linear combination of more than one feature for predicting the target. The general form of linear regression is expressed as:

---

1 Adapted from an image on Wikimedia Commons.

$Y = b_0 + b_1 \times X_1 + b_2 \times X_2 + \ldots + b_n \times X_n + e$, where $b_0 - b_n$ are constants to be learned from training data by minimizing the residual, $e = Y - Y'$.

It is important to note that in a linear model, it is the coefficients ($b_0 - b_n$) that have to be linear, and not the features. Recall from Chapter 4 that a financial analyst, relying on modern portfolio theory and the practice of the frequentist statistical approach, incorrectly assumes that there is an underlying, time-invariant, stochastic process generating the price data of an asset such as a stock.

Market Model

This stochastic process can be modeled as an MM, which is basically a simple linear regression model of the realized excess returns of the stock (target) regressed on the realized excess returns of the overall market (feature), as formulated here:

$$(R - F) = a + b \, (M - F) + e \qquad \text{(Equation 7.1)}$$

- $Y = (R - F)$ is the target, $X = (M - F)$ is the feature.
- R is the realized return of the stock.
- F is the return on a risk-free asset (such as the 10-year US Treasury note).
- M is the realized return of a market portfolio (such as the S&P 500 index).
- a (alpha) is the expected stock-specific return.
- b (beta) is the level of systematic risk exposure to the market.
- e (residual) is the unexpected stock-specific return.

Even though the alpha and beta parameters of this underlying random process may be unknown or unknowable, the analyst is made to believe that these parameters are constant and have "true" values. The assumed time-invariant nature of this stochastic process implies that model parameters can be estimated from any random sample of price data of the various securities involved over a reasonably long amount of time. This implicit assumption is known as the stationary ergodic condition. It is the randomness of sample-to-sample data that creates aleatory uncertainty in the estimates of the true, fixed parameters, according to frequentists. The aleatory uncertainty of the parameters is captured by the residual, $e = (Y - Y')$.

Model Assumptions

Many analysts are generally not aware that in order to make sound inferences about the model parameters, they have to make further assumptions about the residuals based on the Gauss-Markov theorem, namely:

- The residuals are independent and identically distributed.
- The expected mean of the residuals is zero.
- The variance of the residuals is constant and finite.

Learning Parameters Using MLE

If the analyst assumes that the residuals are normally distributed, then it can be shown with basic calculus that the maximum likelihood estimate (MLE) for both parameters, alpha and beta, have the same values as those obtained using the OLS algorithm we learned in high school and applied in Chapter 4 using the Statsmodels library. This is because both algorithms are minimizing the mean squared error or the expected value of the square of the residuals $E[(Y - Y')^2)]$. However, the MLE algorithm is preferred over the OLS algorithm because it can be applied to many different types of likelihood functions.[2]

It is common knowledge that while financial data are abundant, they have very low signal-to-noise ratios. One of the biggest risks in financial ML is that of variance or overfitting of data. When the model is trained on data, the algorithm learns the noise instead of the signal. This results in model parameter estimates that vary wildly from sample to sample. Consequently, the model performs poorly in out-of-sample testing.

In multiple linear regression, overfitting of the data also occurs because the model might have highly correlated features. This is also called multicollinearity and is common in the financial and business world, where most features are interconnected, especially in times of financial distress.

Conventional statisticians have developed two ad hoc methods called regularizations to reduce this overfitting of noisy data by creating a penalty term in the optimization algorithm for reducing the impact of any one parameter. Never mind that this is the antithesis of the frequentist decree of letting "only the data speak for themselves."

There are two types of regularization methods that penalize model complexity:

---

2 Oliver Dürr and Beate Sick, "Building Loss Functions with the Likelihood Approach," in *Probabilistic Deep Learning with Python, Keras, and TensorFlow Probability* (Manning Publications, 2020), 93–127.

Lasso or L1 regularization

Penalizes the sum of the absolute values of the parameters. In Lasso regression, many of the parameters are shrunk to zero. Lasso is also used to eliminate correlated features and improve the interpretation of complex models.

Ridge or L2 regularization

Penalizes the sum of the coefficients squared of the parameters. In ridge regression, all parameters are shrunk to near zero, which reduces the impact of any one feature on the target variable.

In other words, instead of "only letting the data speak for themselves," L2 regularization stifles all the voices, while L1 regularization silences many of them. Of course, models are regularized to make them useful in finance and investing, where data are extremely noisy, and the following Fisher's dictum results in regression models failing abysmally and losing money.

Quantifying Parameter Uncertainty with Confidence Intervals

After estimating the model parameters from training data, the analyst computes the confidence intervals for alpha and beta to quantify their aleatory uncertainty. Most analysts are unaware about the three types of errors of using confidence intervals and don't understand their flaws, as was discussed in Chapter 4. If they did, they would never use confidence intervals in financial analysis except in special cases when the central limit theorem applies.

Predicting and Simulating Model Outputs

Now that the linear model has been built, it is tested on unseen data to evaluate its usefulness for estimating and predicting. The same type of scoring algorithms that are used to evaluate the performance of the model on training data are used on testing data to compute its usefulness. However, to simulate data, the analyst will have to set up a separate Monte Carlo simulation (MCS) model, as discussed in Chapter 3. This is because MLE models are not generative models. They do not learn the underlying statistical structure of the data and so are unable to simulate data.

Probabilistic Linear Ensembles

In MLE modeling, the financial analyst tries to build models that are expected to emulate a "true" model that is supposedly optimal, elegant, and eternal. In probabilistic modeling, the financial analyst is freed from such ideological burdens. They don't have to apologize for their financial models being approximate, messy, and transient because they merely reflect mathematical and market realities. We know that all models are wrong regardless of whether they are treated as prophetic or pathetic. We only evaluate them on their usefulness in achieving our financial goals.

The financial analyst using the probabilistic framework not only applies the inverse probability rule, but also inverts the MLE modeling paradigm. Spurning ideological dictums of orthodox statistics in favor of common sense and the principles of the scientific method, they invert the conventional treatment of data and parameters:

- Training data of excess returns, such as Y = (R − F) and X = (M − F), are treated as constants because their values have already been realized and recorded and will never change. That is the epitome of what a constant means.

- Model parameters, such as alpha (a), beta (b), and the residual (e), are treated as variables with probability distributions since their values are unknown and uncertain. Financial model parameters have aleatory, epistemic, and ontological uncertainty. Their estimates keep changing depending on the sample used, assumptions applied, and the time period involved. That is the quintessence of what a variable means.

The analyst understands that the search for any "true" constant parameter value of a financial model is a fool's errand. This is because the dynamic randomness of markets and their participants ensure that probability distributions are never stationary ergodic. These analysts are painfully aware that creative, free-willed, emotional human beings make a mockery of theoretical, MLE-based "absolutist" financial models almost every day. The frequentist claim that financial model parameters have "true" values is simply unscientific, ideological drivel.

We will use the probabilistic framework to explicitly state our assumptions and assign specific probability distributions to all the terms of the probabilistic framework so far discussed. Each probability distribution has additional parameters that will have to be estimated by the analyst. The analyst will have to specify the reasons for their choices. If the models fail during the testing phase, the analysts will change any and all probability distributions, including their parameters. All financial models are developed based on the most fundamental of heuristic techniques: trial and error.

In a probabilistic framework, we apply the inverse probability rule to estimate our model parameters, as developed in Chapter 5. After we have designed our model, we will develop it in Python using the PyMC library. Based on the terms defined for the MM, the probabilistic linear ensemble (PLE) is formulated as:

P(a, b, e| X, Y) = P(Y| a, b, e, X) P(a, b, e) / P(Y|X) where

- Y = a + b × X + e, as expressed in the MLE linear model, but without its explicit or implicit assumptions. These will be specified explicitly in the PLE.

- P(a, b, e) are the prior probabilities of all model parameters before observing the training data (X, Y).

- P(Y| a, b, e, X) is the likelihood of observing the target training data Y given the parameters a, b, e, and feature training data X.
- P(Y|X) is the marginal likelihood of observing the training values of target Y given the training values of feature X averaged over all possible prior values of the parameters (a, b, e).
- P(a, b, e| X, Y) is the posterior probabilities of the parameters a, b, e given the training data (X,Y).

We now discuss each component of the PLE model in more detail.

Prior Probability Distributions P(a, b, e)

Before the analyst sees any training data (X,Y), they may specify the prior probability distributions of the PLE parameters (a, b, e) and quantify their epistemic uncertainty. All prior distributions are assumed to be independent of one another. These prior distributions may be based on personal, institutional, experiential, or common knowledge. If the analyst does not have any prior knowledge about the parameters, they can express their ignorance with uniform distributions that consider each value between the upper and lower limits equally likely. Remember that having bounds of 0 and 1 should be avoided unless you are absolutely certain that a parameter can take these values. The main objective is to specify one of the most important model assumptions explicitly and quantitatively.

Given the tendency of models to overfit noisy financial data that don't have any persistent structural unity, the analyst is aware that it is foolish to follow the orthodox dictum of "only letting the data speak for themselves." The ad hoc use of regularization methods in MLE models to manage this overfitting risk are merely prior probability distributions in disguise. It can be shown mathematically that L1 regularization is equivalent to using a Laplacian prior, and L2 regularization is equivalent to using a Gaussian prior.[3]

The analyst systematically follows the probabilistic framework and explicitly quantifies their knowledge, or ignorance, about the model parameters with prior probability distributions. This makes the model transparent so it can be changed and critiqued by anyone, especially the portfolio manager. For instance, the analyst could assume that:

---

3 Kevin P. Murphy, "Sparse Linear Models," in *Machine Learning: A Probabilistic Perspective* (Cambridge, MA: The MIT Press, 2012), 421–78.

- alpha is normally distributed: a ~Normal()
- beta is normally distributed: b ~Normal()
- Residual is Half-Student's t-distributed: e ~HalfStudentT()

Likelihood Function P(Y| a, b, e, X)

After the analyst observes the training data (X,Y), they need to formulate a likelihood function that best fits that data and quantifies the aleatory uncertainty of the model parameters (a, b, e). This is the same likelihood function that was used in the MLE linear model. In standard linear regression, the likelihood function for the residuals (e) is assumed to be a Gaussian or normal distribution. However, instead of using a normal probability distribution, the analyst uses Student's t-distribution to model the financial realities of fat-tailed asset price returns. Also, if the likelihood function can accommodate outliers as well as the Student's t-distribution does, the linear regression is termed a robust linear regression.

Student's t-distribution is a family of distributions that can approximate a range of other probability distributions based on its degrees of freedom parameter, v, which is a real number that can range from 0 to infinity. Student's t-distributions are fat-tailed for lower values of v and get more normally distributed as v gets larger. It is important to note that for:

- $v \leq 1$, t-distributions have no defined mean and variance
- $1 < v \leq 2$, t-distributions have a defined mean but no defined variance
- $v > 30$, t-distributions are approximately normally distributed

Say the analyst assigns a Student's t-distribution with $v = 6$ to the likelihood function. Why $v = 6$? Financial research and practice has shown that this t-distribution does a good job of describing the fat-tailed stock price returns. So we are applying prior common knowledge to the choice of the likelihood function. The specific likelihood function can be expressed mathematically as:

- Y ~StudentT(u, e, v = 6) where u = a + b × X and (a, b, e) are as defined by their prior probability distributions

Marginal Likelihood Function P(Y|X)

This is the hardest function to compute given it is averaging the likelihood functions over all the model's parameters. The complexity increases as the types of probability distributions and number of parameters increase. As was mentioned earlier, we need groundbreaking algorithms to approximate this function numerically.

Posterior Probability Distributions P(a, b, e| X, Y)

Now that we have our model specified, we can compute the posterior probabilities for all our model's parameters (a, b, e) given our training data (X,Y). To recap, our model is specified as follows:

- Y ~StudentT(u, e, v = 6)
- u = a + b × X
- a ~Normal(), b ~Normal(), e ~HalfStudentT()
- X,Y are training data pairs in a sample time period that reflect the current market conditions.

Model parameters, their probability distributions, and their relationships are displayed in Figure 7-2.

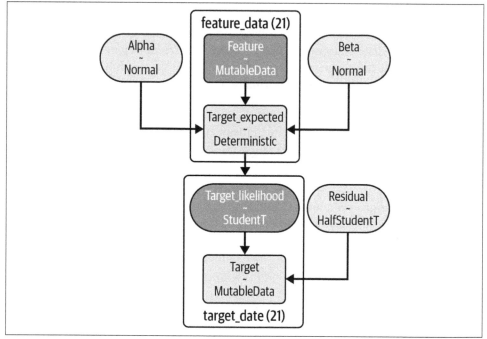

Figure 7-2. Probabilistic market model showing prior distributions used for parameters and the likelihood function used to fit training data

Because of the complexity of any realistic model, especially the marginal likelihood function, we can only approximate the posterior distributions of each of its parameters. PyMC uses the appropriate state-of-the-art MCMC algorithm to simulate the posterior distribution by sampling from it as discussed in Chapter 6. We then use the ArviZ library to explore these samples, enabling us to draw inferences and make predictions from them.

Assembling PLEs with PyMC and ArviZ

Let's now build our PLE in Python by leveraging its extensive ecosystem of powerful libraries. In addition to the standard Python stack of NumPy, pandas, and Matplotlib, we will also be using PyMC, ArviZ, and Xarray libraries. As mentioned earlier, PyMC is the most popular probabilistic machine learning library in Python. ArviZ is a probabilistic language-agnostic tool for analyzing and visualizing probabilistic ensembles. It converts inference data of probabilistic ensembles into Xarray objects, which are labeled, multidimensional arrays. You can search the web for links to the relevant documentation of the previously mentioned libraries.

Building an ensemble of any kind requires a systematic process, and our PLE is no exception. We will follow the high-level ensemble-building process outlined in Figure 7-3. Each phase and its constituent parts will be explained along with the relevant code. It is important to note that even though we will go through our ensemble building process sequentially, this is an iterative, nonlinear process in practice. For instance, you could easily go back and forth from the training phase to the analyze features and target data phase. With that nonlinearity in mind, let's go to the first phase.

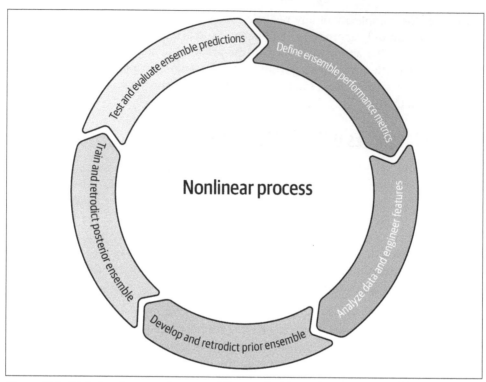

Figure 7-3. High-level process for assembling probabilistic learning ensembles

Define Ensemble Performance Metrics

Our financial objectives and activities should drive the effort of building our PLE. Consequently, this influences the metrics we use to evaluate its performance. Our financial tasks are generally to estimate the parameters of a financial model or to forecast its outputs or both. As you know by now, probabilistic machine learning systems are ideally suited to both these tasks because they do inverse propagation and forward propagation seamlessly. More importantly, these generative ensembles direct us to consider the aleatory and epistemic uncertainties of the problem we are addressing and its possible solutions.

Financial activities

Plausible estimates of the regression parameters alpha and beta in Equation 7.1 are required for several financial activities that are practiced in the industry:

Jensen's alpha
> By regressing the returns of a fund against the returns of its benchmark portfolio, investors evaluate the skill of the fund's manager by estimating the regression's alpha parameter. This metric is known as Jensen's alpha in the industry.

Market neutral strategies

Alpha can also be viewed as the asset-specific expected return regardless of the movements of the market. If a fund manager finds this return significantly attractive, they can try to isolate it and capture it by hedging out the asset's exposure to market movements. This also involves estimating the asset's beta, or sensitivity to the market. The portfolio consisting of the asset and the hedge becomes indifferent or neutral to the vagaries of the market.

Cross-hedging

By assuming constant variance of the residuals in Equation 7.1, the beta parameter can also be shown mathematically to correlate the volatility of one asset (Y) with the volatility of another related asset (X). Cross-hedging programs in corporate treasury departments use this beta-related correlation to hedge a commodity required by their company, say jet fuel, with another related commodity, such as oil. Treasury departments buy or sell financial instruments, such as futures, in the open market to hedge their input costs.

Cost of equity capital

Corporate financial analysts estimate the cost of their company's equity capital by estimating the realized return, R, in the regression Equation 7.1. This is supposedly the expected return on their stock that their public shareholders are demanding. Many analysts still use their stock's CAPM model and estimate R by making alpha = 0 in Equation 7.1.

In this chapter, we will focus on estimating Apple's equity price returns by using its MM, and not its CAPM, for the reasons detailed in Chapter 4. We will estimate the posterior probability distribution of Apple's excess returns (R - F) given the current market regime. The generative linear ensemble can be applied to all the financial activities discussed earlier.

Objective function

A rule that is formulated to measure the performance of a model or ensemble is called an objective function. This function generally measures the difference between the ensemble's estimates or predictions compared with the corresponding realized or observed values. Common objective functions that measure the difference between predicted and observed values in machine learning regression models are mean squared error (MSE) and median absolute errors (MAE). The choice of an objective function depends on the business problem we are trying to solve. An objective function that reduces losses/costs is called a loss/cost function.

Another regression objective function is R-squared. In frequentist statistics, it is defined as the variance of the predicted values divided by the total variance of the data. Note that R-squared can be interpreted mathematically as a standardized MSE objective function that needs to be maximized:

R-squared(Y) = 1 − MSE(Y)/Var(Y)

Since we are dealing with aleatory and epistemic uncertainties in our probabilistic models, this R-squared formula has to be modified so that its value does not exceed 1. The probabilistic version of R-squared is modified to equal the variance of the predicted values divided by the variance of predicted values plus the expected variance of the errors. It can be interpreted as a variance decomposition.[4] We will call this version of the R-squared objective function *probabilistic R-squared*.

Performance metrics

As mentioned earlier, financial data are very noisy, which implies that we need to be realistic about the performance metrics we establish for each development phase. At a minimum, we want our model to do better than random guessing, i.e., we want performance scores greater than 50%. We would like our PLE to meet or exceed the following performance metrics:

- Probabilistic R-squared prior score > 55%
- Probabilistic R-squared training score > 60%
- Probabilistic R-squared test score > 65%
- Highest-density intervals (HDIs): 90% HDI to include almost all training and test data (HDI will be explained shortly)

Keep in mind that all these metrics will be based on personal and organization preferences and are imperfect, as are the models used to produce them. It requires judgment and domain expertise. Regardless, we will use these metrics as another input to help us to evaluate our PLE, critique it, and revise it. In practice, we revise our PLE until we are confident that it will give us a high enough positive expected value in the financial activity we want to apply it to. Only then do we deploy our PLE out of the lab.

Analyze Data and Engineer Features

We have already done data analysis of the target and features in Chapter 4 and in rewriting Equation 7.1.

Data exploration

In general, in this phase you would define your target of interest, such as predicting asset price returns or estimating volatility. These target variables are real valued num-

---

4 Andrew Gelman et al., "R-Squared for Bayesian Regression Models," *The American Statistician* 73, no. 3 (2019): 307–309, *https://doi.org/10.1080/00031305.2018.1549100*.

bers and are termed as regression targets. Alternatively, a target of interest could also be classification of a company's creditworthiness based on predictions of whether it will default or not. These are classification targets that take on discrete numbers like 0 or 1.

You would then identify various sources of data that will enable you to analyze your target and features in sufficient detail. Data sources can be expensive, and you will have to figure out how to get them in a cost-effective manner. Cleaning and processing data from various sources is generally quite time-consuming.

Feature engineering

Recall that a feature is some representation of data that serves as an independent variable enabling inference or prediction of a model's target variable. Feature engineering is the practice of selecting, designing, and developing a useful set of features that work together to enable reliable inferences or predictions of the target variable(s) in out-of-sample data.

To predict a target variable, such as price returns, a model can have many different types of features. Here are examples of various types of features:

Fundamental
> Company sales, interest rates, exchange rates, GDP growth rate

Technical
> Momentum indicators, fund flows, liquidity

Sentiment
> Consumer sentiment, investor sentiment

Other
> Proprietary mathematical or statistical indicators

After you have selected and developed a possible set of features, it is generally a good idea to use relative changes in feature levels, rather than absolute levels, as inputs into your features' dataframe. This reduces the serial autocorrelation endemic in financial time series. Serial correlation occurs when a variable is correlated with past values of itself over time. Traders and investors are generally interested in understanding if a good or bad condition is getting better or worse. So market participants are continually reacting to relative changes in levels in terms of percentages or differences.

If we have more than one feature, we need to check if some of them are highly correlated with one another. Recall that this issue is called multicollinearity. Highly correlated features can unduly amplify the same signal in data, leading to invalid inferences and predictions. Ideally, there should be zero correlation or no multicollinearity among features. Unfortunately, that almost never happens in practice. Coming up with a threshold variance above which you would remove redundant features is a judgment call based on the business context.

Feature engineering is critical to the performance of all ML systems. It requires domain expertise, judgment, experience, common sense, and a lot of trial and error. These are the qualities that enable human intelligence to distinguish correlation from causation, which AI-enabled agents cannot do to this day.

We are going to keep our feature engineering simple in this primer and leverage a vast body of financial knowledge and experience on market models. Our PLE has a single feature: the market as represented by the S&P 500 index.

Data analysis

PLEs demonstrate their strengths when we have small datasets, such that a weak or flat prior is not overwhelmed by the likelihood function. Here we will look at 31 days of data in the last two months of last year, from 11/15/2022 to 12/31/22. This period covers two Federal Reserve meetings and was exceptionally volatile. We will train our PLE on the first 21 days of data and test it on the last 10 days of data. This is called the time series split method of cross-validation. Because financial time series have strong serial correlation, we cannot use the standard cross-validation method, since it assumes that each data sample is independent and identically distributed.

Let's actually download price data for Apple Inc., S&P 500, and the 10-year treasury note, and compute the daily price returns as we did for our linear MM in Chapter 4:

```
# Import standard Python libraries.
import numpy as np
import pandas as pd
from datetime import datetime
import xarray as xr
import matplotlib.pyplot as plt

# Install and import PyMC and Arviz libraries.
!pip install pymc -q
import pymc as pm
import arviz as az
az.style.use('arviz-darkgrid')

# Install and import Yahoo Finance web scraper.
!pip install yfinance -q
import yfinance as yf

# Fix random seed so that numerical results can be reproduced.
np.random.seed(101)

# Import financial data.
start = datetime(2022, 11, 15)
end = datetime(2022, 12, 31)
```

```python
# S&P 500 index is a proxy for the market factor.
market = yf.Ticker('SPY').history(start=start, end=end)
# Ticker symbol for Apple, the largest company in the world
# by market capitalization.
stock = yf.Ticker('AAPL').history(start=start, end=end)
# 10 year US treasury note is the proxy for risk free rate.
riskfree_rate = yf.Ticker('^TNX').history(start=start, end=end)

# Create a dataframe to hold the daily returns of securities.
daily_returns = pd.DataFrame()
# Compute daily percentage returns based on closing prices for Apple and
# S&P 500 index.
daily_returns['market'] = market['Close'].pct_change(1)*100
daily_returns['stock'] = stock['Close'].pct_change(1)*100
# Compounded daily risk free rate based on 360 days for the calendar year
# used in the bond market.
daily_returns['riskfree'] = (1 + riskfree_rate['Close']) ** (1/360) - 1

# Check for missing data in the dataframe.
market.index.difference(riskfree_rate.index)
# Fill rows with previous day's risk-free rate since
# daily rates are generally stable.
daily_returns = daily_returns.ffill()
# Drop NaNs in first row because of percentage calculations
# are based on previous day's closing price.
daily_returns = daily_returns.dropna()
# Check dataframe for null values.
daily_returns.isnull().sum()
# Check first five rows of dataframe.
daily_returns.head()

# Daily excess returns of AAPL are returns in excess of
# the daily risk free rate.
y = daily_returns['stock'] - daily_returns['riskfree']
# Daily excess returns of the market are returns in excess of
# the daily risk free rate.
x = daily_returns['market'] - daily_returns['riskfree']

# Plot the excess returns of Apple and S&P 500.
plt.scatter(x,y)
plt.ylabel('Excess returns of Apple'),
plt.xlabel('Excess returns of S&P 500');

# Plot histogram of Apple's excess returns during the period.
plt.hist(y, density=True, color='blue')
plt.ylabel('Probability density'), plt.xlabel('Excess returns of Apple');

# Analyze daily returns of all securities.
daily_returns.describe()

# Split time series sequentially because of serial correlation
# in financial data.
```

```
test_size = 10

x_train = x[:-test_size]
y_train = y[:-test_size]

x_test = x[-test_size:]
y_test = y[-test_size:]
```

Develop and Retrodict Prior Ensemble

Let's start developing our PLE using the PyMC library. At this point, we explicitly state the assumptions of our ensemble in the prior probability distributions of the parameters and the likelihood function. This also includes our hypothesis about the functional form of the underlying data-generating process, i.e., linear with some noise.

After that, we check to see if the ensemble's prior predictive distribution generates data that is plausible and may have occurred in the past, and are now in our training data sample. A prediction of a past event is called retrodiction and is used as a model check, before and after it is trained. If the data generated by the prior ensemble are implausible, because they don't fall within our highest density interval, we revise all of our model assumptions.

Specify distributions and their parameters

We incorporate our prior knowledge into the ensemble by specifying the prior probability distributions of its parameters, P(a), P(b), and P(e). After that, we specify the likelihood of observing our data given the parameters, P(D | a, b, e).

In the following Python code block, we have chosen a Student's t-distribution with nu = 6 for the likelihood function of our ensemble. Of course, we could also add nu as another unknown parameter that needs to be inferred. However, that would merely increase the complexity without adding much in terms of increasing your understanding of the development process.

```
# Create a probabilistic model by instantiating the PyMC model class.
model = pm.Model()

# The with statement creates a context manager for the model object.
# All variables and constants inside the with-block are part of the model.

with model:
  # Define the prior probability distributions of the model's parameters.
  # Use prior domain knowledge.

  # Alpha quantifies the idiosyncratic, daily excess return of Apple
  # unaffected by market movements.
  # Assume that alpha is normally distributed. The values of mu and
  # sigma are based on previous data analysis and trial and error.
```

```
alpha = pm.Normal('alpha', mu=0.02, sigma=0.10)

# Beta quantifies the sensitivity of Apple to the movements
# of the market/S&P 500.
# Assume that beta is normally distributed. The values of mu and
# sigma are based on previous data analysis and trial and error.
beta = pm.Normal('beta', mu=1.2, sigma=0.15)

# Residual quantifies the unexpected returns of Apple
# i.e returns not predicted by the linear model.
# Assume residuals are Half Student's t-distribution with nu=6.
# Value of nu=6 is based on research studies and trial and error.
residual = pm.HalfStudentT('residual', sigma=0.20, nu=6)

# Mutatable data containers are used so that we can swap out
# training data for test data later.
feature = pm.MutableData('feature', x_train, dims='feature_data')
target = pm.MutableData('target', y_train, dims='target_data')

# Expected daily excess returns of Apple are approximately
# linearly related to daily excess returns of S&P 500.
# The function specifies the linear model and the expected return.
# It creates a deterministic variable in the trace object.
target_expected = pm.Deterministic('target_expected',
alpha + beta * feature, dims='feature_data')

# Assign the training data sample to the likelihood function.
# Daily excess stock price returns are assumed to be T-distributed, nu=6.
target_likelihood = pm.StudentT('target_likelihood', mu=target_expected,
sigma=residual, nu=6, observed=target, dims='target_data')
```

Figure 7-2 was generated by the graphviz method shown in the following code:

```
# Use the graphviz method to visualize the probabilistic model's data,
# parameters, distributions and dependencies
pm.model_to_graphviz(model)
```

Sample distributions and simulate data

Before we train our model, we should check the usefulness of the assumptions of our prior ensemble. The goal is to make sure that the ensemble is good enough for the training phase. This is done by conducting what is called a prior predictive check. We use the ensemble's prior predictive distribution to simulate a data distribution that may have been realized in the past. Recall that this is called a retrodiction as opposed to a prediction, which simulates a data distribution that is most likely to occur in the future.

In the following code block, we simulate 21,000 data samples from the prior predictive distribution. We let ArviZ return the InferenceData object so that we can visualize and analyze the generated data samples. Expand the display after the inference object is returned to examine the structure of the various groups. We will need them for analysis and inference:

```
# Sample from the prior distributions and the likelihood function
# to generate prior predictive distribution of the model.
# Take 1000 draws from the prior predictive distribution
# to simulate (1000*21) target values based on our prior assumptions.
idata = pm.sample_prior_predictive(samples=1000, model=model,
return_inferencedata=True, random_seed=101)

# PyMC/Arviz returns an xarray - a labeled, multidimensional array
# containing inference data samples structured into groups. Note the
# dimensions of the prior predictive group to see how we got (1*1000*21)
# simulated target data of the prior predictive distribution.
idata
```

arviz.InferenceData

▼ prior

    xarray.Dataset

        ▶ Dimensions: **(chain**: 1, **draw**: 1000, **feature_data**: 21)

        ▼ Coordinates:

chain	(chain)	int64 0		🗎 🗄
draw	(draw)	int64 0 1 2 3 4 5 ... 995 996 997 998 999		🗎 🗄
feature_data	(feature_data)	int64 0 1 2 3 4 5 6 ... 15 16 17 18 19 20		🗎 🗄

        ▼ Data variables:

beta	(chain, draw)	float64 1.456 1.142 0.8655 ... 1.335 1.348		🗎 🗄
target_expected	(chain, draw, feature_data)	float64 -0.9134 -0.2484 ... -0.7992 -3.235		🗎 🗄
alpha	(chain, draw)	float64 0.2033 -0.008568 ... 0.06852		🗎 🗄
residual	(chain, draw)	float64 0.633 0.4057 ... 0.251 0.8233		🗎 🗄

        ▶ Indexes: (3)

        ▶ Attributes: (4)

▶ prior_predictive

▶ observed_data

▶ constant_data

Let's plot the marginal prior distributions of each parameter before we conduct prior predictive checks. Note that a kernel density estimate is a smoothed-out histogram of a continuous variable:

```
# Subplots on the left show the kernel density estimates (KDE) of
# the marginal prior probability distributions of model parameters
# from the 1000 samples drawn. Subplots on the right show the parameter
# values from a single Markov chain that were sampled sequentially
# by the NUTS sampler, the default regression sampler.
az.plot_trace(idata.prior, kind='trace',
var_names = ['alpha', 'beta', 'residual'], legend=True);
```

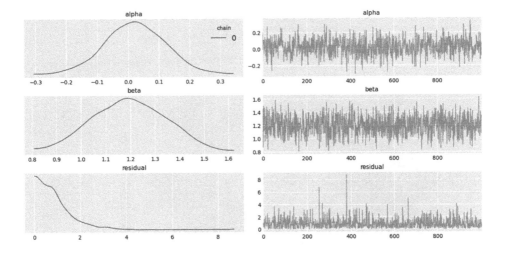

```
# Plot the marginal prior distributions of each parameter with 94%
# highest density intervals (HDI).
# Note the residual subplot shows the majority of probability density function
# within 3 percentage points and the rest extending out into a long tail.
# In Arviz, there is no method to plot the prior marginal distributions but we
# can hack the plot posterior method and use the prior group instead.
az.plot_posterior(idata.prior,
var_names = ['alpha', 'beta', 'residual'], round_to=2);
```

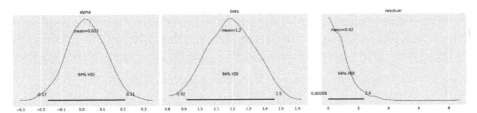

```
# Plot the joint prior probability distribution of alpha and beta with their
# respective means and marginal distributions on the side.
# Hexabin plot below shows little or no linear correlation with the high
# concentration areas in the heat map forming a cloud.
az.plot_pair(idata.prior, var_names=['alpha', 'beta'], kind='hexbin',
marginals=True, point_estimate='mean', colorbar=True);
```

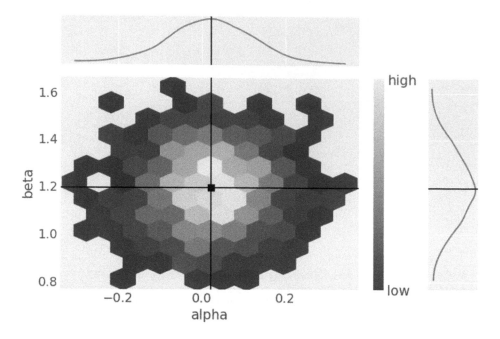

Let's create a prior ensemble of 1000 regression lines, one for each value of the ensemble's parameters (a, b) sampled from its prior distributions, and plot the epistemic uncertainty around the prior mean of the untrained linear ensemble. We also use the prior predictive distribution of the ensemble to simulate data. This displays the epistemic and aleatory uncertainties of the data distributions. Note that the training data is plotted to give us some context and a baseline for the ensemble's retrodictions:

```
# Plot the retrodictions of prior predictive ensemble.

# Retrieve feature and target training data from the constant_data group.
# Feature is now an Xarray instead of a panda's series,
# a requirement for ArviZ data analysis.
feature_train = idata.constant_data['feature']
target_train = idata.constant_data['target']

# Generate 1000 linear regression lines based on 1000 draws from one
# Markov chain of the prior distributions of alpha and beta.
# Prior target values are in 1000 arrays with each array having 21 samples,
# the same number of samples as our training data set.
prior_target = idata.prior["alpha"] + idata.prior["beta"] * feature_train

# Prior_predictive is the data generating distribution of the untrained ensemble.
prior_predictive = idata.prior_predictive['target_likelihood']

# Create figure of subplots
fig, ax = plt.subplots()
```

```
# Plot epistemic and aleatory uncertainties of untrained
# ensemble's retrodictions.
az.plot_lm(idata=idata, x=feature_train, y=target_train,
num_samples=1000, y_model = prior_target,
y_hat = prior_predictive, axes=ax)

#Label the figure.
ax.set_xlabel("Excess returns of S&
P 500")
ax.set_ylabel("Excess returns of Apple")
ax.set_title("Retrodictions of untrained linear ensemble")
ax.legend(loc='upper left');
```

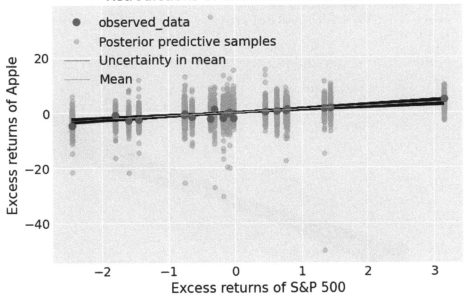

It is very important to observe that the linear ensemble's epistemic uncertainty increases as we move away from the center of the plot. Confessions of ignorance is what we are seeking in any model: it should become increasingly unsure about its expected values as it moves into regions where it has no data and must extrapolate. Our ensemble knows its limitations.

This is seen more clearly in the next plot where we generate and distribute the prior predictive data samples into a 90% high-density interval (HDI) and then conduct a prior predictive check:

```
# Plot 90% HDI of untrained ensemble.
# This will show the aleatory (data related) and epistemic
# (parameter related) uncertainty of model output before it is trained.
```

```
# Create figure of subplots.
fig, ax = plt.subplots()

# Plot the ensemble of 1000 regression lines to show the
# epistemic uncertainty around the mean regression line.
az.plot_lm(idata=idata, x=feature_train, y=target_train,
num_samples=1000, y_model = prior_target, axes=ax)

# Plot the prior predictive data within the 90% HDI band to
# show both epistemic and aleatory uncertainties.
az.plot_hdi(feature_train, prior_predictive, hdi_prob=0.90, smooth=False)

# Label figure.
ax.set_xlabel("Excess returns of S&P 500")
ax.set_ylabel("Excess returns of Apple")
ax.set_title("90% HDI for simulated samples of untrained linear ensemble")
ax.legend();
```

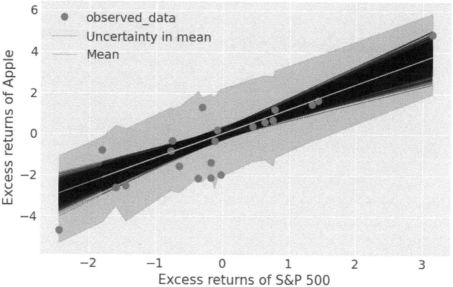

```
# Conduct a prior predictive check of the untrained linear ensemble.
# Create figure of subplots.
fig, ax = plt.subplots()
# Plot the prior predictive check
az.plot_ppc(idata, group='prior', kind='cumulative',
num_pp_samples=1000, alpha=0.1, ax=ax)

# Label the figure.
ax.set_xlabel("Simulated Apple excess returns")
ax.set_ylabel("Cumulative Probability")
ax.set_title("Prior predictive check of untrained linear ensemble");
```

Prior predictive check of untrained linear ensemble

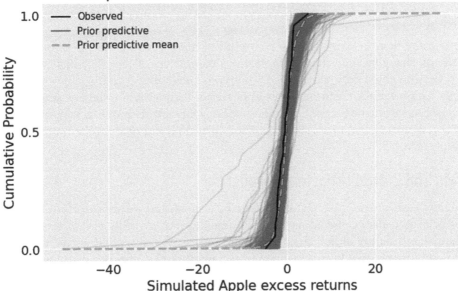

Evaluate and revise untrained model

Specifying a probabilistic model is never easy, and requires many revisions. Let's use qualitative and quantitative prior predictive checks to see if our prior model is plausible and ready for training. From the recent plots, we can see that our ensemble has simulated all the training data within the 90% HDI band. However, the prior predictive check shows some low probability, extreme returns that have not occurred in the recent past. Let's now compute the probabilistic R-squared measure to evaluate the ensemble's retrodictions before it has been trained:

```
# Evaluate untrained ensemble's retrodictions by comparing simulated
# data with training data.

# Extract target values of our training data.
target_actual = target_train.values

# Sample the prior predictive distribution to simulate
# expected target training values.
target_predicted = idata.prior_predictive.stack(sample=("chain", "draw"))
['target_likelihood'].values.T

# Use the probabilistic R-squared metric.
prior_score = az.r2_score(target_actual, target_predicted)
prior_score.round(2)
```

The probabilistic R-squared metric of the prior ensemble is 61%, with a standard deviation of 10%. This exceeds our performance benchmark of 55% for the prior model.

Please note that this performance is a result of many revisions to the prior model I made by changing the values of the various parameters of the prior distributions. I also experimented with different distributions, including a uniform prior for the alpha parameter. All the prior scores were greater than 55%, and the one you see here is closer to the median score. Feel free to make your own revisions to the prior model until you are satisfied that your ensemble is plausible and ready to be trained by in-sample data.

Train and Retrodict Posterior Model

We now have an ensemble that is ready to be trained, and we are confident it reflects our prior knowledge, including the epistemic uncertainty of its parameters and the aleatory uncertainty of the data it might generate. Let's train it with actual in-sample data our ensemble has been anticipating by computing the posterior distribution.

Train and sample posterior

We execute the default sampler of PyMC, the Hamiltonian Monte Carlo (HMC) algorithm, a second-generation MCMC algorithm. PyMC directs HMC to generate dependent random samples from the joint posterior distribution of all the parameters:

```
# Draw 1000 samples from two Markov chains resulting in 2000 values of each
# parameter to analyze the joint posterior distribution.
# Check for any divergences in the progress bar. We want 0 divergences for a
# reliable sampling of the posterior distribution.
idata.extend(pm.sample(draws=1000, chains=2, model=model, random_seed=101))
```

```
100.00% [2000/2000 00:02<00:00 Sampling chain 0, 0 divergences]
100.00% [2000/2000 00:03<00:00 Sampling chain 1, 0 divergences]
```

Evaluating the quality of the MCMC sampling is an advanced topic and will not be covered in this primer. Since we have no divergences in the Markov chains, let's analyze the marginal distribution of each parameter and make inferences about each of them:

```
# Subplots on the left show the kernel density estimates (KDE)
# of the marginal posterior probability distributions of each parameter.
# Subplots on the right show the parameter values
# that were sampled sequentially in two chains by the NUTS sampler
with model:
    az.plot_trace(idata.posterior, kind='trace',
    var_names = ['alpha', 'beta', 'residual'], legend=True)
```

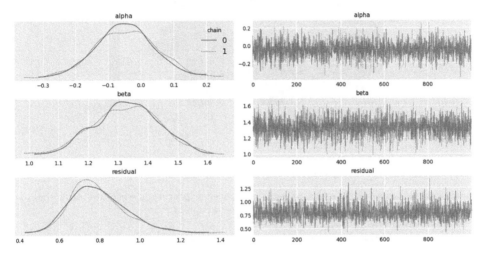

```
# Plot the joint posterior probability distribution of alpha and beta
# with their respective means and marginal distributions on the side.
# Hexabin plot below shows little or no linear correlation with the
# high concentration areas in the heat map forming a cloud.
az.plot_pair(idata.posterior, var_names=['alpha', 'beta'], kind='hexbin',
marginals=True, point_estimate='mean', colorbar=True);
```

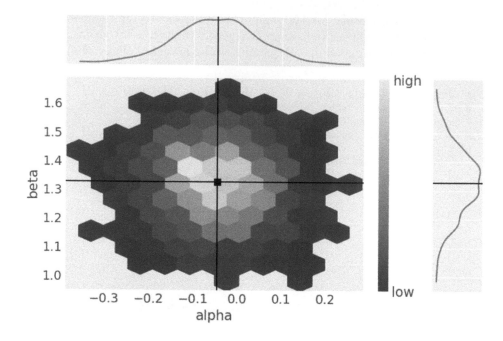

We can summarize the posterior distributions in a pandas DataFrame as follows:

```
# Examine sample statistics of each parameter's posterior marginal distribution,
# including it's 94% highest density interval (HDI).
display(az.summary(idata, kind='stats',
var_names = ['alpha', 'beta', 'residual'], round_to=2, hdi_prob=0.94))
```

	mean	sd	hdi_3%	hdi_97%
alpha	-0.05	0.09	-0.21	0.13
beta	1.33	0.11	1.12	1.54
residual	0.79	0.14	0.54	1.05

This statistical summary gives you the mean, standard deviation, and a 94% credible interval for all our parameters. Note that the 94% credible intervals are computed as the differences between the highest density intervals (HDI): hdi_97% – hdi_3% = hdi_94%.

Unlike the shenanigans of frequentist confidence intervals discussed in Chapter 4, a credible interval is exactly what a confidence interval pretends to be but is not. Credible intervals are a postdata methodology for making valid statistical inferences from a single experiment. This is exactly what we want as researchers, scientists, and practitioners in any field. For instance, the 94% credible interval for beta in the summary table means the following:

- There is a 94% probability that beta is in the *specific interval [1.12 and 1.55]*. It is as simple as that. Unlike confidence intervals, we don't have to deal with some warped definition that defies any semblance of common sense to interpret credible intervals.
- There are no assumptions of asymptotic normality of any distribution.
- There are no underhanded invocations to the central limit theorem.
- Beta is not a point estimate with only aleatory uncertainty.
- We are ignorant of the exact value of beta. It is highly unlikely that we will ever know the exact values of any model parameter for any realistic scenario in the social and economic sciences.
- Parameters like beta are better interpreted as probability distributions with both aleatory and epistemic uncertainties.
- It is much more realistic to model and interpret parameters like beta as unknowable variables rather than as unknowable constants.

It is important to note that credible intervals are not unique within a posterior distribution. Our preferred way is to choose the narrowest interval with the highest probability density within the posterior distribution. Such an interval is also known as the highest-density interval (HDI) and is the method we have been following in this chapter.

You might be wondering why PyMC/ArviZ developers have chosen the default credible interval to be 94%. It is a reminder that there are no physical or socioeconomic laws that dictate that we choose 95% or any other specific percentage. I believe it is a subtle dig at the conventional statistical community for sanctifying the 95% significance level in the social and economic sciences. At any rate, ArviZ provides a method for changing the default interval, as shown in the following code block:

```
# Change the default highest density interval to 90%
az.rcParams['stats.hdi_prob'] = 0.90
```

It helps to visualize the posterior distributions of our model parameters for credible intervals with different probabilities. The following plot shows 70% credible intervals for all three parameters:

```
# Plot the marginal posterior distribution of each parameter displaying
# the above statistics but now within a 70% HDI
az.plot_posterior(idata, var_names = ['alpha', 'beta', 'residual'],
hdi_prob=0.70, round_to=3);
```

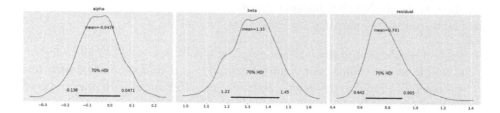

More often than not, we have to evaluate point estimates in making our financial and investment decisions. We can estimate how plausible any point estimate of a parameter is based on where it lies within its posterior probability distribution. For instance, if we want to evaluate the point estimate = 1.15 for beta, we can use it as a reference value and compare it to an HDI, as shown in the following code:

```
# Evaluate a point estimate for a single parameter using its
# posterior distribution.
az.plot_posterior(idata, 'beta', ref_val=1.15, hdi_prob=0.80,
point_estimate='mode', round_to=3);
```

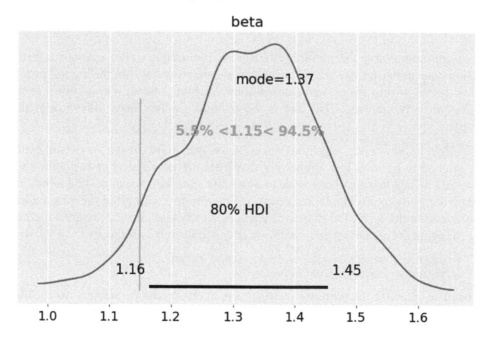

This plot implies that 94.5% of the distribution is above beta = 1.15. Beta = 1.15 is in the left tail of the distribution since only 5.5% of the distribution is below it. Note that the two percentages may not add up to 100% because of rounding errors. So, it is reasonable to conclude that beta = 1.15 is not the best estimate.

Retrodict and simulate training data

We now use the posterior predictive distribution (PPD) to simulate data from the trained ensemble and follow the same steps we did with the ensemble's prior predictive distribution. This will help us to evaluate how well the ensemble has been trained:

```
# Draw 1000 samples each from two Markov chains of the
# posterior predictive distribution.
with model:
  pm.sample_posterior_predictive(idata, extend_inferencedata=True,
  random_seed=101)

# Generate 2000 linear regression lines based on 1000 draws each from
# two chains of the posterior distributions of alpha and beta.
# Posterior target values are in 2000 arrays, each with 21 samples,
# the same number of samples as our training data set.
posterior = idata.posterior
posterior_target = posterior["alpha"] + posterior["beta"] * feature_train

# Posterior_predictive is the data generating distribution of the
# trained ensemble.
posterior_predictive = idata.posterior_predictive['target_likelihood']

# Create figure of subplots.
fig, ax = plt.subplots()

# Plot epistemic and aleatory uncertainties of trained
# ensemble's retrodictions.
az.plot_lm(idata=idata, x=feature_train, y=target_train, num_samples=2000,
y_model = posterior_target, y_hat=posterior_predictive, axes=ax)

# Label the figure.
ax.set_xlabel("Excess returns of S&P 500")
ax.set_ylabel("Excess returns of Apple")
ax.set_title("Retrodictions of the trained linear ensemble")
ax.legend(loc='upper left');
```

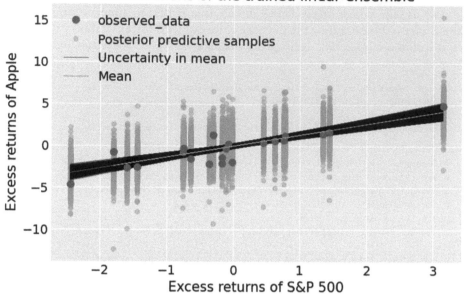

Retrodictions of the trained linear ensemble

```
# Plot 90% HDI of trained ensemble.
# This will show the aleatory (data related) and epistemic
# (parameter related) uncertainty of model output after it is trained.

# Create figure of subplots.
fig, ax = plt.subplots()

# Plot the ensemble of 2000 regression lines to show the epistemic
# uncertainty around the mean regression line.
az.plot_lm(idata=idata, x=feature_train, y=target_train, num_samples=1000,
y_model = posterior_target, axes=ax)

# Plot the posterior predictive data within the 90% HDI band to show both
# epistemic and aleatory uncertainties.
az.plot_hdi(feature_train, posterior_predictive, hdi_prob=0.90, smooth=False)

# Label the figure
ax.set_xlabel("Excess returns of S&P 500")
ax.set_ylabel("Excess returns of Apple")
ax.set_title("90% HDI for simulated samples of trained linear ensemble");
```

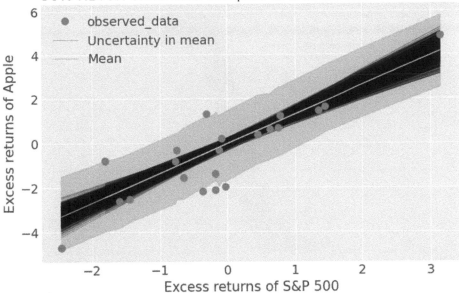

90% HDI for simulated samples of trained linear ensemble

```
# Conduct a posterior predictive check of the trained linear ensemble.

# Create a figure of subplots.
fig, ax = plt.subplots()

# Plot the posterior predictive check.
az.plot_ppc(idata, group='posterior', kind='cumulative',
num_pp_samples=2000, alpha=0.1, ax=ax)

# Label the figure.
ax.set_xlabel("Simulated Apple excess returns given training data")
ax.set_ylabel("Cumulative Probability")
ax.set_title("Posterior predictive check of trained ensemble");
```

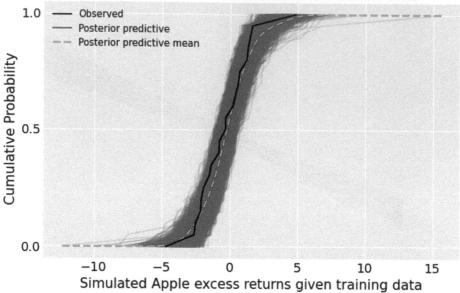

Posterior predictive check of trained ensemble

Evaluate and revise trained model

As we did earlier, let's use qualitative and quantitative checks to see if our posterior model is plausible and ready for testing. The posterior predictive check shows us a range of returns that are more consistent with the recent historical returns of Apple. From its retrodictions, we can see that our ensemble has simulated most of the training data it has been trained on within the 90% HDI band. Let's now compute the probabilistic R-squared measure to evaluate the trained ensemble's performance:

```
# Evaluate trained ensemble's retrodictions by comparing
# simulated data with training data.

# Get target values of our training data
target_actual = target_train.values

# Sample the posterior predictive distribution
# conditioned on training data.
target_predicted = idata.posterior_predictive.stack(sample=("chain", "draw"))
['target_likelihood'].values.T

# Compute probabilistic R-squared performance metric.
training_score = az.r2_score(target_actual, target_predicted)
training_score.round(2)
```

The probabilistic R-squared metric of the posterior ensemble is 65%, with a standard deviation of 8%. This is a performance improvement compared to that of the untrained ensemble. We can make this comparison because we are using the same dataset to make the performance comparison. It also exceeds the training score benchmark of 60%. Our ensemble is ready for its main test: predictions based on out-of-sample or unseen test data.

Test and Evaluate Ensemble Predictions

We are now confident that our trained ensemble reflects both our prior knowledge and new learnings from the in-sample data that were observed. Moreover, the ensemble has updated its parameter probability distributions in light of the training data, including their epistemic uncertainties. Consequently, the data distributions that the ensemble will generate have also been updated, including their aleatory uncertainties.

The various steps that led us here are all necessary but not sufficient for us to decide if we are going to commit hard-earned capital to the predictions of our ensemble. One of the most important tests for any ML system is how well it performs on previously unseen, out-of-sample test data.

Swap data and resample posterior predictive distribution

PyMC provides mutable data containers that enable the swapping of training data for test data without any other changes to the ensemble. We now have to resample the posterior predictive distribution with the new test data for our target and features.

```
# Now we use our trained model to make predictions based on test data.
# This is the reason we created mutable data containers earlier.
with model:
    #Swap feature and target training data for their respective test data.
    pm.set_data({'feature': x_test, 'target': y_test})
    #Create two new inference groups, predictions and predictions_constant_data
    #for making predictions based on features in the test data.
    pm.sample_posterior_predictive(idata, return_inferencedata=True,
    predictions=True, extend_inferencedata=True, random_seed=101)
```

Predict and simulate test data

This creates a new inference group called predictions. We repeat the same steps as we did in the training phase but use test data instead:

```
# Get feature and target test data.
feature_test = idata.predictions_constant_data['feature']
target_test = idata.predictions_constant_data['target']

# Prediction target values are in 2000 arrays, each with 10 samples,
# the same number of samples as our test data set. Predict target values
# based on posterior values of regression parameters and feature test data.
prediction_target = posterior["alpha"] + posterior["beta"] * feature_test
```

```
# Predictions is the data generating posterior predictive distribution
# of the trained ensemble based on test data.
simulate_predictions = idata.predictions['target_likelihood']

# Create figure of subplots.
fig, ax = plt.subplots()

# Plot the 2000 regression lines showing the epistemic and
# aleatory uncertainties of out-of-sample predictions.
az.plot_lm(idata=idata, x=feature_test, y=target_test, num_samples=2000,
y_model = prediction_target, y_hat=simulate_predictions, axes=ax)

# Label figure
ax.set_xlabel("Excess returns of S&P 500")
ax.set_ylabel("Excess returns of Apple")
ax.set_title("Predictions of trained linear ensemble")
ax.legend(loc='upper left');
```

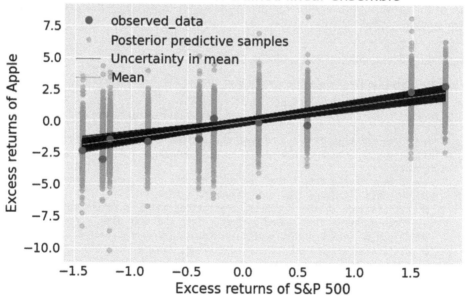

```
# Plot 90% HDI of trained ensemble. This will show the aleatory
# (data related) and epistemic (parameter related) uncertainty
# of trained model's predictions based on test data.

# Create figure of subplots.
fig, ax = plt.subplots()

# Plot the ensemble of 2000 regression lines to show the epistemic uncertainty
# around the mean regression line.
```

```
az.plot_lm(idata=idata, x=feature_test, y=target_test,
num_samples=2000, y_model = prediction_target, axes=ax)

# Plot the posterior predictive data within the 90% HDI band
# to show both epistemic and aleatory uncertainties.
az.plot_hdi(feature_test, simulate_predictions,
hdi_prob=0.90, smooth=False)

# Label the figure.
ax.set_xlabel("Excess returns of S&P 500")
ax.set_ylabel("Excess returns of Apple")
ax.set_title("90% HDI for predictions of trained linear ensemble")
ax.legend();
```

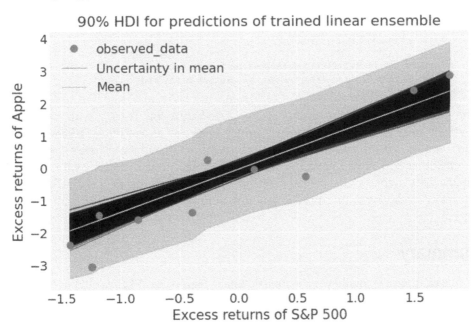

Evaluate, revise, or deploy ensemble

From the recent plot we can see that our ensemble has simulated all of the test data within the 90% HDI band. Let's also compute the probabilistic R-squared measure to evaluate the ensemble's predictive performance:

```
# Evaluate out-of-sample predictions of trained
# ensemble by comparing simulated data with test data.

# Get target values of the test data.
target_actual = target_test.values

# Sample ensemble's predictions based on test data.
target_predicted = idata.predictions.stack(sample=("chain", "draw"))
['target_likelihood'].values.T

# Compute the probabilistic R-squared performance metric.
test_score = az.r2_score(target_actual, target_predicted)
test_score.round(2)
```

The probabilistic R-squared metric of the tested ensemble is 69%, with a standard deviation of 13%. It is better than our training score and exceeds the test score benchmark of 65%. We are ready to deploy our tested ensemble into our paper trading system or other simulated financial system that uses real-time data feeds with fictitious capital. This enables us to evaluate how our ensemble performs in real time before we are ready to deploy it into production and commit real hard-earned capital to our system.

Summary

In this chapter, we saw how probabilistic linear regression (PLE) modeling is fundamentally different from conventional linear regression (MLE) modeling. The probabilistic framework provides a systematic method for modeling physical phenomena in general and financial realities in particular.

Conventional financial models use the MLE method to compute the optimal values of parameters that fit the data. That would be appropriate if we were dealing with time-invariant statistical distributions. It is inappropriate in finance because we don't have such time-invariant distributions. Learning optimal parameter values from noisy financial data is suboptimal and risky. Instead of relying on one expert in such a situation, we are better off relying on a council of experts for the many possible scenarios that are plausible and synthesize their expertise. This is exactly what a probabilistic ensemble does for us. It gives us the weighted average of all the estimates of model parameters.

In probabilistic regression modeling, as opposed to conventional linear modeling, data are treated as fixed and parameters are treated as variables because common sense and facts support such an approach. There is no need for the conventional use of ad hoc methods like L1 and L2 regularization, which are merely prior probability distributions in disguise. Most importantly, in the probabilistic paradigm, we are freed from ideological dictums like "let only the data speak for themselves" and unscientific claims of the existence of "true models" or "true parameters."

Probabilistic ensembles make no pretense to analytical elegance. They do not lull us into a false sense of security about our financial activities with point estimates and bogus analytical solutions fit only for toy problems. Probabilistic ensembles are numerical and messy models that quantify aleatory and epistemic uncertainties. These models are suited for endemic uncertainties of finance and investing. Most importantly, it reminds us of the uncertainty of our knowledge, inferences, and predictions.

In the next chapter, we will explore how to apply our probabilistic estimates and predictions to decision making in the face of three-dimensional uncertainty and incomplete information.

References

Dürr, Oliver, and Beate Sick. *Probabilistic Deep Learning with Python, Keras, and TensorFlow Probability*. Manning Publications, 2020.

Gelman Andrew, Ben Goodrich, Jonah Gabry, and Aki Vehtari. "R-Squared for Bayesian Regression Models." *The American Statistician* 73, no. 3 (2019): 307–309. *https://doi.org/10.1080/00031305.2018.1549100*.

Murphy, Kevin P. *Machine Learning: A Probabilistic Perspective*. Cambridge, MA: The MIT Press, 2012.

Further Reading

Martin, Osvaldo A., Ravin Kumar, and Junpeng Lao. *Bayesian Modeling and Computation in Python*. 1st ed. Boca Raton, FL: CRC Press, 2021.

## CHAPTER 8

Making Probabilistic Decisions with Generative Ensembles

But I realized that the odds as the game progressed actually depended on which cards were still left in the deck and that the edge would shift as play continued, sometimes favoring the casino and sometimes the player.

—*Dr. Edward O. Thorp, the greatest quantitative gambler and trader of all time*

In the previous chapter, we designed, developed, trained, and tested a generative ensemble of linear regression lines. Probabilistic linear regression is fundamentally different from frequentist or conventional linear regression, introduced in Chapter 4. For starters, frequentist linear regression produces a single regression line with parameters optimized to fit a noisy financial dataset generated by a stochastic process that is neither stationary nor ergodic. Probabilistic linear regression generates many regression lines, each corresponding to different combinations of possible parameters, which can fit the observed data distribution with various plausibilities while remaining consistent with prior knowledge and model assumptions.

Generative ensembles have the desirable characteristics of being capable of continually learning and revising model parameters from data and explicitly stated past knowledge. What truly distinguishes generative ensembles from their conventional counterparts are their capabilities of seamlessly simulating new data and counterfactual knowledge conditioned on the observed data and model assumptions on which they were trained and tested regardless of the size of the dataset or the ordering of the data.

Generative ensembles do all these activities consistently with their transparent model assumptions and the rigors of probability calculus, while appropriately scaling the aleatory and epistemic uncertainties inherent in such predictions and counterfactual knowledge. Probabilistic models know their limitations and honestly express their ignorance by widening their highest-density intervals in their extrapolations.

In the previous three chapters, we were primarily focused on inferring the distributions of our ensemble's parameters. In this chapter, we focus our attention on using the simulated outputs of our trained and tested generative ensembles for making financial and investment decisions in the face of three-dimensional uncertainty and incomplete information. In other words, our focus will be on the data-generating posterior predictive distribution of our model instead of the posterior distribution of its parameters. Generally speaking, the ensemble's outputs are what decision makers understand and need for making their decisions. For instance, the distribution of stock price returns is more meaningful to senior management and clients than the distribution of the alpha and beta parameters of the model used to generate them.

After reviewing the probabilistic inference and prediction framework used in this book, we systematize our approach to decision making by using objective functions. In the first example of probabilistic decision making, we explore how you can use the framework to integrate subjective human behavior with the objectivity of data and rigors of probability calculus. Finance and investing involves people, not particles or pendulums, and a decision-making framework that cannot integrate the intrinsic subjectivity of humanity is utterly useless. This also emphasizes the fact that decision making is both an art and a science in which human common sense and judgment are of paramount importance.

Two loss functions that are commonly used by risk managers and corporate treasurers are value at risk (VaR) and expected shortfall (ES). I introduce a new method of computing these risk measures as an integral part of generative ensembles. To use ensemble averages and its simulated data appropriately, we explore the statistical concept of ergodicity to understand why expected value or ensemble average has severe limitations and doesn't work as conventional economic theory will have us believe.

Finally, we explore the complex problem of allocating our hard-earned capital to favorable investment opportunities without the risk of financial ruin at any time. We examine the differences between gambling and investing, making decisions regarding one-off investments and a sequence of investments. The two most important capital allocation algorithms, Markowitz's mean variance and Kelly's capital growth investment criterion, are applied and their strengths and weaknesses are examined.

Probabilistic Inference and Prediction Framework

Let's review and summarize the framework we have used in the second half of the book to make inferences about model parameters, retrodictions about in-sample training data distributions, and predictions about out-of-sample test data distributions. We will illustrate this framework by using the debt default example from Chapter 5—when you were working as an analyst at the hedge fund that invested in high-yielding debt or "junk" bonds:

1. Specify all the possible scenarios or event outcomes that can occur in the sample space. The scenarios S_1 and S_2 are the model parameters that we want to estimate:

   - S_1 is the scenario in which XYZ portfolio company defaults on its debt obligations. S_2 is the scenario in which it doesn't.

   - Scenarios S_1 and S_2 are mutually exclusive and collectively exhaustive, which implies P(default) + P(no default) = 1.

2. Research and use any and all personal, institutional, scientific, and common knowledge about the problem domain that might help you to design your model and assign prior probabilities to the various parameters in the sample space before observing any new data. This is the prior probability distribution of the model.

   - Your hedge fund management team used its experience, expertise, and institutional knowledge to estimate the following prior probabilities for the parameters S_1 and S_2:

     P(default) = 0.10 and P(No default) = 0.90

3. Apply similar prior knowledge and domain expertise to specify likelihood functions for each model parameter. Understand what kind of data might be generated from your parametric model.

   - You used your fund's proprietary ML classification system that leveraged the features of a valuable database about debt defaulters and nondefaulters. In particular, your fund's analysts have found that companies that eventually default on their debt accumulate 70% negative ratings. However, the companies that do not eventually default only accumulate 40% negative ratings.

   - The likelihood functions of the model are: P(negative | default) = 0.70 and P(negative | no default) = 0.40

4. Generate data D′ using the model's prior predictive distribution. The model generates yet-to-be-seen data by averaging the likelihood function over the prior probability distribution of its parameters. The prior predictive distribution serves as an initial model check by simulating data we might have observed in the past based on our current model. The prior predictive distribution is a retrodiction of past data. In general, we can compare the data distribution to our prior knowledge. In particular, we can compare its simulated data to the training data.

   - Based on all your model's assumptions encoded in your prior probability distribution and the likelihood function, you can expect XYZ portfolio company to generate negative and positive ratings with the following probabilities:

     P(negative) = P(negative | default) P(default) + P(negative | no default) P(no default) = (0.70 × 0.10) + (0.40 × 0.90) = 0.43
     P(positive) = P(positive | default) P(default) + P(positive | no default) P(no default) = (0.30 × 0.10) + (0.60 × 0.90) = 0.57

5. Conduct a prior predictive check by observing in-sample data D and comparing it to the simulated data generated in the previous step.

   - If the retrodiction of the data meets your requirements, the model is ready to be trained and you should go to the next step.

   - Otherwise, review the parameters and the functional forms of prior probability distribution and the likelihood function.

   - Repeat steps 2–4 until the model passes your prior predictive check and is ready for training.

6. Apply the inverse probability rule to update the distributions of model parameters. Our model's posterior probability distribution updates our prior parameter estimates, given the actual training data.

   - You observed a negative rating and updated the posterior probability of default of XYZ company as follows:

     P(default | negative) = P(negative | default) P(default) / P(negative) = (0.70 × 0.10)/0.43 = 0.16

7. Generate data D″ using the model's posterior predictive distribution. The trained model simulates yet-to-be-seen data by averaging the likelihood function over the posterior probability distribution of the updated parameters. The posterior predictive distribution serves as a second model check by retrodicting the in-sample data it was trained on and predicting the out-of-sample or test data distribution we might observe later in testing.

- Based on all your model's assumptions encoded in your prior probability distribution, the likelihood function, and the newly observed negative rating, you can expect that XYZ portfolio company will generate new ratings, negative" and positive", with the following updated probabilities:

P(negative" | negative) = P(negative" | default) P(default | negative) + P(negative" | no default) P(no default | negative) = (0.70 × 0.16) + (0.40 × 0.84) = 0.35
P(positive") = 1 − P(negative") = 0.65

We are now faced with one of the most important decisions regarding the outputs of our inferences: how are we going to apply its results to make decisions given incomplete information and three-dimensional uncertainty, so that we increase the odds of achieving our objectives?

Probabilistic Decision-Making Framework

To make systematic decisions in the face of incomplete information and uncertainty, we need to specify an objective function. A loss function is a specific type of objective function where the objective is to minimize the expected value or weighted average loss of our decisions.[1] Simply put, a loss function quantifies our losses for every decision we take based on inferences and predictions we make.

Let's continue working through our debt default example to understand what a loss function does and how to apply it to outcomes that are simulated by our generative ensembles. We will then generalize it so that we can apply it to any decision-making activity that we might face using any type of objective function.

Integrating Subjectivity

The most difficult decisions are the ones that involve a complex interplay between the objective logic of the situation and the equally rational subjective self-interests of various people involved. Of course, the numbers we assign to any loss function for different decisions can be subjective. In such situations, the absolute numbers of the losses are not important. What is important is that we calibrate the losses consistently to reflect the magnitude of the consequences that would result logically from the various decisions that we make.

---

1 Christian P. Robert, *The Bayesian Choice: From Decision-Theoretic Foundations to Computational Implementation* (New York: Springer Science+Business Media, 2007).

Assume that you are working as an analyst at the aforementioned hedge fund. Basically, your job is to excel at data analysis and follow your portfolio manager's directions, especially regarding her risk limits for any portfolio company's bonds. The biggest risk you face at your job is getting fired and losing your main source of income. Here is a scenario you might face in your nascent career in investment management:

- Because of two negative ratings in a row, the probability of default for XYZ company bonds is now 25%.

- Your portfolio manager has directed you to call a risk management meeting when the probability of default of XYZ portfolio company exceeds 30%, her risk limit, which she swears by based on her experiences and expertise.

- You aspire to be a portfolio manager in the near future and need to demonstrate judgment and the ability to bear risk to your manager and colleagues.

The next rating that your ML system assigns XYZ bonds will almost surely not seal the fate of XYZ bonds' default status. But as you see it, the next rating will have dramatic consequences to your life that could rival any Shakespearean tragedy. The outcomes could range from your getting fired to your getting promoted as a portfolio manager. To call a meeting or not to call a meeting with your portfolio manager before the next rating—that is the question. To help you with your dilemma, we need to specify the probability distribution for the next rating, XYZ's probability of default breaching the risk limit, and the loss you might experience based on your decision to call or not to call the meeting with your portfolio manager before observing the rating.

Let's calculate the probability of default for XYZ company if the next rating you observe is a negative one (which would make it three negative ratings in a row):

- P(3 negatives | default) = $0.70 \times 0.70 \times 0.70 = 0.343$
- P(3 negatives | no default) = $0.40 \times 0.40 \times 0.40 = 0.064$
- P(3 negatives) = P(3 negatives | default) P(default) + P(3 negatives | no default) P(no default) = $0.343 \times 0.10 + 0.064 \times 0.90 = 0.0343 + 0.0576 = 0.0919$
- P(default | 3 negatives) = P(3 negatives | default) P(default) / P(3 negatives) = $0.0343/0.0919 = 0.37$

So if the next rating is a negative one, your estimate of the probability of default of XYZ company would be around 37% and would blow past your portfolio manager's risk limit of 30%. But what is the probability that the next rating for XYZ company is a negative one give that we have already observed 2 negative ratings? We have already computed the posterior predictive distribution for the next rating given two consecutive negative ratings for XYZ company:

- P(negative' | 2 negatives) = P(negative' | default) P(default | 2 negatives) + P(negative' | no default) P(no default | 2 negatives) = (0.7 × 0.25) + (0.4 × 0.75) = 0.475
- P(positive' | 2 negatives) = 1 − P(negative' | 2 negatives) = 0.525

It seems that the odds don't favor calling a meeting with your portfolio manager since there is only a 47.5% probability that the next rating for XYZ company is going to be negative. However, these odds don't consider the consequences of your decisions on your career and your colleagues. More specifically, we need to figure out the losses you and your portfolio manager might face based on your decision to call or not to call the risk management meeting with her preemptively.

Estimating Losses

Let's define a loss function, $L(R, D'')$, that quantifies the losses you might experience as a consequence of a decision, R, that you make based on an out-of-sample data prediction, D''.

We now enumerate our outcome data and decision spaces.

The possible ratings of XYZ bonds are $D_1'' = $ negative'' and $D_2'' = $ positive''. Note that these data predictions are mutually exclusive and collectively exhaustive.

Based on the predictions of this future, out-of-sample data, D'' given observed data D, your possible decisions, (R, D''), are enumerated here:

(R_1, D_1'')

Call a meeting with your portfolio manager based on your prediction that the next rating for XYZ bonds is going to be negative and the company's probability of default will breach her risk limit of 30%.

(R_2, D_2'')

Don't call a meeting with your portfolio manager based on your prediction that the next rating for XYZ bonds will be positive and the company's probability of default would be well below her risk limit.

(R_3, D_2'')

Call a meeting with your portfolio manager based on your prediction that the next rating of XYZ company will be positive. Persuade your manager to take advantage of current discounted market prices of XYZ bonds to increase her position size.

(R_4, D_1'')

Don't call a meeting with your portfolio manager based on your prediction that the next rating of XYZ bonds will be negative. Clearly, that would be foolish and not an option you would ever consider. We have merely listed it here for completeness.

Decisions (R_1, D_1''), (R_2, D_2''), and (R_3, D_2'') are the only viable decisions that you can make, and they are mutually exclusive and collectively exhaustive. We need to assign losses to each of these decisions to reflect their consequences to your life.

The possible losses for decision (R_1, D_1'')—in which you call a meeting with your portfolio manager to apprise her of the impending breach of her risk limit by XYZ bonds based on your prediction that the next rating will be negative—are as follows:

- One possible outcome is that the next rating of XYZ company turns out to be negative''. This is a great outcome for you and your portfolio manager. You would have shown sound judgment, anticipation, and risk management—some of the most important qualities of an investment manager. Your portfolio manager would have proactively managed her position risk thanks to your brilliant actions. Consequently, you would make significant progress toward your career goals of becoming a portfolio manager.
  - Your loss function reflects this favorable outcome by giving you a reward or a negative loss. Let's assign it a value of +100 points: $L(R_1, D_1'' \mid \text{negative}'') = +100$

- The only other possible outcome is that the next rating of XYZ company turns out to be positive''. This is not a good outcome for you. Your portfolio manager would take some losses on her hedges that she put on to protect her XYZ bonds based on your previous prediction. She might suspect that you panicked since the probability of a negative rating was 47.5%, less than a coin toss. She could conclude that you might not have the grit and gumption it takes to be a portfolio manager. Your dream of becoming a portfolio manager in the near future would gradually fade away. But let's look at the bright side of such a possible scenario: you would still have your job, and this could turn out to be a good learning experience for you.
  - Your loss function would reflect this by giving you a small loss of say –100 points: $L(R_1, D_1'' \mid \text{positive}'') = -100$

For the decision (R_2, D_2''), where you don't call a meeting based on your prediction of a positive rating for XYZ bonds, your possible losses are as follows:

- One possible outcome is that the next rating of XYZ company turns out to be negative. This is your nightmare scenario. Now the probability that XYZ company is going to default will have blown past your portfolio manager's risk limit. Market prices of bonds of XYZ company would take a hit. Your manager's portfolio would start underperforming her peers and her annual bonus would be in jeopardy. Quite possibly, she would be the one to call a meeting with you. You would be wished the very best in the future and politely escorted out of the door by security personnel.
  - This awful outcome is encoded in your loss function by assigning a large loss to it, say −1000 points: $L(R_2, D_2'' \mid \text{negative}'') = -1000$
- The only other outcome is that the next rating of XYZ company may turn out to be positive''. This would be a good outcome for you. However, it would not be clear to your manager whether it was good judgment or luck that played a role in your decisions and prediction. After all, the probability that the next rating would be a positive one was just 52.5%, a little better than a coin toss. She might conclude that you were cutting it a bit too close for comfort. Contrast this with her reaction to $(R_1, D_1'' \mid \text{positive}'')$. Both are inconsistent but rational viewpoints based on subjective attitudes toward risk that change at any given time for whatever reason. But that's exactly how people and markets can and do behave. We just have to deal with it in the best way we can.
  - Your loss function would reflect this neutral outcome with no loss or 0 points: $L(R_2, D_2'' \mid \text{positive}'') = 0$

Finally, the possible losses for the decision (R_1, D_2'')—where you call a meeting based on your prediction of a positive rating for XYZ bonds and convince your portfolio manager to increase her position size—are as follows:

- One possible outcome after the meeting with your portfolio manager is that the next rating of XYZ bonds turns out to be positive'' as predicted. This is the best outcome for you. Based on your recommendation, your portfolio manager would have already bought more XYZ bonds at discounted market prices. She would most likely have taken the opportunity to make a quick profit as XYZ bond prices rally on the new positive information. You would have demonstrated predictive capabilities and the smarts to monetize it. This would impress everyone at the fund, especially your fund manager, whose bonus check would surely increase. Now it would seem to only be a matter of time until you would be managing a multimillion-dollar portfolio yourself.

— The loss function would calibrate this positive reward by giving you a larger reward or negative loss. Let's assign it a value of +500 points: $L(R_1, D_2'' \mid \text{positive}'') = +500$

- The other outcome after the meeting with your portfolio manager is that the next rating of XYZ company turns out to be negative. This would be the worst outcome for you. Now the probability that XYZ company is going to default has blown past your portfolio manager's risk limit. Market prices of bonds of XYZ company would have taken a big hit while her position size had grown bigger. Your manager's portfolio performance would be bringing up the rear at the fund, and her job would be at risk. There would be nothing to discuss, and you would be escorted out of the door by security personnel.

  — The loss function calibrates this disastrous outcome by assigning a huge loss of –2000 points: $L(R_2, D_2'' \mid \text{negative}'') = -2000$

Minimizing Losses

We can now calculate the expected losses for each of the three decisions (R_1, D_1''), (R_2, D_2''), (R_3, D_2'') by averaging over the posterior predictive probability distribution, $P(D'' \mid D)$, for the next rating of XYZ bonds, given that we have already observed 2 negative ratings:

- $E[L(R_1, D_1'')]$ = P(negative'' | 2 negatives) $L(R_1, D_1'' \mid \text{negative}'')$ + P(positive'' | 2 negatives) $L(R_1, D_1'' \mid \text{negative}'')$ = $0.475 \times +100 + 0.525 \times -100 = -5$ points

- $E[L(R_2, D_2'')]$ = P(negative'' | 2 negatives) $L(R_2, D_2'' \mid \text{negative}'')$ + P(positive'' | 2 negatives) $L(R_2, D_2'' \mid \text{positive}'')$ = $0.475 \times -1000 + 0.525 \times 0 = -475$ points

- $E[L(R_3, D_2'')]$ = P(negative'' | 2 negatives) $L(R_3, D_2'' \mid \text{negative}'')$ + P(positive'' | 2 negatives) $L(R_3, D_2'' \mid \text{positive}'')$ = $0.475 \times -2000 + 0.525 \times +500 = -687.5$ points

In probabilistic decision making, the best decision you can make is the one that minimizes the expected value of your losses averaged over the consequences of your specific decisions. In the formula for minimizing losses, we have averaged the loss function over the posterior predictive distribution of simulated data. Since $E[L(R_1, D_1'')] > E[L(R_2, D_2'')] > E[L(R_3, D_2'')]$, you should decide on (R_1, D_1''). Your best option is to call for a meeting with our portfolio manager as soon as possible and apprise her that XYZ bonds are probably going to blow past her risk limit and that she needs to manage her position appropriately. This choice minimizes your career risks.

It is common knowledge that real-life decision making is an art and a science. Career risks, executive egos, conflicting self-interests, greed, and fear of people are some of the most powerful drivers of financial transactions everywhere in the world—from mundane daily trades to megamergers of the largest companies to the Federal Reserve raising interest rates. You ignore such subjective drivers of decision making at your peril and could miss out on profitable, if not life-changing, opportunities.

At any rate, based on our exercise of minimizing career risks, we can posit that, for discrete distributions, with a posterior predictive distribution $P(D''|D)$ and a loss function $L(R, D'')$, the best decision is the one that minimizes the expected loss, $E[L(R)]$, of predicted outcomes over all possible actions R, as shown here:

$$E[L(R)] = \arg\ \min_R \left(\Sigma_i L\left(R, D''_i\right) \times P\left(D''_i | D\right) \right)$$

This expected loss formula for discrete functions can be extended to continuous functions by substituting summation with integration. We can now apply loss functions to continuous distributions that we encounter in our regression ensembles. As before, we minimize the expected loss over all possible actions R as shown here:

$$E[L(R)] = \arg\ \min_R \left(\int L(R, D'') \times P(D''|D) dD'' \right)$$

These formulas make it look more difficult than it really is in applying our decision framework. What is indeed difficult is understanding and applying the expected value of our ensemble, as we will discuss in the next section.

Risk Management

Investors, traders, and corporate executives aim to profit from risky undertakings in which financial losses are not only expected but inevitable over the investment's holding period. The key to success in these probabilistic endeavors is to proactively and systematically manage losses so that they do not overwhelm profits or impair the capital base in any finite time period. In Chapter 3, we examined the inadequacies of volatility for risk management. Value at risk (VaR) and expected shortfall (ES) are two risk measures that are used extensively by almost all financial institutions, government regulators, and corporate treasurers of nonfinancial institutions.[2] It is very important that practitioners have a strong understanding of the methods used to calculate these measures as they, too, have serious weaknesses that can lead to disastrous mispricing of financial risks. In this section we explore risk management in general and how to apply the aforementioned risk measures to generative ensembles in particular.

---

2 Abdullah Karasan, *Machine Learning for Financial Risk Management with Python* (O'Reilly Media, 2021).

Capital Preservation

Warren Buffett, the greatest discretionary equity investor of all time, has two well-known rules for making investments in risky assets like equities:

- Rule number one: Don't lose money.
- Rule number two: Don't forget rule number one.

Buffett's sage advice is that when making a risky investment, we must focus more on managing the ever-present risks affecting the investment than on its potential future returns. Most importantly, we must never lose sight that the primary objective in investing is the return *of* our capital; the return *on* our capital is a secondary objective. We shouldn't go broke before we get our just deserts, should the investment opportunity actually turn out to be a profitable one in the future. Furthermore, even if the current investment doesn't work out as expected, there will always be others in the future that we can participate in as long as we preserve our capital base. Underlying Buffet's avuncular precept—borne out of decades of exemplary investing experiences—is the important statistical idea of ergodicity, which we explore next.

Ergodicity

Let's go back to the linear ensemble in the previous chapter and analyze the simulated 20,000 posterior predictive samples that our ensemble has generated using our model assumptions and the observed data. It is important to note that the posterior predictive distribution generates a range of possible future outcomes, each of which could have been generated by any combination of parameter values of our ensemble that is consistent with its model assumptions and the data used to train and test it.

While we can easily calculate descriptive statistics of the posterior predictive samples as we do later, we cannot directly associate any sample outcome with specific values of the model parameters. Of course, we can always infer the credible interval of each parameter that might have generated the samples from its marginal posterior distribution, as we did in the previous chapter. Let's use the following Python code to summarize the predicted excess returns of a hypothetical position in Apple stock:

```
# Flatten posterior predictive xdarray into one numpy array of
# 20,000 simulated samples.
simulated_data = target_predicted.flatten()

# Create a pandas dataframe to analyze the simulated data.
generated_data = pd.DataFrame(simulated_data, columns=["Values"])

# Print the summary statistics.
print(generated_data.describe().round(2))

# Plot the predicted samples of Apple's excess returns generated by
```

```
# tested linear ensemble.
plt.hist(simulated_data, bins='auto', density=True)
plt.title("Apple's excess returns predicted by linear ensemble")
plt.ylabel('Probability density'),
plt.xlabel('Simulated excess returns of Apple');
```

```
            Values
count    20000.00
mean        -0.24
std          1.74
min        -10.25
25%         -1.51
50%         -0.43
75%          0.98
max          8.29
```

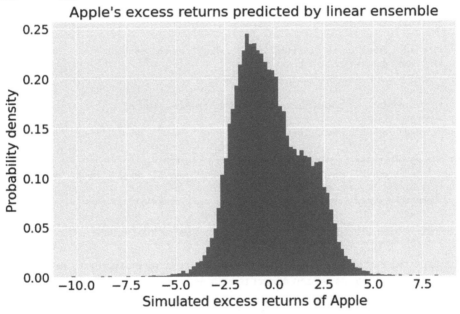

It is more important to note that this posterior predictive distribution of daily excess returns does not predict the specific timing or duration of those returns, only the distribution of possible returns in the future based on our ensemble's model assumptions and data observed during the training and testing periods. Our ensemble average is the expected value of our hypothetical investment in Apple stock. Let's see if it can help us decide whether to hold, increase, or decrease our position size.

A simple loss function, L(R, D″), is simply the market value of our position size multiplied by the daily excess returns of Apple for each simulated data point from the posterior predictive distribution of the ensemble:

- L(R, D″) = R × D″

    — R is the market value of our investment in Apple stock.

    — D″ is a simulated daily excess return generated by our linear ensemble.

In the following Python code, we assume that our hypothetical investment in Apple stock is valued at $100,000 and compute the ensemble average of all simulated excess returns:

```
#Market value of position size in the portfolio
position_size = 100000

#The loss function is position size * excess returns of Apple
#for each prediction.
losses = simulated_data/100*position_size

#Expected loss is probability weighted arithmetic mean of all the losses
#and profits
expected_loss = np.mean(losses)

#Range of losses predicted by tested linear ensemble.
print("Expected loss on investment of $100,000 is ${:.0f}, with max possible
loss of ${:.0f} and max possible profit of ${:.0f}"
.format(expected_loss, np.min(losses), np.max(losses)))

Expected loss on investment of $100,000 is $-237, with max possible loss of
$-10253 and max possible profit of $8286
```

The expected value of –$237 is almost a rounding error based on an investment of $100,000. This suggests we can expect to experience little or no losses if we hold our position, assuming market conditions remain approximately the same as those encoded in our model and reflected in the observed data used to train and test it. Given the large range of possible daily losses and profits our position might incur over time, from –10.25% to +8.29%, isn't the expected value of –0.24% misleading and risky? It seems that an ensemble average or expected value is a useless and dangerous statistic for risk management decisions. Let's dig deeper into the statistical concept of expected value to understand why and how we can apply it appropriately.[3]

---

3 Ole Peters, "The Ergodicity Problem in Economics," *Nature Physics* 15 (2019): 1216–1221; Ole Peters and A. Adamou, "The Time Interpretation of Expected Utility Theory," arXiv.org, February 28, 2021, *https:// arxiv.org/abs/1801.03680*.

Recall that when we estimate the expected value of any variable, such as an investment, we compute a probability weighted average of all possible outcomes and their respective payoffs. We also assume that the outcomes are independent of one another and are identically distributed, i.e., they are drawn from the same stochastic process. In other words, the expected value of the investment is a probability-weighted arithmetic mean. What is noteworthy is that the expected value has no time dependency and is also referred to as the ensemble average of a stochastic process or system. If you have an ensemble of independent and identically distributed investments or trades you are going to make simultaneously, expected value is a useful tool for decision making. Or if you are running a casino business, you can calculate the expected value of your winnings across all gamblers at any given time.

However, as investors and traders, we only observe a specific path or trajectory that our investment takes over time. We measure the outcomes and payoffs of our investment sequentially as a time average over a finite period. In particular, we may only observe a subset of all the possible outcomes and their respective payoffs as they unfold over time. In the unlikely scenario that our investment's trajectory realizes every possible predicted outcome and payoff over time, the time average of the trajectory will almost surely converge to the ensemble average. Such a stochastic process is called ergodic. We discussed this briefly in Chapter 6 in the Markov chain section.

What is special about an ergodic investment process is that the expected value of the investment summarizes the return observed by any investor holding that investment over a sufficiently long period of time. Of course, as was mentioned in Chapter 6, this assumes that there is no absorbing state in the Markov chain that truncates the investor's wealth trajectory. As we will see in this section and the next, investment processes are non-ergodic, and relying on expected values for managing risks or returns can lead to large losses, if not financial ruin.

Even if a process is assumed to be ergodic, the time average of our investment does not take the actual ordering of the sequence of outcomes and payoffs into account. Why should it? After all, it's just another arithmetic mean. What is noteworthy is that this, too, assumes that investors are passive, buy-and-hold investors. The specific sequence of returns that an investment follows in the market is crucial as it leads to different consequences and decisions for different types of investors. An example will help illustrate this point.

A stock trajectory that has a loss of –10.25% followed by a gain of +8.29% entails different decisions and consequences for an investor than a stock trajectory that has a gain of +8.29% followed by a loss of –10.25%. This is despite the fact that in both these two-step sequences the stock ends up down at –2.81% for a buy and hold investor. This up and down returns sequence is called volatility drag as it drags down the expected returns, an arithmetic mean, to the geometric mean, or compounded returns. If the volatility drag is constant, compounded returns = average return - 1/2 variance of returns. But the risks from the volatility drag for an investor could be very different depending on their investment strategy. Let's see why.

Assume that for any stock position in their portfolio, an investor has a daily loss limit of –10% and a daily profit limit of +5%. The former stock sequence (–10.25%, +8.29%) will hit the investor's stop-loss limit order at –10% and force them out of their position. To add insult to injury, the next day the stock comes roaring back +8.29%, while the investor is nursing a –10% *realized* loss on their investment. Now the investor would be down –7.19% compared to their peers who held onto their position or other investors who had a risk limit of –10.26% or lower. Talk about rubbing salt into our investor's wounds! It would now be hard for the investor to decide to re-enter their position after such a bruising whiplash.

Let's now consider what happens if the stock follows the latter sequence (+8.29%, –10.25%). The investor would take a profit of +5% when the stock shoots up +8.29%. They would feel some regret about not selling out of their position at the recent high price. But no one ever times the market perfectly or can do it consistently. However, the next day the investor would feel extremely smart and pleased with themselves when the stock falls –10.25%. They would be outperforming their peers by +7.81% and can gloat about it if they so choose. It would now be quite easy for the investor to re-enter their position in the stock since their break-even price would have been lowered by +5%.

This example demonstrates another reason why volatility, or standard deviation of returns, is a nonsensical measure of risk, as was discussed in Chapter 3. Volatility is just another ensemble average and is non-ergodic. In the first trajectory volatility hurts the investor's returns, and in the second trajectory it helps them.

While the numbers are specific to our probabilistic ensemble, investment trajectories over any time period can be profoundly consequential to most active investors and traders in general. The specific ordering of return sequences impacts an investor's decisions, experiences, and investment success. The concept of the "average investor" experiencing the expected value of returns on an investment is just another financial fairy tale.

Generative Value at Risk

Rather than relying on the ensemble average, a popular loss function called value at risk (VaR) can help us make better risk management decisions for any time period. VaR is a percentile measure of a return distribution, representing the value below which a given percentage of the returns (or losses) fall. In other words, VaR is the maximum loss that is expected to be incurred over a specified period of time with a given probability. See Figure 8-1, which shows VaR and conditional VaR (CVaR), which is explained in the next subsection.

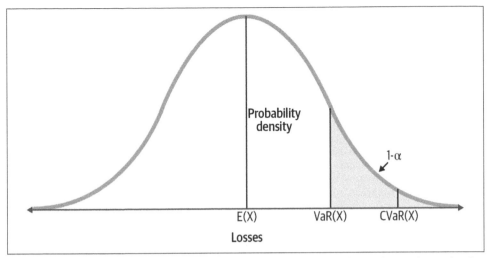

Figure 8-1. Value at risk (VaR) with alpha probability and conditional VaR (CVaR), also known as expected shortfall (ES), with 1-alpha probability shown for a distribution of returns of a hypothetical investment[4]

Unlike volatility, this measure is based on a commonsensical understanding of risk. As an example, say the daily VaR for a portfolio is $100,000, with 99% probability. This means that we estimate that there is a:

- 99% probability that the daily loss of the portfolio will not exceed $100,000
- 1% probability that the daily loss will exceed $100,000

Generally speaking, the time horizon of VaR is often related to how long a decision maker thinks might be necessary to take an action, such as to liquidate a stock position. Longer time horizons generally produce larger VaR values because there is more uncertainty involved the further out you go into the future.

In Chapter 3, we used Monte Carlo simulation to expose the deep flaws of using volatility as a measure of risk. It is common in the industry to use Monte Carlo simulations to estimate VaR for complex investments or portfolios using theoretical or empirical models. The risk estimate is called Monte Carlo VaR. In probabilistic machine learning, this simulation is done seamlessly and epistemologically consistently using the posterior predictive distribution. I use posterior predictive samples to estimate VaR, which I call Generative VaR or GVaR, as follows:

---

4 Adapted from an image on Wikimedia Commons.

- Sort N simulated excess returns in descending order of losses.

- Take the first M of those losses such that 1 − M/N is the required probability threshold.

- The smallest loss in the subset of M losses is your GVaR.

Now let's use Python to compute the GVaR of our linear ensemble from the losses in the tail of its posterior predictive distribution:

```
#Generate a list the 20 worst daily losses predicted
# by tested linear ensemble.
sorted_returns = generated['Values'].sort_values()
sorted_returns.head(20).round(2)
```

```
        4320     -10.25
        2170      -8.71
        14024     -8.35
        6004      -7.32
        9841      -6.74
        1154      -6.59
        19887     -6.34
        4324      -6.24
        16537     -6.21
        11889     -6.06
        234       -6.06
        7062      -5.95
        809       -5.74
        14340     -5.73
        734       -5.54
        14574     -5.49
        11657     -5.40
        4917      -5.39
        15676     -5.38
        18121     -5.34
        Name: Values, dtype: float64
```

```
# Compute the first percentile of returns.
probability = 0.99
gvar = sorted_returns.quantile(1-probability)

print(f"The daily Generative VaR at {probability}% probability is
{gvar/100:.2%} implying a dollar loss of ${gvar/100*position_size:.0f} ")

The daily Generative VaR at 0.99% probability is -3.79% implying a dollar
loss of $-3789
```

Generative Expected Shortfall

After the Great Financial Crisis, it became common knowledge that there is a deep flaw in the VaR measure that was used by financial institutions. It doesn't estimate the heavy losses that can occur in the tail of the distribution beyond VaR's cutoff point. Expected shortfall (ES), also known as conditional VaR, is a loss function that is commonly used to estimate the rare but extreme losses that might occur in the tail of the return distribution. Refer back to Figure 8-1 to see the relationship between VaR and ES. As the name implies, ES is an expected value and is estimated as a weighted average of all the losses after the VaR's cutoff point. Let's compute the generative ES of our linear ensemble and compare it to all the worst returns in the tail of the posterior predictive distribution:

```
# Filter the returns that fall below the first percentile
generated_tail = sorted_returns[sorted_returns <= gvar]

# Expected shortfall is the mean of the tail returns.
ges = generated_tail.mean()

# Generated tail risk is the worst possible loss predicted
# by the linear ensemble
gtr = generated_tail.min()

# Plot a histogram of the worst returns or generated tail risk (GTR)
plt.hist(generated_tail, bins=50)
plt.axvline(x=gvar, color='green', linestyle='solid',
label='Generative Value at Risk')
plt.axvline(x=ges, color='black', linestyle='dashed',
label='Generative expected shortfall')
plt.axvline(x=gtr, color='red', linestyle='dotted',
label='Generative tail risk')

plt.xlabel('Simulated excess returns of Apple')
plt.ylabel('Frequency of excess returns')
plt.title('Simulation of the bottom 1% excess returns of Apple')
plt.legend(loc=0)
plt.show()

print(f"The daily Generative VaR at {probability}% probability is
{gvar/100:.2%} implying a dollar loss of ${gvar/100*position_size:.0f} ")
print(f"The daily Generative expected shortfall at
{1-probability:.2}% probability is {ges/100:.2%} implying a dollar loss
of ${ges/100*position_size:.0f}")
print(f"The daily Generative tail risk is {gtr/100:.2%}
implying a dollar loss of ${gtr/100*position_size:.0f}")
```

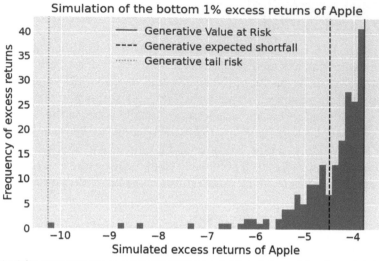

Simulation of the bottom 1% excess returns of Apple

The daily Generative VaR at 0.99% probability is -3.79% implying a dollar loss of $-3789
The daily Generative expected shortfall at 0.01% probability is -4.50% implying a dollar loss of $-4496
The daily Generative tail risk is -10.25% implying a dollar loss of $-10253

From the loss functions of VaR and ES, we can see that there is a 99% probability that the daily losses on our hypothetical investment in Apple stock is not expected to be lower than –3.79%. Should the loss exceed that GVaR threshold, the GES or daily loss in 1% of the scenarios is not expected to be lower than –4.50%.

Generative Tail Risk

The major flaw of ES is that it is yet another expected value or ensemble average that understates the risks due to extreme events. It's an even more dangerous statistic as it is averaging over a subset of the worst losses of the returns of our regression ensemble in a region of the distribution that is even more non-ergodic and fat-tailed as shown in the previous graph of the simulated losses in the tail of the posterior predictive distribution. For our specific ensemble, the worst loss is over twice the GES. If an extreme loss impairs your capital base, you will not be around to observe the expected shortfall. As a volatility trader who is short volatility quite often, I use the worst loss generated by the posterior predictive distribution— –10.25% for our ensemble—as my shortfall and hedge my trades accordingly. I refer to it as the Generative tail risk (GTR) of the ensemble.

If you own a stock, as most people do, you are in essence short volatility and are making a high-probability bet that the stock is not going to make unexpected moves in the future. Based on your risk preferences, position size, and confidence in your regression ensemble, you might choose a different percentile in the tail of the return distribution as a reference point to manage your tail risk. Consequently, you may decide to hold your stock position, reduce it, or hedge it with options or futures or both. Regardless, you should continue to monitor your investment and the overall market by continually updating your regression ensemble with more recent data as it becomes available. As we have discussed in the latter half of this book, continual probabilistic machine learning is the hallmark of generative ensembles.

Capital Allocation

Capital preservation, or return of our capital, is our primary objective. In the previous section, we explored the tools we can use to manage our risky investments to achieve that objective. Now let's focus our attention on the second objective: the return on our capital, or capital appreciation. As investors and traders, we have two related, fundamental decisions to make when faced with investing in risky assets in an environment of three-dimensional uncertainty and incomplete information:

- Evaluate and decide if the investment will appreciate in value over a reasonable time period.
- Decide what fraction of our hard-earned capital to allocate to that opportunity.

Expected value is used extensively for evaluating the attractiveness of investment opportunities. It is applied in almost every situation in finance and investing, from estimating the free cash flows of a company's capital project to valuing its debt and its outstanding equity. However, like all concepts and tools, expected value has its strengths, weaknesses, and limitations. As we have already discussed in the previous section, expected value as an ensemble average is a complex idea. In this section we continue to deepen our understanding of ensemble averages to see if and where they can be applied appropriately by an investor looking to allocate their capital to increase their wealth without risking financial ruin at any time.

Gambling: A Fool's Errand for the Ages

Gambling seems to have fallen into worldwide disrepute at the dawn of civilization. The "Dyuta Sukta" ("Ode to Dice," *Rig Veda*, 1700–1100 BCE) is a psychologically insightful ode to the woes of gamblers in ancient India, where it was a socially accepted activity.[5] The social ills of gambling compelled Chinese authorities to ban or regulate gambling as small-stakes games for most of its long history there. Ancient Jewish authorities suspected the ethics of gamblers and barred them from testifying in court.

No other story captures the ignominy and calamitous consequences of gambling as does the *Mahabharata* (circa 900 BCE), the world's longest epic poem—it is roughly 10 times longer than the *Iliad* and *Odyssey* combined. The seeds of war between two royal families were sown when one of the heroes was invited by his cousin to play a game of dice that were secretly loaded. For complex reasons, the hero was compelled into gambling away his kingdom, his wealth, his four brothers, himself, and finally his wife. The heroes of this great epic plunged from royals to slaves with a few throws of loaded dice. Now that is the epitome of a gambler's ruin!

Gambler's Ruin

It was not until the 17th century that Blaise Pascal, an eminent mathematician and physicist, working with a French aristocrat to improve his gambling skills, proved mathematically what was known to be true for a few millennia: eventually all gamblers go broke. Gambles are useful probabilistic models and have played a pivotal role in the development of probability and decision theories.[6] The classic problem of gambler's ruin is instructive for investors as it emphasizes that a positive expected value is a necessary condition for making investments.

Suppose you decide to play the following coin-tossing game. You start with $M, and your opponent starts with $N. Each of you bets $1 on the toss of a coin, which turns up heads with probability p and tails with probability q = (1 − p). If it's heads, you win $1 from your opponent; if it's tails, you lose $1 to your opponent. The game ends when either player goes broke (i.e., ruined). This is no silly game. It's a stochastic process called an arithmetic random walk and can be used to model stock prices and collisions of dust particles. It is also a Markov chain, since its future state only depends on its current state and not the path it took to get there.

---

5 A. V. Bhide, "Compulsive Gambling in Ancient Indian Texts," *Indian Journal of Psychiatry* 49, no. 4 (2007): 294–95.

6 Ole Peters and Murray Gell-Mann, "Evaluating Gambles Using Dynamics," arXiv.org, June 5, 2015, *https:// arxiv.org/abs/1405.0585.*

The gambler's ruin is a two-part problem in which a gambler makes a series of bets with negative or zero expected value. Using the arithmetic random walk model, it can be shown mathematically that any gambler will almost surely go broke in both of the following scenarios:

1. A gambler makes a series of bets, where the probability of success for each bet is less than 50% and payoff equals the amount staked. In such games the gambler will eventually go broke regardless of their betting strategy since their wager always has negative expectation. It doesn't even matter how big the gambler's bankroll is compared to their opponents. The gambler's probability of ruin P(ruin) is:

$$P(ruin) = \left[1 - \left(\frac{p}{q}\right)^\wedge N\right] / \left[1 - \left(\frac{p}{q}\right)^\wedge(N + M)\right] if\, p < q$$

2. A gambler is given a series of bets where the probability of success of each bet is 50% and the payoff equals the amount staked. These are fair odds, but the gambler's opponent has a bigger bankroll. Surprisingly, the gambler will eventually go broke even in this scenario, if their opponent has a marginally bigger bankroll. If their opponent has a much larger bankroll, such as a casino dealer, the bumpy road to ruin transforms into a highway with no speed limit. The probability of ruin P(ruin) is:

$$P\left(ruin\right) = \frac{N}{(M + N)} if\, P = q \text{ and } M < N$$

Note that in the first scenario, we are assuming that the gambler is not able or allowed to count cards or use the physics of the gambling machine, such as a roulette wheel, as the great Ed Thorp did to beat the dealers in Vegas in the 1960s.[7]

The math is brutally clear. No matter how hard you try or what betting system you invent, because of negative expectations of the bets, gambling is a fool's errand for the ages. Gamblers will take all kinds of random walks that will zig and zag between gains and losses, but all roads will eventually lead to ruin. Games involving equal odds with equal bankrolls are implausible situations for almost all gamblers. So to avoid going broke, a gambler needs to make bets with positive expected values.

But a gamble with positive expectation is commonly known as an investment. In mathematical models, the sign of the expected value of each bet is the main difference between a gamble and an investment, according to John Kelly, the inventor of the optimal capital growth algorithm.[8] By engaging in positive expectation bets, a

---

7 Edward O. Thorp, *A Man for All Markets: From Las Vegas to Wall Street, How I Beat the Dealer and the Market* (New York: Random House, 2017).

8 William Poundstone, *Fortune's Formula: The Untold Story of the Scientific Betting System That Beat the Casinos and Wall Street* (New York: Hill and Wang, 2006).

degenerate gambler morphs into a respectable investor who can now pursue a statistically feasible path of increasing their wealth while avoiding financial ruin. But what fraction of our capital do we allocate to investments with positive expectations? Does it make sense to go all in when we are offered really favorable odds?

Expected Valuer's Ruin

Say you are confronted by a wealthy and powerful adversary who owns a biased coin that has a 76% probability of showing heads. Assume that the probability of this biased coin is known precisely to all, but the physics of any coin toss is always unknown. Your adversary makes you a legally binding offer—an offer you *can* refuse.

If you stake your entire net worth on a single toss of his coin and it shows heads, he will pay you three times the value of your net worth. But if the coin shows tails, you lose your entire net worth except the clothes you are wearing—it's not personal, it's just business. This seems like the wager of a lifetime because it gives you the opportunity to increase your net worth twofold in a blink of an eye:

- Expected value of wager = (3 × net worth × 0.76) – (net worth × 0.24) = 2.04 × net worth.

- Payoffs are in multiples of your net worth, which will get estimated in legal proceedings (or not), so bluffing your net worth won't help.

Do you accept this offer, which clearly has a high expected value, with a 76% probability of success but with a nontrivial 24% probability of financial ruin? Tossing a coin once doesn't really involve time, so can expected value as an ensemble average work here to help us evaluate this opportunity?

Our common sense instinctively raises red flags about relying on any financial rule of maximizing expected value for such high-stakes decision making. It's as if we were the ones staring down the barrel of Detective "Dirty" Harry's famous .44 magnum handgun, wondering whether there is a bullet left, and him warning us: "You've gotta ask yourself one question: 'Do I feel lucky?' Well, do ya, punk?"

Any responsible person, experienced investor, trader, or corporate executive (all of whom, *generally speaking*, are not punks) would refuse this offer because any investment opportunity that even hints at the possibility of financial ruin is a deal-breaker. This is expressed succinctly in a market maxim that says, "There are old traders, there are bold traders, but there are no old, bold traders." Or another one that says, "Bulls make money, bears make money, but pigs get slaughtered." One essential statistical insight of these two aphorisms, built over centuries of collective observations and life experiences, is that maximizing the expected value of investments almost surely leads to heavy losses, if not financial ruin, even if the odds are in your favor.

What about a series of favorable bets where you maximize the expected value of each bet by going all in? Even if your same adversary were to give you a series of independent and identically distributed (i.i.d.) positive expectation bets, it would be ruinous for you to bet everything you have on each successive bet. You don't need mathematical proof to figure out that it only takes one losing bet to wipe out all the accumulated profits and the initial bankroll of any investor who is an expected value maximizer.

So how should you make your decision in one-off binary opportunities with positive expectations that don't involve betting your entire net worth? Let's return to the situation we described in Chapter 6 regarding ZYX technology company and its earnings expectations. Recall that after observing ZYX successfully beat its earnings expectations in the last three quarters, your model's prediction was that there was a 76% probability that it would beat its earnings expectations in the next quarter. Assume that you continue to find the probabilistic model useful, and ZYX is going to announce its earnings after the close of trading today.

Based on prices of options traded on ZYX stock, it seems that the market is pricing a 5% move up in the stock price if ZYX beats its earnings expectations. However, the market is also pricing a 15% move down in ZYX stock price if it does not. For the sake of this discussion, assume that these are accurate forecasts of the move in the stock prices after the earnings event. How can you use this market information and your model's prediction to allocate capital to ZYX stock before the earnings announcement today?

Let's create an objective function $V(F, Y'')$ where F is the fraction of your total capital you want to invest in ZYX and Y'' is the predicted outcome of an earnings beat. Given your objectives of avoiding any possibility of penury, F must be in the interval $[0, 1)$:

- Since F cannot equal 1 for any investment, we avoid the expected value maximizing strategy and the gambler's ruin, as previously discussed.

- Furthermore, leveraging your position is not allowed as F < 1. This means you cannot borrow cash from your broker to invest more capital than the cash in your account. When you borrow money from your broker to invest in stocks, you can end up owing more than your initial capital outlay, which is worse than blowing up your account.

- Since F cannot be negative, you cannot short stocks. Shorting a stock is an advanced trading technique in which you borrow the shares from your broker to sell the stock with the expectation of buying it at a lower price. It's buying low and selling high but in reverse order. Note that stock prices have a floor at $0 because of the limited liability of corporate ownership. However, stocks do not have a theoretical upper limit, which many unfortunate investors have realized in bubbles and manias. This is why shorting stocks can be risky and requires expertise and disciplined risk management. Stocks can burst into powerful rallies, called short covering rallies, for the flimsiest of reasons. These rallies can be twice as powerful, since there are buy orders from buyers and buy orders from short sellers, who are rushing to cover their short positions by buying back the stocks they had previously sold short. I have been on the wrong side of such short covering rallies several times, and the phrase "face-ripping rallies" is a fitting description of these experiences.

Recall that Y'' is our probabilistic model's out-of-sample predictions of ZYX's earnings announcements based on observed in-sample data D, with $P(Y_1'' = 1 \mid D) = 76\%$ when ZYX beats earnings expectations and $P(Y_0'' = 0 \mid D) = 24\%$ when it doesn't. Therefore, the expected value of our objective function, $E[V(F)]$, is the probability weighted average over a profit (W) outcome of 5% and a loss outcome (L) of –15%:

- $E[V(F)] = W \times F \times P(Y_1'' = 1 \mid D) + L \times F \times P(Y_0'' = 0 \mid D)$
- $E[V(F)] = 0.05 \times F \times 0.76 - 0.15 \times F \times 0.24 = 0.002 \times F$
- The trade has an edge or positive expectation of about 0.2%.

It only takes common sense to see that no single investor will observe an increase of 0.2% in the stock value of ZYX, or any other expected value they might have estimated, after the earnings event. Depending on the actual earnings results of ZYX, each investor who is long on the stock will either incur a 5% gain or –15% loss, or vice versa if they are short on the stock. The expected value we have computed is an ensemble average of all the profits and losses of all ZYX stockholders. It is hard to estimate, and it may or may not be within a reasonable range of your estimate.

But why should we care about the ensemble average anyway in this situation? As you can see, it is a completely useless tool for decision making in such one-off binary events for a single investor. A positive expected value of ZYX's earnings event sounds great until you get hit with a –15% loss in a high-frequency microsecond, much faster than your eye can even blink. Mike Tyson, a former heavyweight boxing champion, summarized such hopeful positive expectations eloquently when he said, "Everyone has a plan until they get punched in the mouth."

So what capital allocation algorithm can help you make decisions in one-off binary trades regardless of the amount of capital you are going to allocate to the bet? Unfortunately, there are none. Only your capacity to bear the worst *known* outcome of your decision, which is subjective by definition, can help you make such one-off binary decisions. We have already discussed how to integrate subjectivity into probabilistic decision making. Say you have a daily loss limit of –10% and daily profit limit of +5% for any position in your portfolio. This makes the decision systematic and much easier to make, especially for automated systems:

- Don't invest in ZYX before the earnings announcement, since the non-trivial probability of losing –10% in one day conflicts with the risk limits of your objective function.
- Don't short ZYX stock since that conflicts with your objective function.
- If you already have an investment in ZYX stock, you need to recalibrate your position size and hedge it with options or futures such that the daily loss doesn't exceed –10%. Of course, hedging costs will lower the 5% expected gain, so you will have to recalculate the expected value to make sure it is still positive.

Searching for investment opportunities that have positive expected values over a reasonable time horizon is generally the difficult part of any investment strategy. But in this section, we have learned that making investments with positive expectation is a necessary but not a sufficient condition. Therefore, investors are faced with a dilemma:

- If they allocate too much capital to such a favorable opportunity, they risk bankruptcy or making devastating losses.
- If they allocate too little capital, they risk wasting a favorable opportunity.

This implies that investors need a capital allocation algorithm that computes a percentage of their total capital to a series of investment opportunities with positive expectation such that it balances two fundamental objectives:

- Avoids financial ruin at all times
- Increases their wealth in a finite time period

Some investors have additional objectives that are to be achieved on the capital they manage over a specific time period, generally one year:

- Percentage profits to exceed a defined threshold
- Percentage losses not to exceed a defined threshold

These objectives can be encoded in an investor's objective function that will condition and constrain their capital allocation algorithm. As we have already learned in this chapter so far, applying expected value in investing and finance is neither intuitive nor straightforward, as investment processes are non-ergodic. Let's explore a capital allocation algorithm that is widely used in academia and in the industry.

Modern Portfolio Theory

Modern portfolio theory (MPT), developed by Harry Markovitz in 1952, focuses on quantifying the benefits of diversification using correlations of returns of different assets in a portfolio. It maximizes the expected value of the returns of a portfolio of assets for a given level of variance over a single time period, so volatility (the square root of variance) is used as a constraint on the expected value optimization algorithm. MPT assumes that asset price returns are stationary ergodic and normally distributed.

As we have learned already, these are unrealistic and dangerous assumptions, due to the following factors:

- They ignore skewness and kurtosis of asset price returns, which are known to be asymmetric and fat-tailed even by academics.

- Portfolio diversification is reduced or eliminated in periods of extreme market stress, as we saw recently in 2020 and previously in 2008.

- In normal periods, fat-tailed distributions can introduce large errors in correlations among securities in the portfolio.

- Portfolio weights can be extremely sensitive to estimates of returns, variances, and covariances. Small changes in return estimates can completely change the composition of the optimal portfolio.

MPT portfolios are much riskier than advertised and provide suboptimal returns—diversification leads to "diworsification." Buffet has called MPT "a whole lot of nonsense" and has been laughing all the way to his mega bank ever since.

In an interview, Markowitz admitted to not using his "Nobel prize–winning" mean-variance algorithm for his own retirement funds! If that is not an indictment of the mean-variance algorithm, I don't know what else is.[9] Instead Markowitz used 1/N heuristic or the naive diversification strategy. This is an investment strategy in which you allocate equal amounts of your capital to each of N investments. This naive diversification portfolio strategy has been shown to outperform mean variance and other complex portfolio strategies.[10]

---

9 Bruce Bower, "Simple Heresy: Rules of Thumb Challenge Complex Financial Analyses," *Science News* 179, no. 12 (2011): 26–29.

10 Victor DeMiguel, Lorenzo Garlappi, and Raman Uppal, "Optimal Versus Naïve Diversification: How Inefficient is the 1/N Portfolio Strategy?" *Review of Financial Studies* 22, no. 5 (2009): 1915–53.

We focus our attention on another simpler but equally useless model of MPT to highlight the conceptual blunder of using volatility as a measure of total risk. The capital asset pricing model (CAPM) discussed in Chapter 4 was derived from Markovitz's portfolio theory by his student William Sharpe. It simplifies MPT in terms of thinking about expected return for any risky investment. According to the CAPM, an asset has two types of risks: unsystematic and systematic. Unsystematic risk is idiosyncratic to the asset concerned and is diversifiable. Systematic risk is market risk that affects all assets and is not diversifiable.

The CAPM builds on the heroic assumptions of MPT that all investors are rational and risk-averse and have the same expectations at the same time given the same information, such that markets are always in equilibrium. Such financial fairy tales rival any you might see in Disney's Magic Kingdom. At any rate, these Markovitz investors are supposed to create strongly efficient markets and only hold diversified portfolios that will reduce the correlation among assets and eliminate the idiosyncratic risk of any particular asset. Statistically, this implies that in a well-diversified portfolio, the idiosyncratic risk of any particular asset will be zero, as will the expected value of any error term in the regression line. Therefore, Markovitz investors will only pay a premium for systematic risk of an asset, as it cannot be diversified away.

In such strongly efficient markets, all fairly priced investments will plot on a regression line called the security market line with the intercept equal to the risk-free rate and the slope equal to beta, or systematic risk. An asset's beta gives the magnitude and direction of the movement of the asset with respect to the market. See Figure 8-2 (M is the market portfolio with beta = 1).

The systematic risk term, beta, of the asset's MM is the same as the one calculated using its CAPM. However, note that an asset's market model (MM) is different from its CAPM in three important respects:

- The CAPM formulates expected returns of an asset, while its MM formulates realized returns.

- The MM has both an idiosyncratic risk term (alpha) and an error term in its formulation.

- Based on MPT, the expected value of alpha is zero since it has been diversified away by rational investors. That is the reason it does not appear in the CAPM.

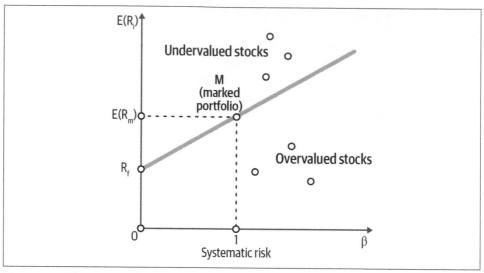

Figure 8-2. The CAPM claims that as you increase the systematic risk of your investment, or beta, its expected return increases linearly. Beta is directly proportional to the volatility of returns of the investment[11]

In simple linear regression, beta quantifies the average change in the target for a unit change in the associated feature. Based on the assumptions of simple linear regression, especially the one about constant variance of the residuals, beta has an analytical formula that is equal to:

- Beta = Rxy × Sy / Sx where:
  - Sy = standard deviation of the target or investment
  - Sx = standard deviation of the feature or market portfolio
  - Rxy = coefficient of correlation between the feature and the target

Beta can also be interpreted as the parameter that correlates the volatility of the risky investment with the volatility of the market.

---

11 Adapted from an image on Wikimedia Commons.

Markowitz Investor's Ruin

As you can see from Figure 8-2, the CAPM claims that you can increase the expected value of returns as much as you want, by selecting risky investments or using leverage or both, as long as you are willing to accept the attendant volatility of the asset's price returns.

Let's test these assumptions about the expected value of returns by generating a very large sample of hypothetical trades with the same probabilities, outcomes, and pay-offs as ZYX's earnings event. In the following Python code, we generate 20,000 samples from our posterior predictive distribution. That should be sufficiently large for the law of large numbers (LLN) to kick in and enable the convergence of any asymptotic property of stochastic processes.

In particular, we will calculate our ensemble average by computing the posterior predictive mean across the 20,000 simulated samples. These samples simulate the two outcomes of ZYX's earnings event. We then provide the same 20,000 outcomes sequentially as a time series to 100 simulated investors. Each simulated investor applies MPT/CAPM theory to their investing process. They allocate anywhere from 1% to 100% of their initial capital of $100,000 to ZYX stock. The profit or loss resulting from each of the simulated outcomes for a specific investor/fraction of the total capital is computed. Our code keeps track of the terminal wealth for each specific fraction/investor iteratively. Finally, we plot the terminal wealth for each fraction/investor and check if the time average of the typical investor equals the ensemble average computed earlier:

```
#Fix the random seed so numbers can be reproduced
np.random.seed(114)

#Number of posterior predictive samples to simulate
N = 20000

#Draw 100,000 samples from the model's posterior distribution
#of parameter p
#Random.choice() selects 100,000 values of p from the
#earnings_beat['parameter'] column using the probabilities in the
#earnings_beat['posterior'] column.
posterior_samples = np.random.choice(earnings_beat['parameter'],
size=100000, p=earnings_beat['posterior'])

#Draw a smaller subset of N random samples from the
#posterior samples of parameter p
posterior_samples_n = np.random.choice(posterior_samples, size=N)

#Generate N random simulated outcomes by using the model's likelihood
#function and posterior samples of the parameter p
#Likelihood function is the Bernoulli distribution, a special case
```

```
#of the binomial distribution where number of trials n=1
#Simulated data are the data generated from the posterior
#predictive distribution of the model
simulated_data = np.random.binomial(n=1, p=posterior_samples_n)

#Plot the simulated data of earnings outcomes y=0 and y=1
plt.figure(figsize=(8,6))
plt.hist(simulated_data)
plt.xticks([0,1])
plt.xlabel('Predicted outcomes')
plt.ylabel('Count')
plt.title('Simulated outcomes of ZYX beating earnings expectations')
plt.show()

#Count the number of data points for each outcome
y_0 = np.sum(simulated_data == 0)
y_1 = np.sum(simulated_data == 1)

#Compute the posterior predictive distribution
print(f"Probability that ZYX will not beat earnings expectations (y=0) is:
{y_0/(y_0+y_1):.3f}")
print(f"Probability that ZYX will beat earnings expectations (y=1) is:
{y_1/(y_0+y_1):.3f}")
```

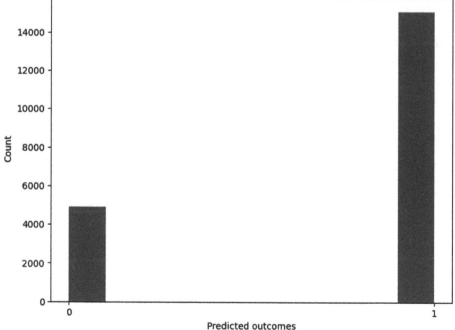

```
Probability that ZYX will not beat earnings expectations (y=0) is: 0.245
Probability that ZYX will beat earnings expectations (y=1) is: 0.755
```

Notice that the probabilities of the outcome variables based on our posterior predictive distribution are almost equal to the theoretical probabilities for y = 0 and y = 1. This validates our claim that the sample size is large enough for asymptotic convergence and the LLN is working as expected. Now we continue to calculate our profits and losses based on a sequence of 20,000 possible outcomes generated by our model to compute the terminal wealth of all investors:

```
#Percentage losses when y=0 and earnings don't beat expectations
loss = -0.15
#Percentage profits when y=1 and earnings beat expectations
profit = 0.05

#Set the starting capital
start_capital = 100000

#Create a list of values for position_size or percentage of total capital
#invested in ZYX by an investor
position_size = np.arange(0.00, 1.00, 0.01)

#Create an empty list to store the final capital values for
#each position_size of an investor
final_capital_values = []

#Loop over each value of position_size f to calculate
#terminal wealth for each investor
for f in position_size:
    #Set the initial capital for this simulation
    capital = start_capital

    #Loop over each simulated data point and calculate the P&L based on y=0 or y=1
    for y in simulated_data:
        if y == 0:
            capital += capital * loss * f
        else:
            capital += capital * profit * f

    # Append the final capital value to the list
    final_capital_values.append(capital)

#Find the value of f that maximizes the final capital of each investor
optimal_index = np.argmax(final_capital_values)
optimal_f = f_values[optimal_index]
max_capital = final_capital_values[optimal_index]

#Plot the final capital values as a function of position size, f
plt.figure(figsize=(8,6))
plt.plot(position_size, final_capital_values)
plt.xlabel('Position size as a fraction of total capital')
plt.ylabel('Final capital values')
plt.title('Growth of total capital as a function of position size in ZYX')
# Plot a vertical line at the optimal value of f
```

```
plt.axvline(x=optimal_f, color='red', linestyle='--')
plt.show()

#Print the optimal value of f and the corresponding final capital
print(f"The optimal fraction of total capital is {optimal_f:.2f}")
print(f"Initial capital of ${start_capital:.0f} grows to a
final capital of ${max_capital:.0f}")
```

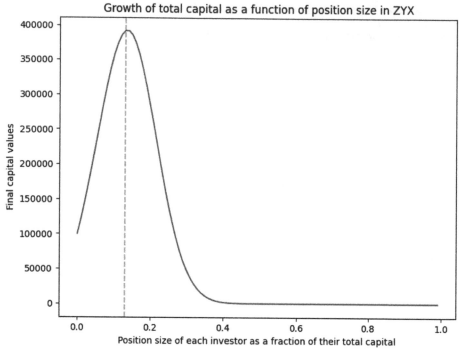

```
The optimal position size of total capital is 0.13
Initial capital of $100000 grows to a final capital of $391438
```

We can make a few obvious observations based on our simulation:

- Investors experience different wealth trajectories based on the fraction of the initial capital they invested in this series of hypothetical positive expectation bets (total of 20,000 i.i.d. bets).

- Investors start losing money if they invested more than 26% of their capital.

- All investors who invested more than 40% of their capital are broke.

- All investors who invested between 1% to 26% of their capital increased their wealth.

- The investor who invested only 13% of their capital had the greatest amount of terminal wealth. In this investment scenario, 13% of total capital is the Kelly optimal position size for growing one's wealth.

- It is important to note that an investor's risk of ruin is closely related to the position size of their initial capital and not to the volatility of returns of the stochastic process, which is the same for every investor.

- Most importantly, even if you are willing to accept the related volatility of your investment, there is a limit to how much capital you should allocate to an investment. This is the fatal flaw of MPT/CAPM and reveals the foolishness of using volatility as a measure of risk.

As shown in our simulation, assuming that investing is an ergodic process and optimizing expected value leads to financial ruin for the majority of the investors applying MPT/CAPM principles of using volatility as a proxy for risk and disregarding position size. This is how LTCM justified leveraging its positions arbitrarily highly and disregarding the possibility of financial ruin.

Kelly Criterion

In 1956, John Kelly, a physicist working at Bell Labs, came up with the groundbreaking solution to the vexing problem of how much is optimal to invest in positive expectation opportunities following a non-ergodic stochastic process. His solution, commonly referred to as the Kelly criterion, is to maximize the expected compound growth rate of capital, or the expected logarithm of wealth.[12] The Kelly position size is the optimal amount of capital allocated to a sequence of positive expectation bets or investments that results in the maximum terminal wealth in the shortest amount of time without risking financial ruin.

Say your wealthy adversary gives you another weighted coin that has a 55% probability of turning up heads. He offers you an infinite series of trades with even odds:

- On heads, you get two times your stake. On tails, you lose your entire stake.

- How much capital do you allocate to maximize your capital in the long term?

Let's run a simulation in Python of a simple series of binary bets with fixed odds to illustrate the power of the Kelly criterion for maximizing your wealth:

```
import numpy as np
import matplotlib.pyplot as plt
```

---

12 J. L. Kelly Jr., "A New Interpretation of Information Rate," *The Bell System Technical Journal* 35, no. 4 (1956): 917–26.

```
np.random.seed(101)

# Weighted coin in your favor
p = 0.55

# The Kelly position size (edge/odds) for odds 1:1
f_star = p - (1 - p)

# Number of series in Monte Carlo simulation
n_series = 50

# Number of trials per series
n_trials = 500

def run_simulation(f):
#Runs a Monte Carlo simulation of a betting strategy with
#the given Kelly fraction.
#Takes f, The Kelly fraction, as the argument and returns a NumPy array
#of the terminal wealths of the simulation.

    # Array for storing results
    c = np.zeros((n_trials, n_series))

    # Initial capital of $100
    c[0] = 100

    for i in range(n_series):
        for t in range(1, n_trials):
            # Use binomial random variable because we are tossing
            # a weighted coin
            outcome = np.random.binomial(1, p)

            # If we win, we add the Kelly fraction to our accumulated capital
            if outcome > 0:
                c[t, i] = (1 + f) * c[t - 1, i]

            # If we lose, we subtract the Kelly fraction from
            # our accumulated capital
            else:
                c[t, i] = (1 - f) * c[t - 1, i]

    return c

# Run simulations for different position sizes
# The Kelly position size is our optimal betting size
c_kelly = run_simulation(f_star)

# Half Kelly size reduces the volatility while keeping the gains
c_half_kelly = run_simulation(f_star / 2)

# Anything more than twice Kelly leads to ruin in the long run
c_3_kelly = run_simulation(f_star * 3)
```

```
# Betting all your capital leads to ruin very quickly
c_all_in = run_simulation(1)

# Plot the expected value/arithmetic mean of terminal wealth
# over all the iterations of 500 trials each
fig, ax = plt.subplots(figsize=(10, 6))

# Overlay multiple plots with different line styles and markers
ax.plot(c_kelly.mean(axis=1), 'b-', lw=2, label='Kelly')
ax.plot(c_half_kelly.mean(axis=1), 'g--', lw=2, label='Half Kelly')
ax.plot(c_3_kelly.mean(axis=1), 'm:', lw=2, label='Three Kelly')
ax.plot(c_all_in.mean(axis=1), 'r-.', lw=2, label='All In')

ax.legend(loc=0)
ax.set_title('Expected Wealth of Bettor With Different Position Sizes')
ax.set_ylabel('Terminal wealth')
ax.set_xlabel('Number of Bets')

plt.show()
```

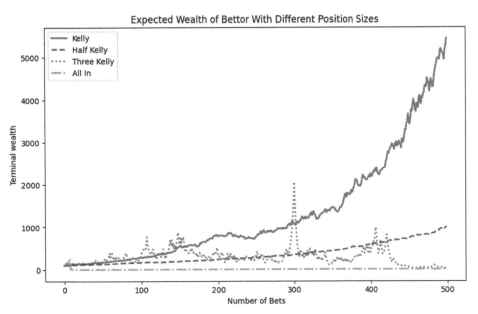

For binary outcomes, an investor can compute the percentage of capital, F, to be allocated to an opportunity with positive expectation in the real world of non-ergodic investing processes. However, the popular literature on the Kelly criterion doesn't provide the general Kelly position sizing formula that you can apply to investments or bets in which you lose a percentage of your stake and not your entire stake. The optimal fraction, F', is:

- $F' = (W \times p - L \times q) / (W \times L)$ where
  - p is the probability of gain and $q = 1 - p$ is the probability of loss.
  - W is percentage gain and L is the percentage loss.
- Note when $L = 1$, you lose your entire stake and you get the popular formula:
  - $F' = (W \times p - q) / W$, or as it is popularly known, edge over odds.
  - This formula is used in sports betting, where you can lose your entire stake.

It is important to note that the Kelly formula relates the ensemble average to the time average of a single trajectory. The expected value, or edge, of the investment is in its numerator. But the denominator modifies the position size implied by the ensemble average by including the multiplicative losses and profits that will be incurred sequentially in the time average. This is the volatility drag we discussed in the ergodicity subsection earlier.

The Kelly formula solves the gambler's ruin problem for multiplicative dynamics quite elegantly. Recall that the gambler's ruin problem involves a series of additive bets. In contrast, the Kelly criterion is used for a series of multiplicative bets. When the expected value or edge of an opportunity is zero, the Kelly formula gives it a zero position size. Furthermore, when the expectation is negative, the position size is also negative. This implies you should take the other side of the bet. In gambling, this would mean betting against gamblers and with the casino dealer. In markets, it means betting that markets will fall and taking a short position in an investment.

The Kelly criterion has many desirable properties for investing in positive expectation investment opportunities:[13]

- It is mathematically indisputable that the Kelly position maximizes the terminal wealth in the shortest amount of time without the risk of going broke.
  - It generates exponential growth since profits are reinvested.
  - It involves a multiperiod, myopic trading strategy where you can focus on the present opportunities without a need for a long-term plan.
- It has risk management built into the formula:
  - Kelly position size is a fraction of your capital.
  - Position size becomes smaller as losses accumulate.

---

13 L. C. MacLean, E. O. Thorp, and W. T. Ziemba, "Long-Term Capital Growth: Good and Bad Properties of the Kelly Criterion," *Quantitative Finance* 10, no. 7 (2010): 681–687.

The Kelly criterion expressed mathematically that evaluating expected values of investment opportunities is necessary but not sufficient. Sizing our investment position to account for the non-ergodic process of investing is of paramount importance and the sufficient condition we need. Unfortunately, capital allocation in financial markets is not that simple, and applying the Kelly criterion is challenging because markets are not stationary.

Kelly Investor's Ruin

As we have mentioned in Chapter 1, financial markets are not only non-ergodic, but they are also nonstationary. The underlying data-generating stochastic processes vary over time. This makes estimating the continually changing statistical properties of these processes hazardous, especially when the underlying structure of the market changes abruptly.

Note that the posterior predictive distribution of the outcome variable Y'', the event that ZYX will beat earnings expectations, has a probability distribution due to the uncertainty of its parameter and data sampling. The 76% probability is just the mean value of its posterior predictive distribution. The expected value of our objective function turns negative if our estimate is less than 75%. There is not much margin for error here, and that should raise red flags. Based on the analytical formula and theoretical probability of an earnings beat of 75%, the Kelly position size should be zero. However, we have overshot the Kelly position, and our capital growth is suboptimal but positive for this simulation. It is quite possible that for another simulation with more samples, the position size changes and the current position size of 13% would lead to ruin.

The Kelly position sizing formula is very sensitive to estimates of both the expected value (the "edge") and the probabilities of gains and losses (the "odds"). The cardinal sin in applying the Kelly formula is to overbet or to have a position size larger than the Kelly size. As an investor's position size goes past the Kelly optimum, the growth rate of their wealth decreases and inexorably moves them toward financial ruin.[14]

---

14 L. C. MacLean, E. O. Thorp, Yonggan Zhao, and W. T. Ziemba, "Medium Term Simulations of the Full Kelly and Fractional Kelly Investment Strategies," in *The Kelly Capital Growth Investment Criterion: Theory and Practice*, eds. L. C. MacLean, E. O. Thorp, and W. T. Ziemba (Hackensack, NJ: World Scientific Publishing Company, 2011), 543–61.

Practitioners of the Kelly criterion use a fraction of the Kelly optimal size, such as half Kelly, to avoid overbetting, as it hedges against:

- Overestimating one's edge
- Misestimating event odds
- Changing edge and odds

Fractional Kelly allocation strategies also reduce the volatility of returns that can accompany full Kelly position sizes. The full application of the Kelly criterion to a portfolio of investments involves nonlinear programming and is beyond the scope of this primer.[15]

Summary

Complex decision making in the real world is an art and a science. Our probabilistic decision framework gives us the perspective and the tools to integrate our prior knowledge and subjective reasons with the objectivity of observed data and the unrelenting rigors of probability calculus. It enables us to make the best decisions that optimize our objectives in the face of uncertainty and incomplete information. To make such systematic decisions that we can entrust to machines, we need to specify an objective function and evaluate the function based on all possible outcomes generated from the posterior predictive distribution of our generative ensembles.

Expected value, also known as an ensemble average, needs to be applied with great caution because finance and investing processes are non-ergodic. Since each investor's wealth trajectory is unique and different from the ensemble average computed across all possible trajectories of all market participants, their time average is not the same as the expected value of the ensemble. Also, different sequences of events lead to different decisions and outcomes even though the time average may be equivalent. In risk management, it is prudent to use value at risk instead of volatility, as VaR is estimated from the distribution of possible returns. Furthermore, it is better to use a tail-risk value instead of expected shortfall as that, too, is an ensemble average. My generative versions of these risk measures are produced seamlessly by probabilistic ensembles as I have demonstrated in this chapter.

---

15 *The Kelly Capital Growth Investment Criterion: Theory and Practice*, eds. L.C. MacLean, E.O. Thorp, and W.T. Ziemba (Hackensack, NJ: World Scientific Publishing Company, 2011).

The expected value of investments is a useful evaluation tool because it separates gambling from investing. However, while positive expectation is a necessary condition for investing, it is not a sufficient condition in a non-ergodic world. You need a capital allocation algorithm to appropriately size your investment so that you don't go broke on any wealth trajectory your investment takes and you have a realistic chance of growing your wealth.

If you are looking to maximize the growth of your capital, you might want to consider the Kelly investment strategy, which outperforms any other capital allocation strategy, especially the suboptimal Markowitz's mean-variance investment strategy. The Kelly criterion investment strategy has been used by the most successful investors of all time, including Warren Buffet, Ed Thorp, and James Simons. It is a travesty that the Kelly criterion is not taught in academia or professional programs. However, the Kelly formula is not a silver bullet and is hard to implement in a nonstationary world. That's why most practitioners like me use fractional Kelly trading strategies to avoid overbetting and the risk of ruin.

Unfortunately, there are no easy formulas or algorithms for success in trading, investing, and finance that can be encoded in any AI system, because markets are not stationary ergodic. Symbolic AI and probabilistic machine learning systems require human common sense and expertise to separate correlation from causation to successfully navigate the aleatory, epistemic, and ontological uncertainties produced by creative, emotional, and free-willed market participants. Now that is a generative ensemble that can almost surely put the odds in your favor.

References

Bhide, A. V. "Compulsive Gambling in Ancient Indian Texts." *Indian Journal of Psychiatry* 49, no. 4 (2007): 294–95.

Bower, Bruce "Simple Heresy: Rules of Thumb Challenge Complex Financial Analyses." *Science News* 179, no. 12 (2011): 26–29.

DeMiguel, Victor, Lorenzo Garlappi, and Raman Uppal. "Optimal Versus Naïve Diversification: How Inefficient is the 1/N Portfolio Strategy?" *Review of Financial Studies* 22, no. 5 (2009): 1915–53.

Karasan, Abdullah. *Machine Learning for Financial Risk Management with Python.* O'Reilly Media, 2021.

Kelly Jr., J. L. "A New Interpretation of Information Rate." *The Bell System Technical Journal* 35, no. 4 (1956): 917–26.

MacLean, L. C., E. O. Thorp, and W. T. Ziemba. "Long-Term Capital Growth: Good and Bad Properties of the Kelly Criterion." *Quantitative Finance* 10, no. 7 (2010): 681–687.

MacLean, L. C., E. O. Thorp, and W. T. Ziemba. "Medium Term Simulations of the Full Kelly and Fractional Kelly Investment Strategies." In *The Kelly Capital Growth Investment Criterion: Theory and Practice*, edited by L. C. MacLean, E. O. Thorp, and W. T. Ziemba, 543–61 (Hackensack, NJ: World Scientific Publishing Company, 2011).

Peters, Ole. "The Ergodicity Problem in Economics." *Nature Physics* 15 (2019): 1216–21.

Peters, Ole, and A. Adamou. "The Time Interpretation of Expected Utility Theory." arXiv.org, February 28, 2021. *https://arxiv.org/abs/1801.03680*.

Peters, Ole, and Murray Gell-Mann. "Evaluating Gambles Using Dynamics," arXiv.org, June 5, 2015. *https://arxiv.org/abs/1405.0585*.

Poundstone, William. *Fortune's Formula: The Untold Story of the Scientific Betting System That Beat the Casinos and Wall Street*. New York: Hill and Wang, 2006.

Robert, Christian P. *The Bayesian Choice: From Decision-Theoretic Foundations to Computational Implementation*. New York: Springer Science+Business Media, 2007.

Thorp, Edward O. *A Man for All Markets: From Las Vegas to Wall Street, How I Beat the Dealer and the Market*. New York: Random House, 2017.

Further Reading

MacLean, L.C., E. O. Thorp, and W. T. Ziemba (eds.). *The Kelly Capital Growth Investment Criterion: Theory and Practice*. World Scientific Publishing Company, 2011.

Index

Symbols

1/N heuristic, 218
α (expected stock-specific return), 100
    code for estimating, 101-103
        confidence intervals, 104
β (systemic risk exposure), 100
    code for estimating, 101-103
        confidence intervals, 104
ε (unexpected stock-specific return), 100

A

AI
    AI systems based on models, 2
    dangers of conventional AI, 129
        causal relationship ignorance, 129, 131
        common sense lacking, 129, 130-132
        maximum likelihood estimation use,
            129, 132-142
        MLE model for earnings expectations,
            133-136
        probabilistic model for earnings expecta-
            tions, 136-142
        spurious correlations, 131
    description of AI, 12-16
    evolution crossroads of AI, xi
    generative AI
        about, 16
        about generative ensembles, 19, 191
        about probabilistic ML, ix, 16
        characteristic of probabilistic ML, 19
        continually learning and revising param-
            eters, 191
        generating data with predictive probabil-
            ity distributions, 123-127

market model, 154
    market model assumptions, 155
    MLE regression models, 153-156
    probabilistic linear ensembles, 156-161
    PyMC library, 152, 161-188
    residual, 153
    simulating new data and counterfactual
        knowledge, 191
    symbolic AI, 13
aleatory uncertainty, 23, 44
    coin tosses, 44
    likelihood function quantifying, 115
    marginal likelihood function, 116
    ML generation of, 45
    posterior probability distribution, 116
    prior and posterior predictive distributions,
        124
algorithmic uncertainty and ML epistemic
    uncertainty, 47
alpha (α) as expected stock-specific return, 100
    code for estimating, 101-103
        confidence intervals, 104
alpha for significance level, 95
Apple Inc. (AAPL)
    code for estimating alpha and beta, 101-103
        confidence intervals, 104
    market model, 100, 108
arbitrage pricing model (APT), 151
arithmetic mean, 66
    average deviation from, 67
    calculating for S&P 500, 73
    central limit theorem, 76-78
    expected value, 67
    law of large numbers, 75, 77

sum of all deviations from, 67
asymmetry of information, 47
axioms of probability, 26-30
    sum rule, 27

B

Bayes, Thomas, 31, 94
Bayesian inference referred to as probabilistic
    inference, 32
Bayesian statistics referred to as epistemic sta-
    tistics, 32, 37
"Bayes's theorem"
    inverse probability rule as proper name, 19,
        31-31, 94
    Laplace as actual discoverer, 31
    proof of, 30
Bernoulli distribution, 134
Bernoulli, Daniel, 31
beta (β) as systemic risk exposure, 100
    code for estimating, 101-103
        confidence intervals, 104
bias as underfitting the training data, 48
    bias-variance balance, 48
bias-free and optimal for all problems as free
    lunch, 38, 51
    about bias in this context, 52
binomial distribution to model interest rates, 7,
    10
    Bernoulli distribution, 135
Black, Fischer, 42
Black-Scholes options pricing model, 42
Black-Scholes-Merton option pricing formula,
    4
    normal distribution basis, 6
book web page, xv
Box, George, 1
Buffet, Warren, 68, 202, 218
Buffon, Georges Louis Leclerc, comte de, 64

C

capital allocation
    about, 211
    gamblers, 212
    gamblers' ruin, 212
    modern portfolio theory, 218-220
    MPT/CAPM investor's ruin, 221-225
capital asset pricing model (CAPM), 101
    dangers of, 219
        investor's ruin, 221-225

    key assumptions wrecked, 109
    modern portfolio theory as basis, 219
        CAPM equally useless, 219
    single-factor market model versus, 101
Carvaka philosophy, 58
cash flows and DCF model, 56
Cauchy distribution, 43, 69
    not having finite mean or variances, 107
central limit theorem (CLT), 76-78
    confidence intervals violating assumptions,
        88, 107
    sampling distributions, 106
central tendency measures, 66
ChatGPT as deep neural network, ix
    probabilistic ML versus, ix
coin tosses as predictable physics, 37, 44
common sense lacking from AI, 130-132
    causal relationships not understood, 129
    probability as common sense reduced to
        calculation, 113
conditional probabilities, 30
    inverting for Monty Hall problem, 30-33
    not commuting, 88
    product rule, 30
confidence intervals (CIs)
    about, 88, 99, 104
        90% CI explained, 99
        95% CI for Apple alpha and beta, 104
        95% CI incorrect interpretation, 105
        95% CI interpretation corrected, 105
    alpha and beta estimation code, 101-103
    central limit theorem assumptions violated,
        88, 107
    CI theory, 98-100
        errors from postdata use, 100, 105-109
        p-values replaced by, 97
        predata theory per Neyman, 99
    errors from postdata use
        about, 100, 105
        probabilistic claims about population
            parameters, 105
        probabilistic claims about sampling dis-
            tributions, 106-109
        probabilistic claims about specific confi-
            dence interval, 106
    key assumptions wrecked
        capital asset pricing model, 109
        market model, 107
    quantifying parameter uncertainty with, 156

single-factor market model for equities, 100
   alpha as expected stock-specific return,
     100
   beta as systemic risk exposure, 100
   capital asset pricing model versus, 101
constants versus variables, 28
conventional AI dangers (see dangers of conventional AI)
conventional view of probability, 24
   (see also dangers of conventional statistical
     methods; frequentist view of probability)
cost of equity capital, 162
credit card interest rate estimation errors, 7-9
cross-hedging, 162

D

dangers of conventional AI
   about, 129
   common sense lacking, 130-132
     causal relationship ignorance, 129, 131
     spurious correlations, 131
   maximum likelihood estimation, 132-142
   flaws of, 129
     MLE model for earnings expectations,
      133-136
     probabilistic model for earnings expecta-
      tions, 136-142
dangers of conventional statistical methods
   about, 87
   confidence intervals
     alpha and beta estimation code, 101-103
     alpha and beta estimation confidence
      intervals, 104
     capital asset pricing model assumptions
      wrecked, 109
     central limit theorem assumptions viola-
      ted, 88, 107
     CI theory as predata, 98
     errors from CI theory used postdata,
      100, 105-109
     market model assumptions wrecked, 107
     single-factor market model for equities,
      100
   frequentist view worse than useless, 24, 97
     impact on financial economics, 100
     null hypothesis significance testing, 87,
      97
     using prosecutor's fallacy, 38, 89

     violating product and inverse probability
      rules, 38
   inverse fallacy, 88-94
   NHST committing prosecutor's fallacy,
     94-97
dangers of modern portfolio theory, 218
   CAPM equally useless, 219
data generated with predictive probability distributions, 123-127
data uncertainty and ML epistemic uncertainty,
   47
DCF (see discounted cash flow model)
de Moivre, Abraham, 31
debt default probability estimation via PML,
   118-123
   ingesting data one point at a time or all at
     once, 123
   learning dynamically, 121
decision making
   probabilistic versus nonprobabilistic, ix
   probabilistic with generative ensembles
     about, 191
     capital allocation, 211-230
     capital preservation, 202
     ergodicity, 202-206
     estimating losses, 197-200
     expected shortfall, 209
     expected valuer's ruin, 214-217
     gamblers, 212
     gamblers' ruin, 212
     integrating subjectivity, 195
     Kelly criterion, 225-229
     Kelly investor's ruin, 229
     loss functions defined, 192, 195
     minimizing losses, 200
     modern portfolio theory, 218-220
     MPT/CAPM investor's ruin, 221-225
     probabilistic decision-making frame-
      work, 195
     probabilistic inference and prediction
      framework, 193-195
     risk management, 201-211
     tail risk, 210
     value at risk, 206-208
   psychology of financial decision making, 26
deductive and inductive reasoning, 54
deep learning as supervised learning, 15
deep neural networks
   misleading marketing term, 132

probabilistic ML models versus, ix
deep Q-learning as reinforcement learning, 15
defense attorney's fallacy, 90
degrees of freedom in variance calculation, 67
dependent/output variables, 2
    target or response in ML systems, 14
deterministic models versus probabilistic, 2, 14
Diaconis, Persi, 44
discounted cash flow model (DCF), 56
    valuing a software project via MCS, 78-82
The Doctrine of Chances (de Moivre), 31
drunkard's search and normal distribution, 7
"Dyuta Sukta" ("Ode to Dice"), 212

E

earnings expectations
    MLE model, 133
    probabilistic model, 136-142
economic recessions and prosecutor's fallacy,
    90-94
Einstein, Albert, 40
Eisenhower, Dwight, 43
endowment effect, 26
epistemic statistics, 37-39
    about, 32
        probability distributions only, 43
    frequentist versus, 39
    image processing requiring probabilistic
        algorithms, 39
    not "Bayesian", 32, 37
    probabilistic ML foundation, 32
    probabilities assigned to any uncertain
        event, 43
    problem of induction, 59
    risk versus uncertainty, 41-43
    subjective probabilities of, 38
epistemic uncertainty, 46-48
    about, 23
    asymmetry of information, 47
    marginal likelihood function, 116
    ML generation of, 47
    point estimate cannot capture, 132
    posterior probability distribution, 116
    prior and posterior predictive distributions,
        124
    probabilistic models versus conventional/
        frequentist, 152
epsilon (ε) as unexpected stock-specific return,
    100

equity single-factor market model, 100
    alpha as expected stock-specific return, 100
    beta as systemic risk exposure, 100
    capital asset pricing model versus, 101
    code for estimating alpha and beta, 101-103
        confidence intervals, 104
    key assumptions wrecked, 107
Erdos, Paul, 25
ergodicity, 202-206
ETF (exchange-traded fund), 71
excess returns for excess risk, 100
expected shortfall (ES), 209
expected stock-specific return (α), 100
    code for estimating, 101-103
        confidence intervals, 104
expected value, 67, 116
expected valuer's ruin, 214-217
expert systems described, 13

F

fat-tailed probability distributions
    Cauchy distribution, 43, 69
        not having finite mean or variances, 107
    low probability events more likely, 69
FCF (free cash flows) in valuing a software
    project, 78-82
feature uncertainty and ML epistemic uncer-
    tainty, 47
the Fed (Federal Open Market Committee)
    interest rate estimation errors, 7-9
feedback in reinforcement learning, 15
Fermi, Enrico, 64
financial data signal-to-noise ratios, 155
    variance risks, 155
        regularizations to reduce, 155
financial theory
    financial markets non-ergodic, 144, 229
        nonstationary also, 229
    flaws of, xi
        book layout, xi
        finance is not physics, 2-4
        inexact instead of precise, 2, 10
        NHST, 87, 97
            (see also dangers of conventional
                statistical methods)
    linear regression's pivotal role, 151
    models wrong but useful, 1
        model failing to adapt to structural
            changes, 10

model parameter estimate errors, 7-9
model specification errors, 6
types of errors, 1, 6-10
models wrong, even dangerous, 4
   conventional AI (see dangers of conventional AI)
   conventional statistics (see dangers of conventional statistical methods)
   Great Financial Crisis reminder, 75
   Long-Term Capital Management, 4
probabilistic financial models, 10
psychology of financial decision making, 26
risk versus uncertainty, 41-43
S&P 500 index normally distributed, 72
   testing, 72-75
what is considered impossible, 115
Fisher, Ronald A., 31, 87, 94, 98, 99
forward propagation quantifying output uncertainty, 11, 123
   Monte Carlo simulation, 63
   prior and posterior predictive distributions enabling, 124
free cash flows (FCF) in valuing a software project, 78-82
frequentist view of probability, 36, 105
   about, 24, 32
     coin tosses, 37
   confidence intervals for alpha and beta, 104
   dangerous (see dangers of conventional statistical methods)
   disparaging epistemic school, 38
   epistemic versus, 39
   free lunch of bias-free and optimal for all problems, 38, 54
   image processing requiring probabilistic algorithms, 39
   long-run frequencies of repeatable events, 106, 107
   maximum likelihood estimation used by, 38
   population parameters constants with "true" values, 105
   regularizations to reduce variance, 155
   worse than useless, 24
     impact on financial economics, 100
     null hypothesis significance testing, 87, 97
     using prosecutor's fallacy, 38, 89
     violating product and inverse probability rules, 38

fundamental analysis, 55, 57

G
gambler's ruin, 212
gambling in history, 212
game theory and Monty Hall problem, 29
Gaus, Carl, 151
Gaus-Markov theorem assumptions, 155
Gaussian distribution (see normal distribution)
generalizing learnings inability in conventional AI, 130-132
generating data with predictive probability distributions, 123-127
generative AI
   about, 16
   about probabilistic ML, ix, 16
     generative characteristic, 19
   generating data with predictive probability distributions, 123-127
   generative ensembles
     about, 19, 191
     continually learning and revising parameters, 191
     market model, 154
     market model assumptions, 155
     MLE regression models, 153-156
     probabilistic linear ensembles, 156-161
     PyMC library, 152, 161-188
     residual, 153
     simulating new data and counterfactual knowledge, 191
geometric Brownian motion (GBM), 67
goal of financial modeling, 1
   flaws of modern financial theory, xi
   model complexity and, 48
Google TensorFlow Probability, 16
gradient-boosted machines as supervised learning, 15
Great Financial Crisis, 75, 209

H
Hastings, William, 148
Hayek, Friedrich, 3
high-frequency traders (HFT) using linear regression models, 151
historical data for parameter values, 10
human intelligence (HI), 16
Hume, David, 58

I

image processing requiring probabilistic algorithms, 39

implementation uncertainty and ML epistemic uncertainty, 47

inaccuracies accommodated by probabilistic models, 10

independent/input variables, 2
    feature or predictor in ML systems, 14

induction problem, 54-59
    about inductive reasoning, 54
    no free lunch theorems in probabilistic framework, 59
    past returns no guarantee of future results, 57
    physics and, 58

information (see knowledge integration)

information asymmetry, 47

input uncertainty quantified via inverse propagation, 11
    enabled by prior and posterior distributions, 124

input/independent variables, 2
    feature or predictor in ML systems, 14

interest rates
    binomial distribution to model, 7, 10
        Bernoulli distribution, 135
    discounted cash flow model, 56
    errors from estimating, 7-9
    impossibility of negative nominal interest rates, 115

inverse fallacy, 88-94
    NHST and rejecting the null hypothesis, 95

inverse probability rule, 30, 114-117
    application to real-world problems, 113
    Bayes's theorem misnomer, 19, 31-31, 94
    dangers of conventional statistical methods, 88-94
    debt default probability estimation, 120
    Monty Hall problem, 33
    probabilistic ML foundation, 32, 113
        debt default probability estimation via PML, 118-123
    product rule reformulation, 30, 88, 113

inverse propagation quantifying input uncertainty, 11
    enabled by prior and posterior distributions, 124

inverting conditional probabilities for Monty Hall problem, 30-33

J

Jensen's alpha, 162

K

k-means clustering algorithm as unsupervised learning, 15

Kelly criterion, 225-229
    Kelly investor's ruin, 229

Kelly, John, 213, 225

Keynes, Maynard, 109

Kipling, Rudyard, 51

knowledge integration
    debt default probability estimation via PML, 118-123
    epistemic uncertainty and, 46
    fundamental analysis, 55, 57
    Markov chains memoryless, 143
    MLE ignoring prior domain knowledge, 133
        MLE model for earnings expectations, 133-136
    no free lunch requiring prior knowledge, 18, 53, 115
    null hypothesis significance testing prohibiting, 18
    prior knowledge and bias-variance balance, 48
    probabilistic ML system characteristic, 17
    problem of induction, 54-59
        about inductive reasoning, 54
        no free lunch theorems in probabilistic framework, 59
    technical analysis, 55, 57

kurtosis, 69
    calculating for S&P 500, 72

L

L1 regularization, 155

L2 regularization, 155

Laplace, Pierre-Simon, 31, 113

lasso regularization, 155

law of large numbers (LLN), 75, 77

LCTM (Long-Term Capital Management), 4

learning dynamically via PML, 121

Legendre, Adrien-Marie, 151

likelihood function P(D|H), 115

aleatory uncertainty quantified by, 115
probabilistic linear ensembles P(Y|a, b, e, X), 159
linear regression
  capital asset pricing model as, 151
  estimating alpha and beta, 101-103
  MLE regression models, 153-156
    learning parameters using MLE, 155
    market model, 154
    market model assumptions, 155
    predicting and simulating model outputs, 156
    quantifying parameter uncertainty with confidence intervals, 156
    residual, 153
  overfitting of data, 155
    regularizations to reduce, 155
  pivotal role in modern finance, 151
    arbitrage pricing model, 151
    capital asset pricing model, 151
    factor models, 151
  probabilistic versus frequentist/conventional, 191
    (see also probabilistic linear ensembles)
  as supervised learning, 15
logistic regression as supervised learning, 15
Long-Term Capital Management (LTCM), 4
Lorentzian distribution (see Cauchy distribution)
loss aversion and endowment effect, 26
loss functions, 192, 195
  expected shortfall, 209
  probabilistic decision making
    estimating losses, 197-200
    integrating subjectivity, 195
    minimizing losses, 200
  value at risk (VaR), 206-208

M

machine learning (ML) models
  description of, ix, 12-16
  probabilistic (see probabilistic financial models; probabilistic machine learning)
  risks of overfitting data, 155
    regularizations to reduce, 155
Macready, William, 52
Mahabharata on gambling, 212
marginal likelihood function P(D), 33, 116

aleatory and epistemic uncertainties combined, 116
debt default probability estimation, 123
prior predictive distribution versus, 125
probabilistic linear ensembles P(Y|X), 159
marginal probability
  Monty Hall problem, 32, 116
  US economy in recession, 93
marginal probability distribution complexity, 130
market bull, bear, stagnant Markov chain, 143
market model for equities (MM), 100
  alpha as expected stock-specific return, 100
  beta as systemic risk exposure, 100
  capital asset pricing model versus, 101
  code for estimating alpha and beta, 101-103
    confidence intervals, 104
  key assumptions wrecked, 107
  linear regression model, 154
    assumptions, 155
market neutral strategies, 162
Markov chain Monte Carlo (MCMC) simulations, 130
  about, 142
  combination origin, 144
  Markov chains, 143
    bull, bear, stagnant financial markets, 143
    conditional independence, 144
    dependent sampling, 143
    memoryless, 143
    Metropolis MCMC algorithm, 145-148
    Metropolis-Hastings MCMC algorithm, 148
    stationary ergodic, 144
  Student's t-distribution simulation, 145-148
Markowitz, Harry, 218, 218
maximum likelihood estimation (MLE)
  about, 20
  dangers of conventional AI, 129
    MLE model for earnings expectations, 133-136
    probabilistic model for earnings expectations, 136-142
    why MLE models fail in finance, 132-142
  flaws for finance and investing, 129
  frequentists using, 38
  probabilistic linear regression model versus, 152

regression models, 153-156
    learning parameters using MLE, 155
    market model, 154
    market model assumptions, 155
    predicting and simulating model outputs, 156
    quantifying parameter uncertainty with confidence intervals, 156
    residual, 153
MCS (see Monte Carlo simulation)
mean, 66
    average deviation from, 67
    calculating for S&P 500, 73
    central limit theorem, 76-78
    expected value, 67
    law of large numbers, 75, 77
    sum of all deviations from, 67
measurement uncertainty and ML aleatory uncertainty, 45
median, 67
method uncertainty and ML epistemic uncertainty, 47
Metropolis MCMC algorithm, 145-148
Metropolis, Nicholas, 64, 144
Metropolis-Hastings MCMC algorithm, 148
Mitchell, Tom, 14
MLE (see maximum likelihood estimation)
mode, 67
models
    about, 2
        deterministic models, 2, 14
        input/independent variables, 2
        output/dependent variables, 2
        parameters, 2
        probabilistic models, 2, 14
    bias-variance balance, 48
    goal of financial modeling, 1
        flaws of modern financial theory, xi
        model complexity and, 48
    limitations must be known, 129
        (see also dangers of conventional AI)
    ML and AI explained, 12-16
        ML defined by Tom Mitchell, 14
        parameters from in-sample data, 14
        performance via out-of-sample data, 14
        types of ML systems, 15
    model uncertainty and ML epistemic uncertainty, 47
    PML models

debt default probability estimation, 118-123
    ingesting data one point at a time or all at once, 123
probabilistic financial models, 10
    about, 2
    model uncertainty quantified, 10
    training a linear ML system, 14
stochastic processes modeled by Markov chains, 143
uncertainty incorporated, 50
uncertainty must be quantified, 10, 87
wrong but useful, 1, 43
    model failing to adapt to structural changes, 10
    model parameter estimate errors, 7-9
    model specification errors, 6
    types of errors, 1, 6-10
wrong, even dangerous, 4
    dangers of conventional statistics, 87
        (see also dangers of conventional statistical methods)
    Great Financial Crisis reminder, 75
    Long-Term Capital Management, 4
modern portfolio theory (MPT)
    about, 218
    based on normal distribution, 6
    capital allocation, 218-220
    dangers of, 218
        investor's ruin, 221-225
    excess returns for excess risk, 100
    price data generated by underlying, time-invariant, stochastic process, 101
    S&P 500 index normally distributed, 72
    testing, 72-75
Moivre, Abraham de, 31
Monte Carlo simulation (MCS)
    about, 11, 33
        independent sampling, 142
        sampling error, 78
    building a sound MCS, 83
        challenges of, 83
    history of, 64
    importance of, 63
    Markov chain Monte Carlo simulations
        about, 130, 142
        combination origin, 144
        Markov chains, 143
        Markov chains stationary ergodic, 144

Metropolis MCMC algorithm, 145-148
    Metropolis-Hastings MCMC algorithm,
      148
    Student's t-distribution simulation,
      145-148
  Monty Hall solution via, 33-35
  output uncertainty quantified via forward
    propagation, 11, 63
  pi estimation, 64
  statistical concepts of, 66-76
  theoretical underpinnings of, 77
  valuing a software project, 78-82
Monty Hall problem, 24-26
  about, 23
  axioms of probability, 26-30
  epistemic uncertainty, 46
  game theory and, 29
  inverting conditional probabilities, 30-33
    inverse probability rule, 114-117
  Monte Carlo simulation for solution, 33-35
  ontological uncertainty, 49
  psychology of financial decision making, 26
  relative probability, 40-41
  types of uncertainty, 23
MPT (see modern portfolio theory)
multicollinearity, 155

N

naive diversification strategy, 218
Nash equilibrium, 30
Nash, John, 30
net present value (NPV), 78-82
Newton, Isaac, 3, 4
Neyman, Jerzy, 87, 98, 98
NFL (see no free lunch (NFL) theorems)
NHST (see null hypothesis significance testing)
no free lunch (NFL) theorems, 51-54
  about, 24
  bias-free and optimal for all problems as
    free lunch, 38
  free lunch per Rudyard Kipling, 51
  frequentist claims disputed by, 38
  prior knowledge necessary for optimization,
    18, 53, 115
  problem of induction in probabilistic
    framework, 59
"Nobel Prize in Economics", 3
Nobel, Alfred, 3
nonprobabilistic ML models described, ix

normal (Gaussian) distribution, 70
  financial theories using, 6, 71
  S&P 500 index, 72
    testing, 72-75
  skewness of zero, 69
null hypothesis (H0) in NHST, 95
null hypothesis significance testing (NHST)
  about, 87
  conditional probabilities not commuting, 88
  knowledge integration prohibited by, 18
  must be rejected, 87, 97
  path to "worse than useless", 98
  prosecutor's fallacy, 18, 88, 94-97
    proof by contrapositive, 95
NumPy random number generator, 73

O

objective function, 163
objectivity per NHST, 18
"Ode to Dice" ("Dyuta Sukta"), 212
ontological uncertainty, 49-50
  about, 23
  ML generation of, 50
optimal capital growth algorithm, 213
option pricing models, Thorp versus Black and
  Scholes, 42
ordinary least squares (OLS), 151
outliers, 67
  median unchanged by extremes of, 67
  mode unaffected by, 67
output uncertainty quantified via forward
  propagation, 11
  Monty Hall problem, 33-35
  PML models, 11, 123
    Monte Carlo simulation, 63
  prior and posterior predictive distributions
    enabling, 124
output/dependent variables, 2
  target or response in ML systems, 14

P

p-values
  CI theory replacing, 97
  conditional probabilities not commuting, 88
  flaws and abuses, 88
    prosecutor's fallacy, 95
parameters of a model, 2
  errors from estimating, 7-9
  in-sample data providing, 14

learning using MLE, 155
  quantifying uncertainty with confidence intervals, 156
parameter inference by ML systems, 19
  probalistic models, 152, 191
parameter uncertainty
  ML epistemic uncertainty and, 47
  quantifying with confidence intervals, 156
  point estimate not capturing epistemic uncertainty, 132
  prior and posterior distributions, 124
  zero probability value, 115
Pareto distribution not having finite mean or variances, 107
Pascal, Blaise, 212
Pearson, Egon, 98
Pearson, Karl, 94
performance of a model
  learning algorithms averaged across problem domains all the same, 52
  optimal and bias-free for all problems as free lunch, 38, 51
    about bias in this context, 52
    optimal because of prior knowledge and assumptions, 54
  out-of-sample data providing, 14
  performance metrics, 164
physics
  coin tosses following laws of, 37, 44
  finance is not physics, 2-4
    inexact instead of precise, 2
  problem of induction, 58
  special relativity, 40
pi estimation via Monte Carlo simulation, 64
plans useless, planning indispensable, 43
PML (see probabilistic machine learning)
policy-gradient methods as reinforcement learning, 15
population parameters
  error from postdata use of confidence intervals, 105
  frequentist view as constants with "true" values, 105
posterior predictive distribution P(D**|D), 125
posterior probability distribution P(H|D), 116
  probabilistic linear ensembles P(a, b, e|X, Y), 160
predictions

MLE regression models, 156
  prior and posterior predictive distributions, 114, 124
    generating data with predictive probability distributions, 123-127
  training a linear ML system, 14
Price, Richard, 31
principal component analysis as unsupervised learning, 15
prior and posterior distributions, 124
prior and posterior predictive distributions
  about, 114, 124
  generating data with predictive probability distributions, 123-127
  posterior predictive distribution, 125
  prior predictive distribution, 124
prior knowledge (see knowledge integration)
prior predictive distribution P(D*), 124
  marginal likelihood function versus, 125
prior probability distributions P(a, b, e), 158
probabilistic decision making with generative ensembles
  about, 191
  capital allocation, 211
    expected valuer's ruin, 214-217
    gamblers, 212
    gamblers' ruin, 212
    Kelly criterion, 225-229
    Kelly investor's ruin, 229
    modern portfolio theory, 218-220
    MPT/CAPM investor's ruin, 221-225
  loss functions defined, 192, 195
  probabilistic decision-making framework
    about, 195
    estimating losses, 197-200
    integrating subjectivity, 195
    minimizing losses, 200
  probabilistic inference and prediction framework, 193-195
  risk management
    about, 201
    capital preservation, 202
    ergodicity, 202-206
    expected shortfall, 209
    tail risk, 210
    value at risk, 206-208
probabilistic financial models, 10
  debt default probability estimation, 118-123
  deterministic versus, 2, 14

earnings expectations, 136-142
as generative models, 16, 123
  about, 191
  generating data with predictive probability distributions, 123-127
  market model, 154
  market model assumptions, 155
  MLE regression models, 153-156
  probabilistic linear ensembles, 156-161
  residual, 153
inaccuracies accommodated by, 10
ingesting data one point at a time or all at once, 123
model uncertainty quantified, 10
probabilistic linear ensembles, 156-161
  about, 156
  assembling with PyMC and ArviZ, 161-188
  likelihood function $P(Y|a, b, e, X)$, 159
  marginal likelihood function $P(Y|X)$, 159
  posterior probability distributions $P(a, b, e|X, Y)$, 160
  prior probability distributions $P(a, b, e)$, 158
PyMC library for assembling probabilistic linear ensembles, 161-188
  about PyMC library, 16, 152
  analyzing data and engineering features, 164-166
  defining ensemble performance metrics, 162-164
  developing and retrodicting prior ensemble, 168-176
  testing and evaluating ensemble predictions, 185-188
  training and retrodicting posterior model, 176-185
probabilistic inference, not "Bayesian", 32
probabilistic linear ensembles
  assembling with PyMC and ArviZ, 161-188
  about PyMC library, 16, 152
  analyzing data and engineering features, 164-166
  defining ensemble performance metrics, 162-164
  developing and retrodicting prior ensemble, 168-176

testing and evaluating ensemble predictions, 185-188
training and retrodicting posterior model, 176-185
frequentist linear regression versus probabilistic, 191
likelihood function $P(Y|a, b, e, X)$, 159
marginal likelihood function $P(Y|X)$, 159
posterior probability distributions $P(a, b, e|X, Y)$, 160
prior probability distributions $P(a, b, e)$, 158
probabilistic machine learning (PML)
  about, ix, 16
  deep neural networks versus, ix
  generative AI, ix, 16, 123
  PyMC library, 16
  Stan library, 16
aleatory uncertainty generation, 45
characteristics of, 16-20
  generative ensembles, 19
  knowledge integration, 17
  parameter inference, 19
  probability distributions, 17
  uncertainty awareness, 20
debt default probability estimation, 118-123
  ingesting data one point at a time or all at once, 123
  learning dynamically, 121
epstemic statistics foundation, 32
finance is not physics, 2-4
  inexact instead of precise, 2
generating data with predictive probability distributions, 123-127
generative ensembles
  about, 19, 191
  continually learning and revising parameters, 191
  market model, 154
  market model assumptions, 155
  MLE regression models, 153-156
  probabilistic linear ensembles, 156-161
  PyMC library, 152, 161-188
  residual, 153
  simulating new data and counterfactual knowledge, 191
inverse probability rule foundation, 32, 113
  application to real-world problems, 113
  debt default probability estimation, 120
  detail about, 114-117

ML and AI explained, 12-16
  ML defined by Tom Mitchell, 14
  parameters from in-sample data, 14
  performance via out-of-sample data, 14
  types of ML systems, 15
point estimate zero probability for probability density functions, 27
prior and posterior distributions, 124
prior and posterior predictive distributions
  about, 114
PyMC library for assembling probabilistic linear ensembles, 161-188
  about PyMC library, 16, 152
  analyzing data and engineering features, 164-166
  defining ensemble performance metrics, 162-164
  developing and retrodicting prior ensemble, 168-176
  testing and evaluating ensemble predictions, 185-188
  training and retrodicting posterior model, 176-185
training a linear ML system, 14
  dependent variable as target or response, 14
  independent variable as feature or predictor, 14
  ML defined by Tom Mitchell, 14
  types of ML systems, 15
probability
  axioms of, 26-30
    sum rule, 27
  common sense reduced to calculation, 113
  conditional probabilities, 30
    inverting for Monty Hall problem, 30-33
    product rule, 30
  deterministic and random variables, 27
  epistemic school of thought, 37-39
    about, 32
    frequentist versus, 39
    probabilities assigned to any uncertain event, 43
    problem of induction, 59
    subjective probabilities of, 38
  frequentist conventional view, 36, 105
    about, 24, 32
    coin tosses, 37

confidence intervals for alpha and beta, 104
  dangerous (see dangers of conventional statistical methods)
  disparaging epistemic school, 38
  epistemic versus, 39
  free lunch of bias-free and optimal for all problems, 38, 54
  impact on financial economics, 100
  long-run frequencies of repeatable events, 106, 107
  maximum likelihood estimation used by, 38
  null hypothesis significance testing, 87, 97
  population parameters constants with "true" values, 105
  regularizations to reduce variance, 155
  using prosecutor's fallacy, 38, 89
  violating product and inverse probability rules, 38
meaning of, 35
probability density functions, 27
probability mass functions, 27
relative probability, 40-41
risk versus uncertainty, 41-43
subjective probabilities, 38
uncertainty quantification and analysis, 24
probability density functions (PDF), 27
  probability of point estimate as zero, 27, 37
probability distributions
  Bernoulli same as binomial for single trial, 135
  errors from model not adapting to structural changes, 10
  errors in model parameter estimations, 8
  fat-tailed Cauchy distribution, 43, 69
    not having finite mean or variances, 107
  generating data with predictive probability distributions, 123-127
  Markov chain Monte Carlo simulation, 130
  Monte Carlo simulations sampling randomly from, 33
  prior and posterior distributions, 124
    posterior predictive distribution, 125
  prior and posterior predictive distributions
    about, 114, 123
    generating data with predictive probability distributions, 123-127

prior predictive distribution, 124
probabilistic ML system characteristic, 17
    learning from in-sample data, 19
    parameter's entire probability distribution, 20
probability distribution functions, 27
    zero probability parameter value, 115
probability mass functions (PMF), 27
probability-weighted average sum, 67, 116
product rule for conditional probabilities, 30
    frequentist inference methods violating, 38
    inverse probability rule derived from, 30, 88, 113
    Bayes's theorem pejorative, 31, 94
proof by contrapositive, 95
prosecutor's fallacy, 88-94
    about, 87
    frequentist inference methods using, 38, 89
    null hypothesis significance testing committing, 18, 88, 94-97
psychology of financial decision making, 26
PyMC library
    about, 16, 152
    used in this book, 16
    assembling probabilistic linear ensembles, 161-188
    analyzing data and engineering features, 164-166
    defining ensemble performance metrics, 162-164
    developing and retrodicting prior ensemble, 168-176
    testing and evaluating ensemble predictions, 185-188
    training and retrodicting posterior model, 176-185
Pyro extending PyTorch platform, 16

Q

Q-learning as reinforcement learning, 15

R

random forests as supervised learning, 15
random number generator (NumPy), 73
random sampling
    dependent sampling, 142
    (see also Markov chain Monte Carlo (MCMC) simulations)
    independent sampling, 142

(see also Monte Carlo simulation)
    leading to stable solution, 63
    (see also Monte Carlo simulation)
recessions and prosecutor's fallacy, 90-94
regression (see linear regression)
regularizations to reduce variance, 155
    lasso regularization, 155
    ridge regularization, 155
reinforcement learning ML systems, 15
relative probability, 40-41
    relativity principle in physics, 40
Renaissance Technologies, 6
residual, 153
reward-to-risk ratio, 67
ridge regularization, 155
risk
    excess returns for excess risk
        single-factor market model for equities, 100
    risk management, 201
        capital preservation, 202
        ergodicity, 202-206
        expected shortfall, 209
        tail risk, 210
        value at risk, 206-208
    systemic risk exposure (β), 100
        code for estimating, 101-103
        estimation confidence intervals, 104
    uncertainty versus, 41-43
    unsystematic and systematic of CAPM, 219
    volatility as nonsensical measure, 68
        underestimating financial risk, 71-75
Rosenbluth, Arianna W., 144
Rosenbluth, Marshall, 144
Rumsfeld, Donald, 23
Russian government default on local currency bonds, 4

S

S&P 500
    normally distributed, 72
        testing, 72-75
    volatility underestimating risk, 71-75
SAI (symbolic AI), 13
sampling distributions of sample mean, 106
    errors from confidence interval postdata use, 106-109
sampling error of Monte Carlo simulations, 78

sampling uncertainty and ML aleatory uncertainty, 45
scenario analysis, 11
Scholes, Myron, 4, 42
Selvin, Steve, 24
sensitivity analysis, 11
Sharpe ratio, 68
Sharpe, William, 219
significance level (alpha)
    about, 95
Simpson, O. J., 90
single-factor market model for equities, 100
    alpha as expected stock-specific return, 100
    beta as systemic risk exposure, 100
    capital asset pricing model versus, 101
    code for estimating alpha and beta, 101-103
        confidence intervals, 104
    key assumptions wrecked, 107
skewness, 69
    calculating for S&P 500, 72
Smith, Adam, 2
software project valuation via MCS, 78-82
Stan library
    about, 16
standard deviation, 67
    calculating for S&P 500, 73
stationary ergodic as time invariant, 72
stationary ergodic stochastic process, 144
statistical decision theory of Neyman, 98
statistical inference
    flaws in conventional methodology, xi
        book layout, xi
    key concepts behind Monte Carlo simulation, 66-76
    probability as soul of, 35
    (see also probability)
Statsmodels linear regression to estimate alpha and beta, 101-103
stochastic processes
    modeled by Markov chains, 143
        stationary ergodic, 144
stock single-factor market model, 100
    alpha as expected stock-specific return, 100
    beta as systemic risk exposure, 100
    capital asset pricing model versus, 101
    code for estimating alpha and beta, 101-103
        confidence intervals, 104
    key assumptions wrecked, 107

Student's t-distribution MCMC simulation, 145-148
subjective probabilities of epistemic probabilities, 38
subjectivity integrated into probabilistic decision making, 195
sum rule of probability, 27
supervised learning ML systems, 15
Sveriges Riksbank Prize in Economic Sciences in Memory of Alfred Nobel, 3
symbolic AI (SAI), 13
systematic risk of CAPM, 219
systemic risk exposure (β), 100
    code for estimating, 101-103
        confidence intervals, 104

T

t-distribution MCMC simulation, 145-148
target distribution equal probabilities, 53
technical analysis, 55, 57
Teller, Augusta H., 144
Teller, Edward, 144
TensorFlow Probability (Google), 16
Thorp, Edward O., 42, 191, 213
time
    financial time series as asymmetric and fat-tailed, 75
    stationary ergodic as time invariant, 72
        Markov chains as stationary ergodic, 144
    stochastic processes modeled by Markov chains, 143
time-variant distribution parameter values from historical data, 10
total probability rule for Monty Hall problem, 33
training a linear ML system, 14
    dependent variable as target or response, 14
    independent variable as feature or predictor, 14
    ML defined by Tom Mitchell, 14
    objective of ML systems, 14
    "training" as feeding sample data, 14
    types of ML systems, 15
training data overfit as variance, 48
training data underfit as bias, 48
transposed conditional fallacy (see prosecutor's fallacy)
type I and type II error control by Neyman, 98

U

Ulam, Stanisław, 64
uncertainty quantification and analysis
  all models should quantify uncertainty, 10
  input uncertainty via inverse propagation, 11
    prior and posterior distributions enabling, 124
  MLE models failing in finance, 132
  Monty Hall problem, 24-26
    about, 23
    axioms of probability, 26-30
    epistemic uncertainty, 46
    game theory and, 29
    inverting conditional probabilities, 30-33
    inverting conditional probabilities detail, 114-117
    Monte Carlo simulation for solution, 33-35
    ontological uncertainty, 49
    psychology of financial decision making, 26
    relative probability, 40-41
    types of uncertainty, 23, 44-50
  output uncertainty via forward propagation
    about, 11, 63
    Monte Carlo simulation, 63
    Monty Hall problem, 33-35
    PML models, 11, 123
    prior and posterior predictive distributions enabling, 124
  probability for, 24
    probabilistic AI for, 20, 50
  problem of induction, 54-59
    about inductive reasoning, 54
    no free lunch theorems in probabilistic framework, 59
    physics and, 58
  risk versus uncertainty, 41-43
  types of uncertainty, 23, 44-50

unconditional probability
  Monty Hall problem, 32, 116
  US economy in recession, 93
unexpected stock-specific return (ϵ), 100
uniform distributions have no tails, 69
unsupervised learning ML systems, 15
unsystematic risk of CAPM, 219

V

value at risk (VaR), 206-208
  expected shortfall, 209
valuing a software project via MCS, 78-82
variables
  constants versus, 28
  continuous variables of probability density functions, 27
  deterministic and random variables, 27
  discrete variables of probability mass functions, 27
  input/independent, 2
    feature or predictor in ML systems, 14
  output/dependent, 2
    target or response in ML systems, 14
variance, 67
  financial data signal-to-noise ratios, 155
    regularizations to reduce overfitting, 155
  as overfitting the training data, 48
    bias-variance balance, 48
  standard deviation via, 67
volatility, 67
  modern portfolio theory, 218
  nonsensical measure of risk, 68
    underestimating financial risk, 71-75
von Neumann, John, 64

W

web page for book, xv
Wolpert, David, 51

About the Author

Deepak K. Kanungo is an algorithmic derivatives trader, instructor, and CEO of Hedged Capital LLC, an AI-powered proprietary trading company that he founded in 2009. Since 2019, Deepak has taught tens of thousands of O'Reilly Media subscribers worldwide the concepts, processes, and machine learning technologies for algorithmic trading, investing, and finance with Python.

In 2005, long before machine learning was an industry buzzword, Deepak invented a probabilistic machine learning method and software system for managing the risks and returns of project portfolios. It is a unique probabilistic framework that has been cited by IBM and Accenture, among others.

Previously, Deepak was a financial advisor at Morgan Stanley, a Silicon Valley fintech entrepreneur, a director in the Global Planning Department at Mastercard International, and a senior analyst with Diamond Technology Partners. He was educated at Princeton University (astrophysics) and the London School of Economics (finance and information systems). He is the instructor for the O'Reilly course *Hands-On Algorithmic Trading With Python* (*https://oreil.ly/hands-on-algorithmic-trading*).

Colophon

The animal on the cover of *Probabilistic Machine Learning for Finance and Investing* is a Cape girdled lizard (*Cordylus cordylus*), a native of the southern Cape region in South Africa. Known for their golden-brown color and spiny scales, girdled lizards can often be found sunbathing on top of large rocks with other members of their colonies.

Cape girdled lizards inhabit crags, rocky outcrops, and mountain summits. To protect themselves against predators, these lizards wedge themselves firmly in the cracks of the rocks by inflating their lungs, making it extremely difficult for their predators to pry them out. Their thorny tails also serve as extra protection. Cape girdled lizards spend their mornings and evenings foraging for food (mostly insects) before returning to the safety of the rocky cracks.

Many of the animals on O'Reilly covers are endangered; all of them are important to the world.

The cover illustration is by Karen Montgomery, based on an antique line engraving from Routledge's *Picture Natural History*. The cover fonts are Gilroy Semibold and Guardian Sans. The text font is Adobe Minion Pro; the heading font is Adobe Myriad Condensed; and the code font is Dalton Maag's Ubuntu Mono.